General Counsel in the 21st Century

Challenges and Opportunities

Consulting Editors **Christoph H Vaagt** and **Wolf-Peter Gross**

Consulting editors
Christoph H Vaagt
Wolf-Peter Gross
On behalf of the International Bar Association

Managing director
Sian O'Neill

General Counsel in the 21st Century: Challenges and Opportunities
is published by
Globe Law and Business Limited
3 Mylor Close
Horsell
Woking
Surrey GU21 4DD
Tel: +44 20 3745 4770
www.globelawandbusiness.com

Print and bound by CPI Antony Rowe

General Counsel for the 21st Century: Challenges and Opportunities
ISBN 9781909416772

Table of contents

Introduction: challenges and opportunities for general counsel in the 21st century

Wolf-Peter Gross
Christoph H Vaagt
Law Firm Change Consultants

Until recently, the legal department has been left outside the consideration of general management theories and thus the focus for change. The legal department was sacrosanct within companies – with its own language, its own way of doing things, particular IT needs and cumbersome processes, it existed in a world of its own for all non-legal parties.

But the world has changed, and it has changed dramatically. Nowadays, legal processes are analysed, just like any other process in the business. Finance departments no longer accept the view that legal costs are necessary costs to companies; instead, they are looking for cost reduction. Moreover, they want to see a profitable business case behind the legal department. DuPont has set the example: with its Six Sigma approach (ie, continual process optimisation), it has become clear that improvement is possible. Paul Smith argues for this in a very simple manner in a later chapter: the legal department has to be managed. This is the new mantra for general counsel.

Therefore, there are several areas in which legal departments are to be reorganised, and some do it successfully already:

- The way the legal department is run in terms of leadership and management;
- How the role of the general counsel changes and thus how he must improve his skills;
- The way in which technology impacts on the work of the legal department, both regarding how it is run internally and how it must be aware of the IT department as more and more businesses are based on an IT infrastructure, leading to numerous implications for the legal field;
- The scope of the legal department when it comes to general legal affairs or, defined more broadly, in regard to risk assessment;
- The strategy a legal department may employ and the effect this has on the competitive position of the company;
- The interaction with internal and external clients; and
- The management of its resources (people, competences, time, money).

It used to be that the general counsel would be the most senior corporate counsel in the legal department, commanding an overview of the legal issues of the company and focusing on the major issues around litigation and company structure. This certainly was true – until today. Dealing with a company's legal issues is still one of the primary tasks of the general counsel, but it is no longer the sole area of concern.

Thus, we consider the job of the general counsel as being based around the four primary roles shown in Figure 1.

Figure 1: Primary roles of a general counsel

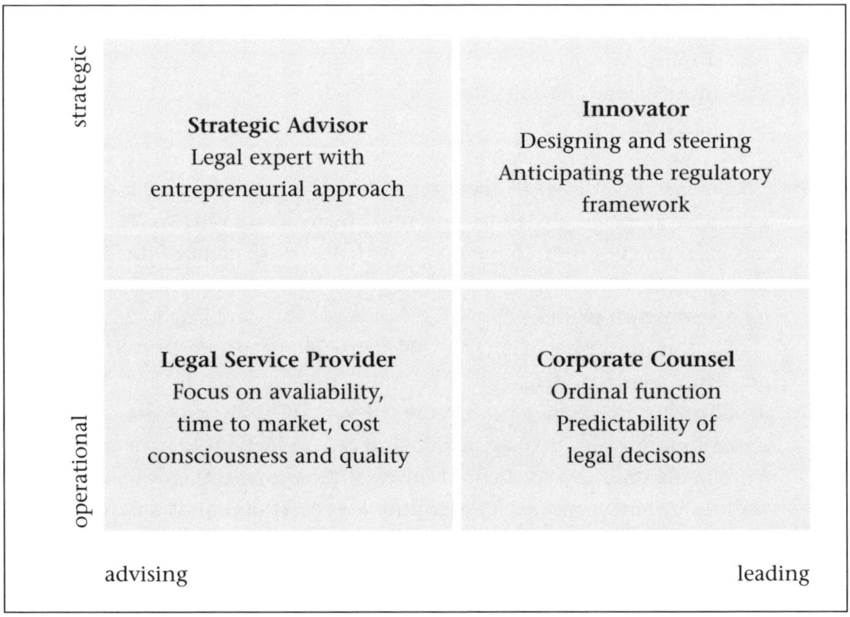

Today the general counsel and his team have to encompass far more. He is the legal service provider for the line management operating within the (internal) clients' supply chain processes. He is the strategic legal adviser for the top management team with respect to strategic and business-critical decisions and projects. And not least, he is an innovator in the sense of anticipating the regulatory framework for doing business. All of these aspects of the legal function are equally vital and necessary for the company. Today, we ask general counsel the following key questions:

- Does the organisational structure support the role and positioning of the legal department in the best possible way and is it orientated in line with the strategy, core competencies and needs of the overall organisation?
- Is there sufficient space for the areas of leadership, consultation and implementation?
- Does the structure ensure efficiency and effectiveness?
- Is an appropriate handling of the basic paradoxes possible?
- Is sufficient consideration given to the exchange of knowledge, cooperation and quality insurance?
- Are the roles, responsibilities and interface functions clarified?
- Are the resources available in sufficient flexibility?

- Are the procedures efficient, effective and robust?
- Which mechanisms are intended to maintain the organisation's vitality and to allow it to adapt to changing needs?

To fill all these roles, the general counsel must be a manager who:
- understands business strategy;
- manages people from diverse backgrounds;
- understands information technology;
- makes use of business process re-engineering techniques;
- calculates and executes budgets;
- considers key performance indicators; and
- assesses and documents risks including financial implications.

Above all that, he has to keep ahead of major legal developments with which the company might be confronted.

The general counsel still provides legal services, which means that he integrates the legal work custom-fitted into purely operational processes. He needs to understand exactly what is needed when and in which format in order to help the line management do business. Being as close as possible to the business is the paradigm in this respect. He must be accepted by the business line managers, and trying to influence decision making in order to avoid pitfalls long before they may become manifest is necessary to avoid costly legal disputes further down the road. This requires a new way of interacting with business and often a different methodology from that learned at law school. The goal is not to look for legal problems, but rather to guide the managers without a legal background through the legal frameworks. By doing so, he must focus on the value to be generated.

The general counsel also needs to provide leadership. Apart from the line management and top management team, the company is the general counsel's client. What he deems appropriate for those in charge might not necessarily be good for the company in general. The general counsel has the utmost responsibility for everything associated with compliance with the laws of the land (and those of other jurisdictions, legal regimes, regulatory frameworks etc) in the organisation – a task he cannot delegate. In the end, he provides the framework for a legally sound organisation. This requires stamina, backbone and independence, as well as communication skills that go beyond the techniques learned at law school.

Obviously, the base skills of a legal counsel need to be much broader than they used to be. Besides a legal education with a necessary understanding of the major jurisdictions in which businesses deal today (ie, EU, UK and US laws), having knowledge of business administration is fundamental. In addition, a solid understanding of information technology is needed as computer literacy is considered a basic skill these days. The skills he needs in today's world are discussed later by Leigh Dance and Christian Rau. The role of the general counsel is also the focus of the chapters by Bruno Cova, who argues that the role is heavily affected by the need for compliance, and Peter Kurer, who proposes that a general counsel must redefine himself as a risk manager in the broadest of terms.

Since doing business is to a large extent determined by legal provisions, it is no surprise that managers nowadays need a basic understanding of the legal environment in which they are operating. Their legal strategies must be 'astute' to minimise risk and create value, attain core business objectives, identify and resolve legal issues and effectively handle disputes, as described hereafter by Professor Bagley.

Robert Bird describes the basic strategic options a company can choose regarding its legal behaviour. These range from an avoidance approach on the one hand – dealing with legal issues only in reaction to outside pressures – to a rather transformational attitude on the other – using the law to create competitive advantages. All of this has a long-term effect on the competitiveness of a company. Each legal strategy may have its advantages and disadvantages; it might be adequate for a particular case, but not necessarily for the company as a whole. Thus, it is worthwhile to make a conscious decision about which basic legal strategy to pursue. Furthermore, it has an impact on the positioning of the legal department, its role and its primary tasks.

The general counsel has a major influence on this strategic positioning. Max Hübner's chapter provides a key finding here: no one but the general counsel is in charge of driving the change in the legal department and thus influencing both the legal culture and the legal strategy within the company. In his personal reflections, Hübner illustrates how the general counsel constantly adapts and reinvents the legal department by using leadership techniques and decision-making methods.

The general counsel as an agent of innovation is Paul Lippe's perspective, reflecting on one of the four primary roles stated above. A company will not change the way it perceives the law unless the general counsel integrates innovation with his job – both in how his team does its work and how the legal department enables innovation across the company. The proper clue towards this attitude is provided by Felix Rackwitz and Filip Corveleyn: instead of focusing on the legal issues at hand, innovative law firms focus on the business problem the client is facing rather than only the legal ones.

Kent Walker from Google goes a step further. He predicts the lawyer being at the heart of the revolution. Indeed, in today's rapidly changing world, the law must adapt to the age of the internet. Lawyers must understand the logic of the new industrial revolution currently under way, allowing the creation of a new set of rules on top of everything we have considered to be the core of our societies for the last 200 years or so.

For most companies exploiting the innovations of the digital revolution, the efficient handling of customer data is fundamental to their commercial success, but also represents their Achilles' heel if measured against the increasingly complex contractual and international statutory restrictions. Compliant handling of their customer data represents a major issue for legal as well as IT departments. A thorough understanding of the related problems is a must-have for every in-house counsel involved. Dennis Grabherr looks at these issues from the point of view of an IT service provider operating in the business-to-business space, as it is fair to assume that with an increasingly complex delivery infrastructure, many IT service providers are not yet in a position to ensure that their 24/7, follow-the-sun global service delivery models handle entrusted corporate customer data in compliance with all applicable contractual, legal, regulatory or governance obligations. In order to avoid contractual liability for breach of contract and fines (eg, for information security breaches and related reputational damage), every IT service provider must ensure that its customer data is handled with integrity and in a compliant and safe manner. In order to frame future business models which are capable of compliant customer data handling, it is imperative not only for the legal and IT teams to join up and be brutally transparent in their processes, but also that buy-in and the full backing of top management is unconditionally required.

The role of the general counsel – and the legal department – has shifted from being observational to proactive. Abhijit Mukhopadhyay traces this development and provides a number of examples to illustrate what makes the difference. He also explores what is meant by 'adding value'.

Paul Smith from Eversheds argues that in large corporations the 'more for less' mantra is being chanted ever louder, bringing pressure to bear on internal legal departments in many ways. He examines these pressures and provides solutions for greater operational efficiency. These include the preparation of an operational strategy; the optimisation of internal resources; the management of external resources; and the demonstration of success through metrics and measures.

The job is to deliver high-quality service and work products against increasing time and budgetary constraints, thus highlighting the challenges faced by general counsel. A key to success is strategically categorising work according to priority and importance, and then applying consistent standards for the actual product. Jochen Deister and Carsten Reimann use a real-life case to describe how using an International Organization for Standardization (ISO)-based process approach can help general counsel to fulfil his tasks more effectively and efficiently. The authors describe how the legal department of a major German corporation put this approach into practice. Deister and Reimann build their case for a 'lean and mean' legal department, based on a set of quality guidelines and standards to cope with this challenge.

This understanding is the basis of Peter Kurer's observation when it comes to risk assessment. The scope of the legal department may be more difficult to define in the future, as it has already been quite difficult in the past. Other departments often refer work to the legal department when, in fact, they are hoping to avoid making a decision themselves – most likely for political reasons. 'Compliance' as the new buzzword for legal astuteness is also less clearly defined than 'legal' and some companies have started to build up compliance organisations alongside, or even in competition with, the legal department. Thus, as Bruno Cova argues, in the 21st century corporate governance will increasingly become a key proving ground for general counsel (more so than for any other corporate officer).

The standing of the legal department can only be as good as the human resources doing the work. Christian Rau's chapter provides a hands-on, best-practice overview of this fundamental aspect of the general counsel's responsibility. Having the right people in place is the key to the acceptance of legal support from the business. Or as Rau puts it in his 10 takeaways: it is all about the right people and the right mindset.

Finally, Steven Rosenberg's input on the role of information technology in shaping and supporting global legal operations certainly provides an incentive for breaking new ground or continuing on the path of using information and communications technology proactively for the day-to-day work of handling legal work flow, communicating and administrating data.

All of these aspects represent challenges and opportunities for today's general counsel. We hope that our authors and ourselves have identified if not all, at least some of those which matter in the 21st century.

Integrating law and strategy: the value of legal astuteness

Constance E Bagley
Yale Law School

1. Introduction

According to a 2012 KPMG survey of 320 general counsel: "The role of general counsel is moving from one of 'fire-fighting' and reacting to events to being more strategic and proactively anticipating risks at an earlier stage."[1] Because failure to comply with applicable laws can subject a firm to crushing government fines, the payment of billions in damages, termination of entire lines of business and imprisonment of its executives, any discussion of law and strategy must begin with compliance with law.[2]

Yet staying out of trouble is only part of the picture. Lawyers can do more than help firms to anticipate and manage risk.[3] They can create value by serving as 'transaction cost engineers'[4] and 'enterprise architects'.[5] Business lawyers: craft complex contractual relationships; structure joint ventures, licensing arrangements and other strategic alliances; organise and reorganise firms; practise preventive law; protect intellectual property; and handle regulatory matters.[6]

But too often, managers view lawyers as a necessary evil, not a strategic partner. They treat law purely as a constraint, something to comply with and react to.[7] In contrast, legally astute managers work with strategically astute counsel to solve complex problems and to marshal, protect and leverage resources.[8] They possess a valuable dynamic managerial capability[9] that may be a source of sustained competitive advantage under the resource-based view of the firm.[10]

1 KPMG International Cooperative, 'Beyond the Law: KPMG's Global Study of How General Counsel are Turning Risk to Advantage' (2012).

2 Constance E Bagley, *Winning Legally: Using the Law to Create Value, Marshal Resources and Manage Risks* (2005).

3 S L Schwarcz, 'Explaining the Value of Transactional Lawyering', 12 *Stanford Journal of Law, Business & Finance* 486 (2007).

4 Ronald J Gilson, 'Value Creation by Business Lawyers: Legal Skills and Asset Pricing', 94 *Yale Law Journal* 239, 255 (1984).

5 G W Dent, Jr, 'Business Lawyers as Enterprise Architects', 64 *Business Lawyer* 279, 289–93 (2009).

6 *Ibid.*

7 Constance E Bagley, 'Winning Legally: The Value of Legal Astuteness', 33 *Academy of Management Review* 378, 378–79 (2008).

8 Constance E Bagley & Mark Roellig, 'The Transformation of General Counsel: Setting the Strategic Legal Agenda' in *Legal Risk Management, Governance and Compliance: A Guide to Best Practice from Leading Experts* 45–66 (Charles Wild & Stuart Weinstein, eds, 2013).

9 David J Teece, Gary Pisano & Amy Shuen, 'Dynamic Capabilities and Strategic Management', 18 *Strategic Management Journal* 509, 515 (1997) ("Winners in the global marketplace have been firms that can demonstrate timely responsiveness and rapid and flexible product innovation, coupled with the management capability to effectively coordinate and redeploy internal and external competences.")

10 Bagley, *supra* note 7.

The resource-based view posits that "a firm develops competitive advantage by not only acquiring, but also developing, combining and effectively deploying its physical, human, and organisational resources in ways that add unique value and are difficult for competitors to imitate."[11] Like failure to implement the correct corporate governance practices,[12] failure to implement appropriate legal measures can prevent firms from fully realising the benefits of the other resources they control.[13]

While recognising that "competitive advantage can flow at a point in time from the ownership of scarce but relevant and difficult-to-imitate assets, especially know-how", Teece made it clear that "in fast-moving business environments open to global competition, and characterized by dispersion in the geographical and organizational sources of innovation and manufacturing, sustainable advantage ... requires unique and difficult-to-replicate dynamic capabilities."[14] Teece divides dynamic capabilities "into the capacity (1) to sense and shape opportunities and threats, (2) to seize opportunities, and (3) to maintain competitiveness through enhancing, combining, protecting, and, when necessary, reconfiguring the business enterprise's intangible and tangible assets."[15] There are legal components of each.[16]

For example, because "the locus of world-class research/productive capability might lie external to the enterprise", firms may need to outsource at least aspects of their research and development to compete effectively.[17] Legally astute top management teams can use a variety of legal structures to engage in research and development activities with others, such as university and company researchers, licensors and joint venture partners.[18] Similarly, social media offer powerful means for discerning, anticipating and exploring customer needs, but the collection and use of personal data require adherence to the applicable laws and regulations governing privacy protection, which are particularly strict in the European Union.

Section 2 below sets forth the five elements of the dynamic capability of legal astuteness. Section 3 explains how legally astute top management teams and their strategically astute lawyers create realisable value while managing the attendant risks by:

---

11 Barry A Colbert, 'The Complete Resource-Based View: Implications for Theory and Practice in Strategic Human Resource Management', 29 *Academy of Management Review* 341, 343 (2004). See generally Jay B Barney, 'Firm Resources and Sustained Competitive Advantage', 17 *Journal of Management* 99, 106–11 (1991) (firm resources have the potential of providing sustained competitive advantage if they are valuable, rare and imperfectly imitable by competitors, and have no strategically equivalent substitutes); Birger Wernerfelt, 'A Resource-Based View of the Firm', 5 *Strategic Management Review* 171 (1984).

12 Jay B Barney, Mike Wright and David J Ketchen Jr, 'The resource-based view of the firm: Ten years after 1991', 27 *Journal of Management* 625, 625 (2001).

13 Bagley, *supra* note 7, at 385.

14 David J Teece, 'Explicating Dynamic Capabilities: The Nature and Microfoundations of (Sustainable) Enterprise Performance', 28 *Strategic Management Journal* 1319, 1319 (2007).

15 *Ibid.*

16 See Constance E Bagley, 'The Dynamic Capability of Legal Astuteness' in *Oxford Handbook of Dynamic Capabilities* (David J Teece, ed, forthcoming).

17 Teece, *supra* note 14, at 1331; Gary Pisano, W Shan & David J Teece, 'Joint Ventures and Collaboration in the Biotechnology Industry', in *International Collaborative Ventures in US Manufacturing* 183, 202 (D Mowery, ed, 1998).

18 Constance E Bagley & Christina D Tvarno, 'Promoting "Academic Entrepreneurship" in Europe and the United States: Creating an Intellectual Property Regime to Facilitate the Efficient Transfer of Knowledge from the Lab to the Patient', *Duke Journal of Comparative & International Law* (forthcoming); Constance E Bagley & Christina D Tvarno, 'Pharmaceutical Public-Private Partnerships in the United States and Europe: Moving from the Bench to the Bedside', 4 *Harvard Business Law Review* 301 (2014).

- using formal contracts as complements to relational governance;
- protecting, redeploying and enhancing the value of knowledge assets and other firm resources;
- using legal tools to create valuable options and to combat risk/loss aversion and overconfidence bias;
- practising "strategic compliance management"[19] and thereby converting regulatory constraints into opportunities; and
- helping shape the 'rules of the game'[20] governing business.

Section 4 explains that there are degrees of legal astuteness; Section 5 concludes with the systems approach to law and strategy, a descriptive integrating framework for understanding law and strategy.

2. Elements of legal astuteness

Legal astuteness requires:

- a set of value-laden attitudes about the importance of law and ethical behaviour to firm success;
- a proactive approach to management, regulation and risk;
- the ability to exercise informed judgement when managing the legal and business aspects of business;
- context-specific knowledge of the law and the appropriate use of legal tools;[21] and
- strategically astute lawyers.[22]

2.1 Value-laden attitudes

Legally astute top management teams understand that "business decisions consist of continuous, interrelated economic and moral components".[23] When dealing with conflict, business leaders and their counsel "should keep trying to reframe issues and refine tactics until they are satisfied that the firm's legitimate business objective of 'winning' in the marketplace is being advanced in an effective, legal, and above board manner."[24] In short, they acknowledge that the moral aspects of choice are the final component of strategy.[25]

The general counsel "is sometimes viewed as the 'ethics police person,' who catches inappropriate activities and institutes corrective actions to bring the rule-breaker into compliance with corporate governance standards. The GC is [usually] also a key member of the committees that examine the adequacy of internal controls

---

19 Bagley, *supra* note 2, at 50.

20 Douglass C North, *Institutions, Institutional Change and Economic Performance* (1990) (the 'rules of the game' include both formal, explicit rules, such as constitutions, laws and property rights, as well as informal, often implicit rules, such as conventions, norms of behaviour and codes of conduct).

21 Bagley, *supra* note 7, at 379.

22 Bagley & Roellig, *supra* note 8.

23 D L Swanson, 'Addressing a Theoretical Problem in Reorienting the Corporate Social Performance Model', 20 *Academy of Management Review* 43, 51 (1995).

24 Bagley & Roellig, *supra* note 8.

25 Edmund P Learned, C Roland Christensen, Kenneth R Andrews & William D Guth, *Business Policy: Texts and Cases* 578 (1969).

and compliance with regulatory rules."[26] Or, as Bond Pearce, managing partner Victor Tettmar, put it, general counsel should be the "guardian of moral capital".

Bagley[27] and Bagley and Roellig[28] assert that every manager has a responsibility to ensure ethical behaviour and compliance with law. 'Creative compliance' – that is, "complying with the letter of the law but defeating its spirit and purpose"[29] and taking advantage of unintended legal loopholes[30] – can lead to ethical and unlawful behaviour down the road.

Especially when discussing values, "management communicates as much by what it doesn't do or say as by what it says and does. In fact, behavioral forms of communication are apt to have more credibility than spoken or written forms."[31] As Ben Heineman, former general counsel of General Electric, explained: "The stirring call for performance with integrity at the large company meeting can be eroded by the cynical comment an executive makes at a smaller meeting, by the winks and nods that implicitly sanction improprieties, by personal actions (dishonesty, lack of candor) that contradict company values."[32]

The ethical business leader's decision tree (see Figure 1) is an example of a tool that legally astute managers can use to assess not only the legality but also the ethics of their proposed actions.[33] Managers are encouraged to ask first whether the action complies with the letter and spirit of the law. If it does, then the next inquiry is whether it would enhance shareholder value. Even if it would not, legally astute managers will go on to ask whether it would be unethical to refrain from acting. This reflects not only the importance of meeting the manager's and the firm's ethical standards, but also the need to meet societal expectations, which directly affect a firm's licence to operate, the application and interpretation of existing laws and regulations, and the adoption of new laws and regulations. If the management team elects to take an action that is not legally mandated and does not enhance shareholder value, then it should disclose the reasons behind its decision to shareholders so they can take them into account when casting their votes for the board of directors at the next election. This transparency prevents management from using its professed concern for other constituencies or broad societal welfare to mask poor performance.[34]

---

26 A D Jagolinzer, D F Larcker & D J Taylor, 'Corporate Governance and the Information Content of Insider Trades', 49(5) *Journal of Accounting Research* 1249, 1249 (2011).

27 Bagley, *supra* note 7.

28 Bagley & Roellig, *supra* note 8.

29 Timothy P Terrell, 'Professionalism on an International Scale: The Lex Mundi Project to Identify the Fundamental Shared Values of Law Practice', 23 *Emory International Law Review* 469, 536 (2009) (defining "creative compliance" as "complying with the letter of the law but defeating its spirit and purpose").

30 Daniel T Ostas, 'Legal Loopholes and Underenforced Laws: Examining the Ethical Dimensions of Corporate Legal Strategy', 46 *American Business Law Journal* 487, 487 (2009) (noting that "using the law for private gain raises a number of potentially thorny ethical issues").

31 Philip P Drotning, 'Organizing the Company for Social Action', in *The Unstable Ground: Corporate Social Policy in a Dynamic Society* 260 (S Prakash Sethi, ed, 1974).

32 Ben W Heineman, Jr, 'Avoiding Integrity Land Mines', *Harvard Business Review*, April 2007, at 102.

33 Constance E Bagley, 'Forethought: The Ethical Leader's Decision Tree', *Harvard Business Review*, February 2003, at 18–19 (2003).

34 Constance E Bagley & Karen Page, 'The Devil Made Me Do It: Replacing Corporate Directors' Veil of Secrecy with the Mantle of Stewardship', 36 *San Diego Law Review* 897 (1999).

Figure 1: The ethical business leader's decision tree

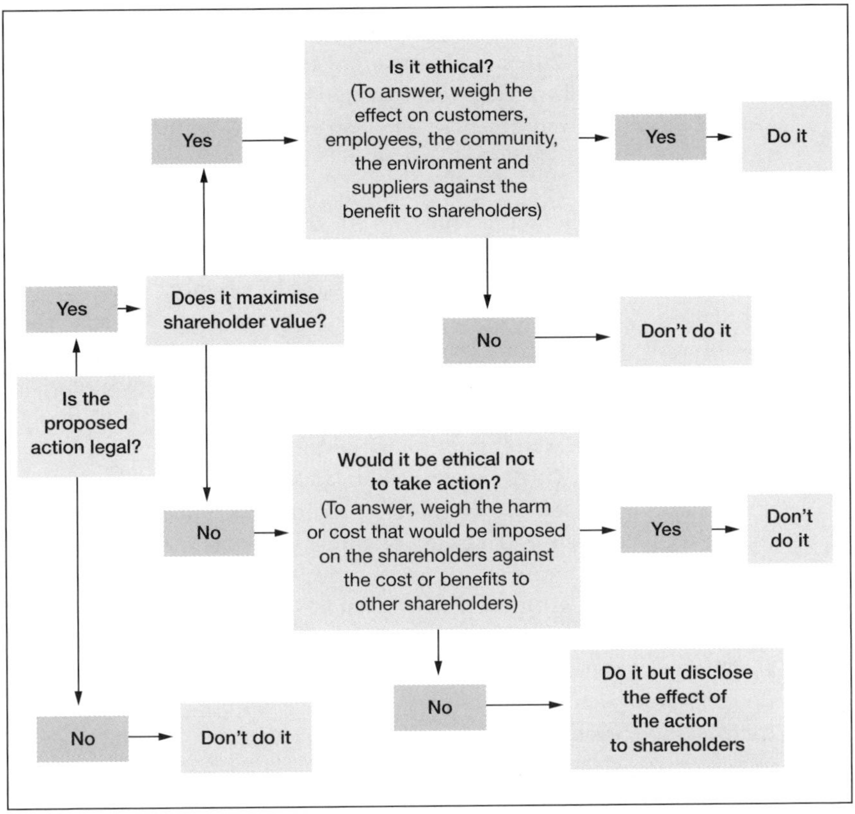

2.2 Proactive approach

Legally astute top management teams recognise that "[b]usiness corporations do not have legal problems. They have business problems where legal considerations may be more or less important, depending on the specific circumstances."[35] Taking a proactive approach fosters threat and opportunity identification, learning and experimentation, key processes in dynamic environments.[36] For example, a proactive strategy for reducing pollution and addressing other environmental matters that "anticipate[s] future regulations and social trends and design[s] or alter[s] operations, processes, and products to prevent (rather than merely ameliorate) negative environmental impacts" is a dynamic capability that can offer competitive advantage.[37] According to Nehrt,

---

35 Marshall Clinard & Peter C Yeager, *Corporate Crime* 20 (1980).

36 Teece, Pisano, & Shan, *supra* note 17.

37 J Alberto Aragón-Correa & Sanjay Sharma, 'A Contingent Resource-Based View of Proactive Corporate Environmental Strategy,' 28 *Academy of Management Review* 71, 73 (2003). See also William Q Judge & Thomas J Douglas, 'Performance Implications of Incorporating Natural Environmental Issues Into The Strategic Planning Process: An Empirical Assessment', 20 *Academy of Management Review* 1015, 1015 (1998); Robert D Klassen & D Clay Whybark, 'The Impact of Environmental Technologies on Manufacturing Performance', 42 *Academy of Management Review* 599, 599 (1999).

firms' ability to reduce pollution became a source of competitive advantage only after firms replaced the mindset of reducing pollution to meet government end-of-pipe restrictions with a search for ways to use environmentally friendly policies to create value.[38] General Electric's ecomagination campaign, designed to promote the development and sale of energy-efficient products and to reduce its own emissions, reduced expenses by more than $100 million and increased the revenues generated by its environmentally friendly products, such as hybrid locomotives and more efficient jet engines.[39]

Proactive strategies for dealing with the interface between a firm's business and the natural environment that went beyond environmental regulatory compliance were associated with improved financial performance.[40] The continuum of approaches to managing the interface between business and the natural environment that Aragon-Correa and Sharma describe – which ranges from a reactive posture that responds "to changes in environmental regulations and stakeholder pressures via defensive lobbying and investments in end-of-pipe pollution control measures" to proactive postures – can be extended to the interface between business and other aspects of the legal environment.[41]

Managers who view the law purely as a constraint, something to react to rather than to use proactively, will miss opportunities to use the law and legal tools to sense opportunities and threats, to seize opportunities, and to protect, marshal, leverage and redeploy tangible and intangible assets.[42] As Siedel explained: "law plays an important role in both reducing costs and creating value for your customers – by enabling you to offer either lower prices or products that provide unique benefits."[43] He provided examples from lawsuits dealing with product liability, workers' compensation, wrongful discharge, sexual harassment and environmental regulation to support this claim.[44]

Managers who fail to be proactive will also lose the benefits provided by strategically astute lawyers, who can help to drive business success.[45] As Bagley and Roellig explain, "the later a lawyer is brought into the planning of a transaction, the more likely it is that the lawyer will have to say 'no.' Anticipating this, business managers may provide counsel with a skewed set of facts in hopes of improving the

---

38 Chad Nehrt, 'Maintainability of First Mover Advantages When Environmental Regulations Differ Between Countries', 23 *Academy of Management Review* 77, 77 (1998).

39 Martin LaMonica, 'Newsmaker: Stirring GE's Ecomagination', CNET News.com, October 26 2007, available at http://news.cnet.com/Stirring-GEs-Ecomagination/2008-11392_3-6215496.html.

40 William Q Judge & Thomas J Douglas, 'Performance Implications of Incorporating Natural Environmental Issues Into The Strategic Planning Process: An Empirical Assessment', 20 *Academy of Management Review* 1015, 1015 (1998); Robert D Klassen & D Clay Whybark, 'The Impact of Environmental Technologies on Manufacturing Performance', 42 *Academy of Management Review* 599, 599 (1999).

41 Aragon-Correa & Sharma, *supra* note 37, at 73.

42 Bagley, *supra* note 16.

43 George J Siedel, *Using the Law for Competitive Advantage* 5 (2002).

44 See also George J Siedel & Helena Haapio, 'Using Proactive Law for Competitive Advantage', 47 *American Business Law Journal* 641, 656–57 (2010) (drawing parallels between the US literature on using law for competitive advantage and the European Proactive Law Movement, which "'[i]n addition to avoiding disputes, litigation and other hazards' ... 'seeks ways to use the law to create value, strengthen relationships and manage risk.'")

45 Bagley & Roellig, *supra* note 8.

likelihood of receiving the go-ahead."[46] To avoid this dynamic and promote not only compliant corporate behaviour but also value creation and capture, general counsel should act as strategic partners and encourage managers to take an active role in legal matters from the outset – that is, to be legally astute.[47]

2.3 Exercise of informed judgement

Legal astuteness requires the ability to exercise informed judgement. Law is not an exact science – legal rules are not applied formulaically. Seemingly minor changes in facts can result in dramatically different legal outcomes. Often, there is no clear precedent to serve as a guide. Dealing effectively with the uncertainties inherent in many decisions having legal aspects require the exercise of informed judgement. Legally astute managers – even those with formal legal training – do not purport to advise themselves on legal matters of importance. They appreciate the importance of selecting a true counsellor at law who combines knowledge of the black-letter law with judgement and wisdom. As (former Yale Law School Dean) Kronman explained: "wisdom is more than technical skill; it is the capacity to offer deliberative advice – that is, to go beyond merely supplying whatever means are needed to achieve the client's goals and to deliberate with the client about the wisdom of the client's ends."[48] Certain courses of action may be legal but not wise.[49]

2.4 Context-specific knowledge of the law and the application of legal tools

The non-lawyers on the top management team need context-specific knowledge of the law and the application of legal tools – that is, 'legal literacy'[50] – so they can communicate in a meaningful way with counsel. Just as "[a] person trained as a scientist may have a difficult time understanding the point of view of a lawyer",[51] top management teams lacking legal expertise cannot be expected to understand the legal subtleties underlying complex relationships and transactions in today's global economy. Managers and lawyers speak distinct professional dialects, further enhancing the potential for misunderstanding. To work together effectively, the lawyer and business leader must be able to understand what the other is concerned about; they must share a common vocabulary to "typify and stabilize experiences and integrate those experiences into a meaningful whole."[52]

For example, in what Warren Buffett of Berkshire Hathaway called "the most successful managerial performance in bankruptcy I've ever seen",[53] USG Corporation, manufacturer of Sheetrock® wall board and other building materials, successfully shed its asbestos liability pursuant to an orchestrated strategy that combined:

---

46 Constance E Bagley & Mark Roellig, 'General Counsel: Strategic Partners or Hired Guns?' in European Company Lawyers Association, *Company Lawyers: Independent by Design* (2014).

47 Bagley & Roellig, *supra* note 8.

48 Anthony T Kronman, *The Lost Lawyer* 132–33 (1995).

49 Bagley, *supra* note 8.

50 *Ibid.*

51 Richard L Daft & Robert H Lengel, 'Organizational Information Requirements, Media Richness and Structural Design', 32 *Management Science* 554, 564 (1986).

52 Andrew M Pettigrew, 'On Studying Organizational Cultures', 24 *Administrative Science Quarterly* 570, 575 (1979).

53 Karen Richardson, 'Years Into Filing, USG Is Smiling', *Wall Street Journal*, Feb 15, 2006.

- filing for bankruptcy under Chapter 11 so it could obtain a 'channelling injunction' whereby the plaintiffs suing for asbestos-related disease would be required to seek redress solely from a dedicated trust funded by USG and approved by 75% of the claimants;
- lobbying for federal legislation to create a multi-firm fund for the payment of asbestos personal injury claims in accordance with accepted medical standards for determining the existence and severity of asbestos-related disease;
- litigating dubious claims;
- a human resource strategy that valued both factory workers and up-and-coming managers;
- transparency with both investors and employees;
- a reputation for reliability and honest dealing with suppliers, customers and employees; and
- the ability to shift resources from primarily manufacturing Sheetrock® and other building materials to distributing other firms' products as well.[54]

USG emerged from bankruptcy five years after filing with a channelling injunction in effect pursuant to a reorganisation plan that was approved by 98% of the asbestos claimants and a shareholder committee led by Warren Buffett, whose holding company Berkshire Hathaway owned about 15% of USG's stock and back-stopped a $1 billion rights offering, with all debts paid in full with default interest, shareholder equity intact, and more than a 50% increase in revenues. Although USG chief executive Bill Foote conducted this 'orchestration'[55] and played a critical role lobbying for changes in the law, USG's success would not have been possible but for Foote's own personal knowledge of law and legal tools, and his close relationship with general counsel Stan Ferguson and other in-house lawyers along with the outside lawyers who helped to litigate the asbestos claims and advised on the bankruptcy proceedings. It also would not have been possible absent USG's ability to restructure its business to include counter-cyclical lines, such as distribution, and to grow the company through acquisitions.[56]

2.5 Strategically astute counsel

General counsel (also known as chief legal officers) perform a multiplicity of roles, including manager of the legal department, legal adviser and educator, negotiator, crisis manager and strategic planner.[57] They are "the 'Swiss army knife' of the legal profession."[58] Legally astute managers acknowledge the "right and responsibility [of

---

54 Constance E Bagley & Eliot Sherman, 'USG Corporation (A)', Harvard Business School Publishing Case No 807-090 (2007); Constance E Bagley & Eliot Sherman, 'USG Corporation (B)', Harvard Business School Publishing Case No 807-120 (2007); Constance E Bagley & Eliot Sherman, 'USG Corporation (C)', Harvard Business School Publishing Case No 807-121 (2007).

55 David J Teece, 'Dynamic Capabilities: Routines versus Entrepreneurial Action', 49(8) *Journal of Management Studies* 1395, 1397 (2012).

56 Bagley, *supra* note 16.

57 S H Duggin, 'The Pivotal Role of the General Counsel in Promoting Corporate Integrity and Professional Responsibility', 51 *St Louis University Law Journal* 989 (2007).

58 O S Simmons, 'The Under-Examination of In-House Counsel', 11(1) *Transactions: The Tennessee Journal of Business Law* 145, 146 (2009).

inside counsel] to insist upon early legal involvement in major transactions".[59] They call on their lawyers to play an active role in formulating the corporation's strategy as a whole rather than just bringing them in to serve as technical consultants after a legal problem has arisen or the management team has already decided what to do.[60]

The lawyers have to earn the respect and trust of the non-lawyers on the top management team to get a seat at the table from the outset.[61] Trust is a firm-specific relationship,[62] which cannot be readily recreated when a lawyer or manager leaves to join another firm.

Directors "expect their [chief legal officer] to be commercially aware and to combine this awareness with their legal knowledge and experience".[63] The firm's lawyers need to understand the firm's value proposition, resources, industry, customers, business plan and overall strategy. In short, the lawyers must be strategically astute.[64]

Legal advice needs to be business-oriented and tailored to the needs of each firm. Both internal and external counsel must be able to translate legal cases, regulations, briefs, memoranda and jargon into understandable business terms, concepts and communications.[65] As one company president put it: "The [general counsel] should make us aware of what we should be doing and tell us this in a straightforward manner, not in complex legal language."[66]

In environments in which a high degree of legal astuteness is needed, it is necessary to form what Clark and Wheelwright call 'heavyweight teams', comprising managers and in-house lawyers.[67] Unlike representatives governed by Graham Allison's notion of "where you stand depends on where you sit",[68] members of heavyweight teams do not just represent their functional group. Instead, they act as general managers with responsibilities for the success of the entire project.

Al Spies, the chief financial officer of US West, used to say: "I have no use for lawyers who talk in the third person. This is not about what you can do; this is about what we can do."[69] Indra Nooyi, PepsiCo's president and chief financial officer then its chief executive, encouraged the PepsiCo lawyers to use both their legal expertise and their business judgement when working with managers, stating: "We can't afford this separation of church and state."[70]

Bringing together individuals, such as lawyers and managers, from different

---

59 Abram Chayes & Antonia H Chayes, 'Corporate Counsel and the Elite Law Firm', 37 *Stanford Law Review* 277, 281 (1985).

60 Bagley, *supra* note 7.

61 Bagley & Roellig, *supra* note 8.

62 Jay B Barney & Mark H Hansen, 'Trustworthiness as a Source of Competitive Advantage', 15 *Strategic Management Journal* 175, 175 (1994).

63 KPMG, *supra* note 1, at 53.

64 Bagley and Roellig, *supra* note 8.

65 *Ibid.*

66 KPMG, *supra* note 1, at 10.

67 Kim B Clark & Steven C Wheelwright, 'Organizing and Leading Heavyweight Development Teams', *California Management Review*, Winter 1992, at 9.

68 See generally Graham Allison & Philip Zelikow, *Essence of Decision: The Cuban Missile Crisis* 307, 325–47 (2nd edn 1999) (explaining that the recommendations of key decision makers involved in the Cuban missile crisis were highly correlated with their functional responsibilities).

69 Quoted in Bagley & Roellig, *supra* note 8.

70 Quoted in Bagley, *supra* note 2, at 227.

'thought-worlds' may increase access to historical perspectives and multiple functional areas,[71] enhance problem solving by widening scanning activities,[72] and reduce group-think by prompting greater disagreement,[73] but at the cost of increasing team conflict as different people use their own specialised languages, images and stories.[74] It may also decrease interpersonal communication and reduce perceived effectiveness.[75]

Managers and lawyers employ distinct mental models,[76] which impedes their ability to take advantage of each other's area of professional expertise. While managers tend to focus on value creation and capture (ie, maximising the potential upside), lawyers tend to focus on risk management (ie, minimising the potential downside).[77]

To achieve internal integration, problem solving must be tightly connected across departmental boundaries,[78] and the costs associated with functional diversity must be overcome.[79] The team must find a way to garner the positive process effects of diversity and reduce the negative direct effects.[80] To bridge this kind of professional gap, managers and counsel must learn how to make explicit the key assumptions underlying their reasoning and engage in meaningful face-to-face interactions to address complex and conflicting issues.[81] Decisions in one function can then take into account the skills and concerns of the other function.

Although there are many benefits of involving in-house counsel at an early stage, there is a risk that involving the inside lawyers in shaping major transactions and corporate policy will result in their being co-opted by the non-lawyer managers.[82] The possible loss of professional objectivity is particularly acute "when the question of legality is tinged in shades of gray as opposed to black and white"[83] and when the in-house lawyers "actively seek to join the ranks of senior management and leave the legal department altogether."[84] As Bagley and Roellig explain:

---

71 Deborah G Ancona & David P Caldwell, 'Demography and Design: Predictors of New Product Team Performance', 3 *Organization Science* 321, 323 (1992).

72 Sara L Keck, 'Top Management Team Structure: Differential Effects by Environmental Context', 8 *Organization Science* 143, 143 (1997).

73 C Chet Miller, Linda M Burke & William H Glick, 'Cognitive Diversity Among Upper-Echelon Executives: Implications for Strategic Decision Processes', 19 *Strategic Management Journal* 39, 39 (1997).

74 *Ibid.*

75 Keck, *supra* note 72, at 145.

76 See generally Chris Argyris, *Reasoning, Learning and Action: Individual and Organizational* (1982).

77 Matthew Parsons, *Effective Knowledge Management for Law Firms* 107 (2004).

78 Clark & Wheelwright, *supra* note 67.

79 Ancona & Caldwell, *supra* note 71, at 336–38.

80 *Ibid* at 338.

81 Peter M Senge, *The Fifth Discipline: The Art and Practice of the Learning Organization* 6–7 (1990).

82 Of course, even outside counsel are susceptible to client capture. See Hugh P Gunz & Sally P Gunz, 'Client Capture and the Professional Service Firm', *American Business Law Journal* 685, 688 (2008) (explaining that capture occurs when "clients become so important to the professionals serving them that they lose the professional independence that is presumed by the profession to govern the relationship").

83 Deborah A DeMott, 'Colloquium Ethics in Corporate Representation: The Discrete Roles of General Counsel', 74 *Fordham Law Review* 955, 955 (2005).

84 Susanna M Kim, 'Dual Identities and Dueling Obligations: Preserving Independence in Corporate Representation', 68 *Tennessee Law Review* 179, 206 (2001). Auerbach argued that this potential loss of objectivity makes it inappropriate for inside counsel to be involved in strategic planning unless the plans are vetted by independent outside counsel. Joseph Auerbach, 'Can Inside Counsel Wear Two Hats?', *Harvard Business Review*, Sept–Oct 1984, at 80.

One of the most challenging roles of a general counsel is to have the courage and foresight to respond to the assertion, 'Everyone else does it this way,' with 'But we don't,' then to move the dialogue to a discussion of how the firm might otherwise accomplish the business objective with less risk. In fact, every business leader has an obligation to ensure that the enterprise does not make irrational business decisions (including breaking the law) and should appropriately escalate any decision that falls within this area.[85]

General counsel should be a trusted counsellor,[86] not a hired gun.[87] Strategically astute lawyers never lose sight of the fact that they are members of a profession that has at its core an obligation to uphold the law. As Dan Cooperman, Stanford Law School professor and former general counsel at Oracle and Apple, put it: "There is a professional duty not to be complicit in a criminal act, so if you believe that the corporation is violating the law, you really have no choice but to resign."[88]

The problem of co-option may make it necessary to ensure that certain in-house and outside lawyers are kept separate from the top management team so they can objectively evaluate the legality of proposed actions.[89] This important monitoring function is akin to that performed by internal and external auditors. Thus, it may be appropriate to locate in-house lawyers geographically near the business units for purposes of contract negotiation and most other legal matters, but to centralise regulatory functions, such as antitrust, environmental and securities law compliance, at the firm's executive headquarters to avoid undue identification with any given business unit.[90]

Nelson and Nielsen found that roughly 25% of the responding in-house counsel were members of senior management, based on their titles.[91] When the general counsel is a member of the top management team, it may be necessary to appoint an independent chief compliance officer or chief risk officer who vets all courses of action to ensure legal and regulatory compliance, especially in highly regulated industries.[92] Although it may be appropriate for the chief compliance officer or chief risk officer to report to the chief legal officer for routine matters, he should have direct access to and a reporting relationship with the audit committee as well.[93] For example, at MassMutual Financial Group, the chief compliance officer reports functionally to the chair of the audit committee, with administrative and informational (as defined by resolution) 'dotted-line' reporting to the general counsel.[94] In addition, Bagley and Roellig recommend that the audit committee be

---

85 Bagley & Roellig, *supra* note 8.

86 S M Linowitz & M Mayer, *The Betrayed Profession: Lawyering at the End of the Twentieth Century* 4 (1994).

87 Bagley & Roellig, *supra* note 46.

88 Quoted in R Lowe, 'Compliant Counsel', 8(2) *In-House Perspective* 13, 15 (2012).

89 Constance E Bagley, 'What's Law Got to Do With It? Integrating Law and Strategy', 47 *American Business Law Journal* 587 (2010).

90 *Ibid.*

91 Robert L Nelson & Laura B Nielsen, 'Cops, Counsel, and Entrepreneurs: Constructing the Role of Inside Counsel in Large Corporations', 34 *Law & Society Review* 457, 461 (2000).

92 Bagley & Roellig, *supra* note 47. See also Sung Hui Kim, 'The Banality of Fraud: Re-Situating the Inside Counsel as Gatekeeper', 74 *Fordham Law Review* 983, 998 (2005) (discussing the difficulty for inside counsel who are part of senior management to serve as adequate gatekeepers).

93 Bagley & Roellig, *supra* note 47.

94 *Ibid.*

involved in the selection, objectives, appraisal and compensation of the chief compliance officer/chief risk officer, with advice of a non-binding nature from the chief executive or general counsel, and, therefore, determine the officer's performance and prospects.[95]

This would appear to be a significant change from current practice. Although most of the 619 participants in the 2008 Chief Legal Officer Survey conducted by the Association of Corporate Counsel indicated that the 'next big issue' was "maintaining appropriate compliance programs and internal controls in the face of increasing economic concerns" and "doing more with less",[96] there is little evidence that firms are in fact creating internal legal compliance auditing functions independent from the general counsel or chief legal officer. Indeed, general counsel may be loath to give up the power inherent in his role as the top legal cop in the organisation.

3. The value of legal astuteness

Legally astute top management teams can:

- use formal contracts as complements to relational governance to reduce transaction costs[97] and strengthen relationships;
- protect, redeploy and enhance the realisable value of knowledge assets and other firm resources;
- use legal tools to create valuable options and combat risk/loss aversion and overconfidence bias;
- practise "strategic compliance management"[98] and thereby convert regulatory constraints into opportunities; and
- help shape the 'rules of the game'.

3.1 Using contracts to reduce transaction costs and strengthen relationships

The law makes it possible for parties to agree on their own private rules and will enforce those rules as long as they do not conflict with fundamental public policies embodied in the public rules. Managers who are highly skilled in managing contractual forms of governance, such as complete contingent claims contracts that specify the economic costs that will be imposed on parties engaging in opportunistic behaviour,[99] will have a competitive advantage over those who must use more costly immediate market forces of governance (such as equity joint ventures) or hierarchical forms of governance to protect against exchange vulnerabilities, such as moral hazard, adverse selection and hold-up.[100]

Relational norms, such as trust, can serve "as substitutes for complex, explicit

---

95 Bagley & Roellig, *supra* note 21.

96 'Corporate Counsel Face "Doing More With Less"', 17 *Corporate Counsel Weekly* (BNA) 133 (Apr 29, 2009).

97 For a discussion of transaction cost economics see Oliver E Williamson, *The Economic Institutions of Capitalism: Firms, Markets and Relational Contracting* (1985); Oliver E Williamson, *Markets and Hierarchies* (1975).

98 Bagley, *supra* note 2, at 50.

99 See Williamson (1985), *supra* note 97.

100 Jay B Barney & Mark H Hansen, 'Trustworthiness as a Source of Competitive Advantage', 15 *Strategic Management Journal* 175, 175 (1994).

contracts or vertical integration".[101] Indeed, certain relational governance experts "contend that formal contracts may even undermine a firm's capacity to develop relational governance",[102] by signalling distrust of the other party and thereby encouraging opportunistic behaviour.[103]

Poppo and Zenger used data on outsourcing relationships in information services during the early 1990s as evidence for their alternative argument that well-specified contracts may actually promote more competitive long-term, trusting exchange relationships.[104] Contrary to the assertion that formal contracts undermine relational governance, they argued: "The presence of clearly articulated contractual terms, remedies, and processes of dispute resolution as well as relational norms of flexibility, solidarity, bilateralism, and continuance may inspire confidence to cooperate in interorganizational exchanges."[105] Their research revealed that relational governance and contract customisation both directly and indirectly increased exchange performance as measured by satisfaction with the cost, quality and responsiveness of the outsourced service. This is consistent with one lawyer's statement that he was "sick of being told 'we can trust old Max' when the problem is not one of honesty but one of reaching an agreement that both sides understand".[106] Poppo and Zenger further found that increases in the level of relational governance were associated with greater levels of contractual complexity and that increases in the level of contractual complexity were associated with greater levels of relational governance.[107]

Conversely, poorly structured contracts can destroy value, as evidenced by Apple Computer's 1985 licence agreement with Microsoft Corporation, which gave Microsoft the right to use "the visual displays in Windows 1.0 and the named application programs [which embodied certain aspects of the Macintosh graphical user interface] in current and future software products."[108] When Microsoft released Windows 2.03, which more closely resembled the 'look and feel' of the Macintosh graphical user interface (GUI) than Windows 1.0, Apple sued Microsoft for infringing its copyrights on the Mac GUI. Microsoft asserted that the 1985 agreement entitled it to use all of the aspects of the Mac GUI embodied in Windows 1.0 in all future versions of its operating system. In response, Apple claimed that the 1985 agreement

---

101 Laura Poppo & Todd Zenger, 'Do Formal Contracts and Relational Governance Function as Substitutes or Complements?', 23 *Strategic Management Journal* 707, 707 (2002). See generally Benjamin Klein & Keith B Leffler, 'The Role of Market Forces in Assuring Contract Performance', 89 *Journal of Political Economy* 615 (1981); Charles Hill, 'Cooperation, Opportunism, and the Invisible Hand: Implications for Transaction Cost Theory', 15 *Academy of Management Review* 500 (1990); Jeffrey Dyer, 'Effective Interfirm Collaboration: How Firms Minimize Transaction Costs and Maximize Transaction Value', 40 *Strategic Management Journal* 687 (1997); Jeffrey Dyer & Harbir Singh, 'The Relational View and Cooperative Strategy and Sources of Interorganizational Competitive Strategy and Sources of Interorganizational Competitive Advantage', 23 *Academy of Management Review* 660 (1998).

102 Poppo & Zenger, *supra* note 101, at 707.

103 *Ibid* (citing Sumantra Ghoshal & Peter Moran, 'Bad for Practice: A Critique of the Transaction Cost Theory', 21 *Academy of Management Review* 13, 24, 27 (1996)); Stewart Macauly, 'Non-Contractual Relatives in Business: A Preliminary Study', 28 *American Sociological Review* 55, 64 (1963)).

104 Poppo & Zenger, *supra* note 101.

105 *Ibid* at 712. This makes sense given the difficulty of providing for all contingencies in a written contract for a strategic alliance. See Dent, *supra* note 5, at 290–92.

106 Macauly, *supra* note 103, at 58–59.

107 Poppo & Zenger, *supra* note 101, at 721.

108 *Apple Computer, Inc v Microsoft Corp*, 709 F Supp 925, 931–32 (ND Cal 1989).

was only "a license of the interface of Windows Version 1.0 as a whole, not a license of broken out 'elements' which Microsoft could use to create a different interface more similar to that of the Macintosh."[109]

The term 'visual display' was not defined in the agreement and the court declined to give it a specific, technical meaning. The court reasoned: "Had it been the parties' intent to limit the license to the Windows 1.0 interface, they would have known how to say so."[110] Of the 189 aspects of the Mac GUI that Apple claimed Microsoft had infringed, the court concluded that 179 were covered by the 1985 agreement.[111] Aside from Apple's use of a trash can for deleted files, the court ultimately concluded that none of the remaining aspects of the Mac GUI was protectable under the copyright laws.[112]

This was not the first time Microsoft chief executive Bill Gates had succeeded in negotiating highly favourable contract terms. Gates negotiated a contract with IBM that allowed Microsoft to retain the rights to MS-DOS, the operating system Microsoft designed for IBM's personal computer. In the words of a prominent software executive: "IBM thought they had Gates by the balls. He's just a hacker, they thought. A harmless nerd. What they actually had by the balls was an organism which has been bred for the accumulation of great power and maximum profit, the child of a lawyer, who knew the language of contracts and who just ripped those IBM guys apart."[113]

3.2 Protecting, redeploying and enhancing the value of knowledge assets and other firm resources

The sources of firm value and future growth opportunities are many and varied;[114] however, it is increasingly difficult to identify significant sources of firm value wherein legal rights are not important factors in realising that value. For example, intellectual property (IP) law provides managers with various techniques to realise the value of knowledge.[115] These include trademarks, copyrighting works, patenting inventions and processes, and protecting proprietary information as trade secrets. IP rights can differentiate products, erect barriers to entry, reduce costs and be a source of licensing revenues.

Brand-association trademarks, such as slogans, packaging, colours, scents and shapes, increase cash flow and decrease cash-flow variability.[116] Brand-association trademark activity is positively associated with return on assets, stock returns and Tobin's q (the ratio of a firm's market value to the replacement cost of its assets).[117]

Apple Inc coupled the innovative design of its iPod device with a well-executed

---

109 *Ibid.*
110 *Apple Computer, Inc v Microsoft Corp*, 717 F Supp 1428, 1430–32 (ND Cal 1989).
111 *Ibid* at 1435.
112 *Apple Computer, Inc v Microsoft Corp*, 799 F Supp 1006, 1041 (ND Cal 1992).
113 John Seabrook, 'A Reporter at Large: E-Mail from Bill', *New Yorker*, January 10 1994, at 48, 59.
114 See, eg, Carl W Kester, 'Today's Options for Tomorrow's Growth', *Harvard Business Review*, Mar–Apr 1984 (explaining that firms can use a variety of resources to create value and generate growth), at 153.
115 See Boualem Aliouat, 'Patents and Trademarks: From Business Law to Legal Astuteness', in *Legal Strategies: How Corporations Use Law to Improve Performance* 293 (Antoine Masson & Mary J Shariff, eds, 2010) (explaining how legally astute firms can use IP protection to increase realisable value).
116 Alexander Krasnikov, Saurabh Mishra & David Orozco, 'Evaluating the Financial Impact of Branding Using Trademarks: A Framework and Empirical Evidence', 73 *Journal of Marketing* 154, 161 (2009).
117 *Ibid.*

trademark strategy[118] and a copyright licensing strategy that avoided the pitfalls that had filled earlier entrants, such as MP3.com.[119] Apple registered both the iPod product name and the iPod product shapes as trademarks.[120] Unlike MP3.com, which made digital copies of the music on its customers' compact discs in reliance on what turned out to be an erroneous interpretation of the fair-use exemption,[121] like Spotify, Apple negotiated licensing contracts with the music copyright owners before offering digital downloads of their music.

Similarly, Bram Cohen, the developer of a new way to use the internet to transfer very large computer files, successfully negotiated a licensing agreement between his firm BitTorrent and Warner Brothers for the lawful peer-to-peer distribution of movies.[122] Cohen understood the importance of not promoting the use of his software for illegal purposes and hired as the firm's lawyer Clive Davis, who had represented the record and film industry and had a reputation for protecting their IP rights.

IP rights can be used both offensively to shut down a competing line of business (as happened when Polaroid used its patents to shut down Kodak's instant camera and film business)[123] and defensively as bargaining chips (as happened when Amgen and Chiron settled their interleukin-2 patent infringement case by giving each other cross-licences).[124] The founders of PrimeSense, an Israeli firm that had developed cutting-edge gestural human-computer interface technology, understood the critical importance of protecting the firm's proprietary technology.[125] After Apple refused to sign PrimeSense's nondisclosure agreement, which included a no-reverse-engineering clause, PrimeSense struck a deal with Microsoft. PrimeSense became Microsoft's original equipment manufacturer for the system-on-a-chip and certain optics used in Microsoft's X-Box Kinect, but only after Microsoft agreed not to appropriate PrimeSense's trade secrets or to attempt to reverse-engineer its product.[126] Because PrimeSense did not give Microsoft an exclusive licence to its technology, it kept aspects secret and its engineers continued to innovate by reducing the size of its product to the size of a pack of chewing gum while adding additional functionalities, the founders and their venture-capital investors were ultimately able to sell the firm as a whole to Apple in 2014 for roughly $350 million. Apple would have had access to PrimeSense's technology earlier had its lawyers and engineers been willing to be

---

118 David Orozco & James G Conley, 'Shape of Things to Come', *Wall Street Journal*, May 12 2008, at R6.

119 Constance E Bagley & Reed Martin, 'BitTorrent', Harvard Business School Case No 806–169 (2004).

120 Orozco & Conley, *supra* note 118, at R6.

121 *UMG Recordings, Inc v MP3.com, Inc*, 92 F Supp 2d 349, 352 (SDNY 2000). MP3.com had made digital copies of the music on its customers' compact discs, which customers could access from personal computers, using the internet, after demonstrating that they owned a copy of the music to be downloaded. The company argued that this 'space shifting' was protected fair use. The US District Court for the Southern District of New York rejected this argument and held MP3.com liable for direct infringement. *UMG Recordings*, 92 F Supp 2d at 352–53.

122 Constance E Bagley & Reed Martin, 'Warner Brothers and BitTorrent', Boston: Harvard Business School Case No 807-012 (2006).

123 Lawrence Ingrassia & James S Hirsch, 'Polaroid's Patent Case Award, Smaller than Anticipated, Is a Relief for Kodak', *Wall Street Journal*, October 15 1990, at A3.

124 Constance E Bagley, *Managers and the Legal Environment: Strategies for the 21st century* 387 (4th edn 2002).

125 Constance E Bagley & Reed Martin, 'PrimeSense Ltd', Yale School of Management Case No 12-023 (2012).

126 Constance E Bagley & Reed Martin, 'PrimeSense Ltd and the Microsoft Kinect', Yale School of Management Case No 13-016 (2013).

more flexible when first approached by PrimeSense about the firm's legitimate interests in protecting its proprietary technology.

IBM earned $1.5 billion in licensing fees and patent royalties in 2001.[127] Licensing both provided a way to capture the value of the discoveries that IBM did not have the ability to commercialise and distributed IBM's technology more broadly, thereby increasing its ability to influence the development of industry standards and protocols.[128]

Taken alone, IP rights are rarely sufficient to create sustained competitive advantage. They must be part of an ongoing stream of innovative products and processes. As Jay Walker, founder of Priceline.com, explained, no one piece of intellectual property will protect a firm from competitors.[129] Even firms with a strong product position must continually innovate.[130]

3.3 Creating options and combating decision-making biases

The law offers a variety of tools that legally astute managers can use to create valuable options[131] and overcome decision-making biases. An option is the right, but not the obligation, to defer a decision until a future date.[132] Examples include an option to purchase or lease real property, the right to terminate a joint venture, and securing co-investment rights in future venture-capital rounds.[133]

Managers suffer from a variety of decision-making biases when they have to make choices with imperfect information and under risk.[134] Legally astute managers skilled in the adoption and application of flexible legal rules (eg, choice of business entity) and the use of legal tools are better equipped to combat both overconfidence bias and risk/loss aversion, each of which can impede innovation.[135]

The excessive optimism inherent in overconfidence bias "leads to investment in low or negative return projects",[136] including the pursuit of litigation when settlement would be the wiser choice. For example, Texaco could have settled the tortious-interference-with-contract case brought by Pennzoil after Texaco bought Getty Oil for far less than the $10.5 billion awarded by the jury or the subsequent $3 billion Texaco had to pay to settle the case. The Texaco lawyers were so sure of victory on the merits, they did not deign to even put on a damages expert.[137] As a result, the only evidence of damages was testimony from the plaintiff's expert, who

---

127 Louis V Gerstner, *Who Says Elephants Can't Dance?* 149 (2002).
128 *Ibid.*
129 Michael J Roberts & Constance E Bagley, 'Priceline.com and Microsoft (B)', Harvard Business School Case No 802–82 (2001).
130 Priceline.com successfully sued Microsoft Corporation and Expedia for violating its patent on using bidder-driven commerce to sell airline seats, hotel rooms and other services. *Ibid.*
131 Bagley, *supra* note 7, at 386.
132 Real options theory posits that there is value inherent in the right to defer decisions characterised by uncertainty. See, eg, Bruce Kogut & Nalin Kulatilaka, 'Capabilities as Real Options', 12 *Organization Science* 744 (2001).
133 For a discussion of co-investment rights, see Constance E Bagley & Craig E Dauchy, *The Entrepreneur's Guide to Business Law* (3rd edn 2008).
134 D Kahneman & A Tversky, 'Prospect Theory: An Analysis of Decisions under Risk', 47(2) *Econometrica* 263–291 (1979).
135 Teece, supra note 14, at 1328.
136 *Ibid* at 1327.
137 James Kinnear, *The Man Who Wore the Star – Real-Time Perspectives on a Business Leader's Changing World* (2001).

testified that it would cost Pennzoil $7 billion to find an equivalent amount of oil to what it would have obtained had its agreement to acquire Getty been consummated. Had Texaco called its expert, he would have testified that the proper measure of damages was roughly $500 million – the amount of Texaco's overbid.

Another bias, namely risk/loss aversion:

> *can cause individuals to overly discount the possibility that an uncertain result will be positive, that is, to be overly timid.*[138] *The former head scientist at the Xerox Palo Alto Research Center (Xerox PARC) attributed Xerox's failure to reap the rewards of its researchers' path-breaking inventions, such as object-based computing, the computer mouse, and the Ethernet, to a corporate aversion to risk. Had Xerox patented its technology, it could have created an option to commercialize the technology itself, license it to another firm, or abandon it when the needs of the personal computer market became more clear.*[139]

Unlike Hitachi and other competitors that were unwilling to take the litigation risk, EMC Corporation decided to acquire VMware, a pioneer in x86 software virtualisation technology, even though VMware was embroiled in a patent infringement lawsuit with Microsoft at the time.[140] EMC's chief executive Joe Tucci and its general counsel Paul Dacier convinced the board of directors that the benefits of the acquisition outweighed the risks. This calculus was based in part on EMC's ability to use its own patents as bargaining chips, its own internal expertise litigating patent cases, its ability to limit its enterprise risk by doing a reverse triangular merger so VMware would be a separate subsidiary, and its relationship with Microsoft, which was both a competitor and a partner. About a year after the acquisition, Microsoft chief executive Steve Ballmer called Tucci proposing that both sides dismiss their claims because "friends do not sue friends". A company that EMC acquired in 2004 for roughly $635 million had market capitalisation of more than $43 billion on August 15 2014. (EMC spun off 20% of VMware's shares in an initial public offering in 2007; as of August 15 2014, EMC's 80% stake was worth roughly $34 billion, roughly 45% of EMC's total market capitalisation of $60 billion). Had EMC been unable to transform itself from primarily a commodity hardware manufacturer into a data solution provider, it would not be trading at its current multiple of roughly 24 times earnings.

Similarly, by subjecting the founders' shares to vesting and requiring approval by the preferred shareholders, voting as a class, for certain major transactions, such as the sale of assets outside the ordinary course of business or borrowing above a certain threshold amount, venture-capital investors preserve the right to modify the management team and the business plan as needed to reflect emerging realities, including technological discoveries.[141] Staged preferred stock investments both reduce the risk of failure and diminish the overconfidence that might accompany exposure to a novel, but not necessarily commercially viable, idea.

Properly advised corporate directors can make corporate investments, borrow

---

138 Kahneman & Tversky, *supra* note 134; D Kahneman & D Lovallo, 'Timid Choices and Bold Forecasts: A Cognitive Perspective on Risk Taking', 39(1) *Management Science* 17 (1993).

139 Bagley, *supra* note 14.

140 Constance E Bagley, C I Knoop & C I Lombardi, 'EMC Corp: Proposed Acquisition of VMware', Boston, Mass: Harvard Business School Publishing Case No 806-153 (2006).

141 Constance E Bagley & Craig E Dauchy, *The Entrepreneur's Guide to Business Law* (4th edn 2011).

money or complete acquisitions knowing that the business judgement rule will protect them from personal liability if the venture fails as long as they make informed and disinterested decisions in good faith.[142] As the Delaware Court of Chancery explained: "absent an allegation of interestedness or disloyalty to the corporation, the business judgment rule prevents a judge or jury from second guessing director decisions if they were the product of a rational process and the directors availed themselves of all material and reasonably available information."[143] These protections are "designed to allow corporate managers and directors to pursue risky transactions without the specter of being held personally liable if those decisions turn out poorly."[144]

3.4 Strategic compliance management

Failure to comply with the law can result in massive fines and penalties, imprisonment and, at the outer bounds, the demise of the firm. In 2015 five banks pleaded guilty to criminal price-fixing of LIBOR and other lending rates and agreed to pay billions in fines.[145] By August 2014 financial institutions had paid more than $95 billion to resolve criminal and civil suits arising out of the sale of faulty subprime mortgages and toxic securities backed by such mortgages.[146] GlaxoSmithKline paid $3 billion to resolve criminal and civil charges that it had promoted certain prescription drugs for uses not approved by the US Food and Drug Administration.[147] Raj Rajaratnam, head of Galleon Funds, was sentenced to prison for insider trading.[148] Regulators mandated the closing of the SAC Capital Advisors hedge fund after the firm was convicted of illegal insider trading.[149] In addition to the direct costs of sanctions (eg, fines and punitive damages) and the legal costs associated with litigation and appeals, illegality can divert funds from strategic investments, tarnish a firm's image with customers and other stakeholders, raise capital costs and reduce sale volume.[150] Convicted firms earned significantly lower returns on assets than unconvicted firms.[151] In the case of WorldCom, $200 billion of shareholder value was lost in fewer than 12 months, making it the largest corporate fraud in history.[152]

A firm with three or more violations is more likely to act illegally than a firm

---

142 Bagley, *supra* note 16.

143 *In re Citigroup Inc Shareholder Derivative Litigation*, 964 A 2d 106, 124 (Del Ch 2009).

144 *Ibid* at 125.

145 B Protess & M Corkery, 'Tempered Penalties for Guilty Pleas', *New York Times.Com/Dealbook*, May 14 2015.

146 B Protess & M Corkery, 'Bank of America Offers U.S. Biggest Settlement in History Over Toxic Mortgage Loans', *New York Times.Com/Dealbook*, August 6 2014.

147 US Dept of Justice, 'GlaxoSmithKline to Plead Guilty and Pay $3 Billion to Resolve Fraud Allegations and Failure to Report Safety Data' (2012), available at http://www.justice.gov/opa/pr/2012/July/12-civ-842.html (accessed August 15 2014).

148 'Ship of Knaves', *Economist*, June 1 2013.

149 P Lattman & B Protess, '$1.2 Billion Fine for Hedge Fund SAC Capital in Insider Case', *New York Times.Com/Dealbook*, November 4 2013.

150 Melissa S Baucus & David A Baucus, 'Paying the Piper: An Empirical Examination of Longer-Term Financial Consequences of Illegal Corporate Behavior', 40 *Academy of Management Review* 129, 139–41 (1997).

151 *Ibid.*

152 Richard Breedan, 'Restoring Trust', report to the Hon Jed S Rakoff, US District Court for the Southern District of New York, submitted in connection with the WorldCom bankruptcy proceeding on August 26 2003.

with only one.[153] In fact, three or more prior violations may be the best predictor of illegal behaviour.[154] Thus, compliance is path dependent.

To promote compliance, legally astute managers practise "strategic compliance management".[155] There are 10 steps:

1. Start with ethics and start with the 'tone at the top'.
2. Help shape the rules of the game.
3. Look for opportunities to convert constraints into opportunities.
4. Understand duties and anticipate risks.
5. Benchmark both accidents and violations and near-misses.
6. Avoid conflicts of interest and fully disclose.
7. Implement appropriate controls and processes.
8. Compete hard but fairly.
9. Educate all employees and distribute written policies.
10. Be prepared to deal with compliance failures.[156]

This is not a case of one size fits all, however. "Each firm must tailor its controls, processes, policies, and practices to the noncompliance risks that are most salient for that firm."[157]

Of course, it is not enough for top management to give lip service to the need for corporate compliance. "If an employee is held accountable for traditional corporate tasks whose performance will determine his success or failure, and is also urged to undertake social objectives on which his performance is not measured, the result is inevitable. Even the most well-intentioned employee will devote his time and attention to the functions on which his career progress depends."[158] In an opinion highly critical of the chief executive of Kidde plc, Judge Doumar commented after a jury found Kidde liable for misappropriating trade secrets belonging to X-It, a start-up that had developed an innovative fire escape ladder: "This case is the very epitome of corporate governance in the last decade of the twentieth century – where greed and the resultant pressure on corporate officers to produce results out of line with the actual value of the assets they manage turns those officers into vultures, devouring the very businesses which they are trying to enhance."[159]

3.5 Helping shape the public rules

Firms can help to shape the rules governing their conduct.[160] As Justice Stevens stated in his dissent in *Citizens United v Federal Election Commission*: "Business corporations must engage the political process in instrumental terms if they are to maximize shareholder value."[161]

153 Melissa S Baucus & Janet P Near, 'Can Illegal Corporate Behavior Be Predicted: An Event History Analysis', 34 *Academy of Management Journal* 9, 27 (1991).
154 *Ibid.*
155 Bagley, *supra* note 2, at 50.
156 *Ibid* at 47–50.
157 Bagley, *supra* note 16.
158 Drotning, *supra* note 31, at 259.
159 *X-It Products, LLC v Walter Kidde Portable Equipment, Inc*, 227 F Supp 2d 494, 546 (ED Va 2002).
160 G Richard Shell, *Make the Rules or Your Rivals Will* 1–31 (2004).
161 130 S Ct 876, 963 (2010).

Instead of just reacting to regulations after they are adopted, firms can propose rules that would be favourable to them by lobbying and engaging in other political activities.[162] Cummins Engine lobbied to prevent the US Environmental Protection Agency from backing away from tighter emission controls for diesel engines in part to capture the value of its investment in cleaner engines.[163] Yoffie and Bergenstein called on firms to replace *ad hoc*, reactive and issue-by-issue approaches to government regulation with a proactive entrepreneurial strategy for creating and sustaining political advantage.[164] Frederick W Smith, founder of Federal Express, explained that deregulation, "much of which we induced", was "a very big part of the FedEx story which has hardly ever been commented upon".[165] Instead of trying to weaken the Foreign Corrupt Practices Act of 1978, General Electric lobbied for a global ban on bribes,[166] thereby reducing the competitive disadvantage General Electric faced when competing for government contracts with non-US firms.

4. Degrees of legal astuteness

As depicted in Table 1, there are degrees of legal astuteness.

Table 1: Degrees of legal astuteness[167]

	Degree of legal astuteness		
Characteristics	**Low ——————————► High**		
Attitude of top management team towards legal dimensions of business	Not my responsibility		Important part of my job
Top management team view of lawyers	Necessary evil		Partner in value creation and risk management

continued on next page

162 Shell, *supra* note 160; Barry M Mitnick, *The Political Economy of Regulation: Creating, Designing and Removing Regulatory Forms* 434-42 (1980); Barry M Mitnick, 'The Strategic Uses of Regulation – and Deregulation', in *Corporate Political Agency: The Construction of Competition in Public Affairs* 67–78 (Barry M Mitnick ed, 1993) (arguing that firms can seek or exploit regulation to gain competitive advantage).

163 Geoff Paradise, 'Cummins up to Standards', *Daily Telegraph* (Sydney, Australia), April 20 2002, at 38.

164 David B Yoffie & Sigrid Bergenstein, 'Creating Political Advantage: The Rise of The Corporate Political Entrepreneur', *California Management Review*, Fall 1985, at 126–29.

165 Bloomberg Business, 'Fred Smith on the Birth of FedEx', September 19 2004, available at www.bloomberg.com/bw/ stories/2004-09-19/online-extra-fred-smith-on-the-birth-of-fedex.

166 Ben W Heineman Jr, *High Performance with High Integrity* 135–36 (2008).

167 Bagley, *supra* note 7, at 384.

168 *Ibid* at 383.

	Degree of legal astuteness		
Characteristics	**Low →**		**High**
Frequency of general counsel contact with chief executive	Low		High
Flow of business information and legal queries	On a discrete issue-by-issue basis		Ongoing
General counsel is member of top management team	No		Yes
Top management team approach to legal issues	Reactive		Proactive
Involvement of top management team in managing legal aspects of business	Hands off		Hands on
Top management team approach to regulation	Do minimum to comply		Exceed regulatory requirements as a result of operational changes that increase realisable value
Involvement of lawyers in strategy formation	Low		High

continued on next page

	Degree of legal astuteness		
Characteristics	**Low → High**		
Involvement of managers in resolving business disputes	Low		High
Involvement of managers in contract negotiation	Low		High
Involvement of lawyers in striking deals	Low		High
Legal literacy of managers	Low		High
Business acumen of lawyers	Low		High

"Firms that attain a degree of legal astuteness that 'fits' with their strategic posture and their external environment should realize greater value from this managerial capability than those who do not."[168]

5. An integrating framework for understanding law and strategy

Firms do business within a broader societal context, which affects firm resources,[169] the value proposition and various activities in the value chain,[170] the competitive environment,[171] public law,[172] and thus the options available to the top management team.[173] Society grants rights and powers to private firms, which society can revoke if

169 Bagley, *supra* note 7.

170 Michael E Porter, 'How Competitive Forces Shape Strategy' in Michael E Porter, *On Competition* 21 (1996); Bagley, *supra* note 16.

171 Michael E Porter & Mark R Kramer, 'Strategy and Society: The Link Between Competitive Advantage and Corporate Social Responsibility', *Harvard Business Review*, Dec 2006, at 78 (societal conditions form a key part of the competitive context and affect the firm's ability to improve productivity and to execute strategy over the long term). See generally Michael E Porter, *Competitive Strategy: Techniques for Analyzing Industries and Competitors* 3–33 (1980); Shell, *supra* note 160, at 1–31 (2004).

172 Brady Dennis, 'Obama Ushers in New Financial Era', *Washington Post*, July 22 2010, at A13.

173 Christine Oliver, 'Sustainable Competitive Advantage: Combining Institutional and Resource-Based Views', 18 *Strategic Management Journal* 697, 699 (1997) (conformity to social expectations contributes to organizational success and survival).

174 See, eg, Donna J Wood, 'Corporate Social Performance Revisited', 16 *Academy of Management Review* 691 (1991).

firms do not act responsibly.[174] As Tom Stephens, chief executive of Manville Corporation put it, when explaining Manville's decision to add labels warning of the potential carcinogenic effect of fiberglass: "The laws of society are more powerful than any law that Congress can put on the books. Woe to any businessman who doesn't read the law of society and understand them."[175]

Law and organisations are "endogenously coevolutionary".[176] Public laws will change both in response to firm conduct – especially unethical behaviour or managerial misconduct – and in response to the firm's lobbying and other political activities.[177] For example, conduct by Goldman Sachs and other investment banks involved in the meltdown of the subprime mortgage market contributed to the passage of the Dodd-Frank Wall Street Reform and Consumer Protection Act of 2010, the most sweeping financial reform since the Great Depression,[178] and to the tighter banking rules imposed by Basel III.

The systems approach to law and strategy, depicted in Figure 2,[179] builds on Cohen and Cyert's characterisation of the firm and the environment as "parts of a complex interactive system"[180] and rejects the false dichotomy in the traditional literature between the market and nonmarket environments of business.[181] The unit of analysis is the top management team, "one of the most critical resources for a successful corporate strategy",[182] which is embedded within the societal context of business. The top management team defines the value proposition and selects and performs the activities in the value chain, while also helping to shape the rules of the game, the competitive environment and the resources of the firm.

---

175 William Glaberson, 'Of Manville, Morals and Mortality', *New York Times*, October 9 1988, at F1.

176 Lauren B Edelman & Mark C Suchman, 'The Legal Environments of Organizations', 23 *Annual Review of Sociology* 479, 501 (1997).

177 See, eg, Lee Preston & James E Post, *Private Management and Public Policy: The Principle of Public Responsibility* 12 (1975).

178 Brady Dennis, 'Obama Ushers in New Financial Era', *Washington Post*, July 22 2010, at A13.

179 An earlier version of this figure appeared in Bagley, *supra* note 89.

180 Kalman J Cohen & Richard M Cyert, 'Strategy: Formulation, Implementation, and Monitoring', 46 *Journal of Business* 349, 352 (1973).

181 See, eg, David Baron, *Business and its Environment* 2 (2003). Baron defines 'market environment' as encompassing "those interactions between firms, suppliers, and customers that are governed by markets or private agreements such as contracts". *Ibid.* In contrast, the non-market environment "encompasses those interactions between the firm and individuals, interest groups, government entities, and the public that are intermediated not by markets but by public and private institutions." *Ibid.* Non-market issues of importance to firms include "environmental protection, health and safety, technology policy, regulation and deregulation, human rights, international trade policy, legislative politics, regulation and antitrust, activist pressures, media coverage of business, stakeholder relations, corporate social responsibility, and ethics." *Ibid.* Baron proposed a framework for 'non-market strategy' that looks at the impact of government on business separately from market forces and then attempts to develop integrated strategies that explicitly address both market and non-market relationships. David P Baron, 'Integrated Strategy: Market and Nonmarket Components', *California Management Review*, Winter 1995. For a literature review, see Jean J Boddewyn, 'Understanding and Advancing the Concept of "Nonmarket"', 42 *Business & Society* 297 (2003).

182 Mark Shanley & Margaret Peteraf, 'Deploying, Leveraging, and Accessing Resources Within and Across Firm Boundaries: Introduction to the Special Issue', 25 *Managerial & Decision Economics* 291, 293 (2004). See generally Donald E Hambrick & Phyllis A Mason, 'Upper Echelons: The Organization as a Reflection of its Top Managers', 9 *Academy of Management Review* 193 (1984) (positing that organisations are a reflection of their top management team); Mason A Carpenter, Marta A Geletkanycz & William Gerard Sanders, 'Upper Echelons Revisited: Antecedents, Elements, and Consequences of Top Management Team Composition', 30 *Journal of Management* 749 (2004) (reviewing research on upper echelons perspective).

Figure 2: The systems approach to law and strategy

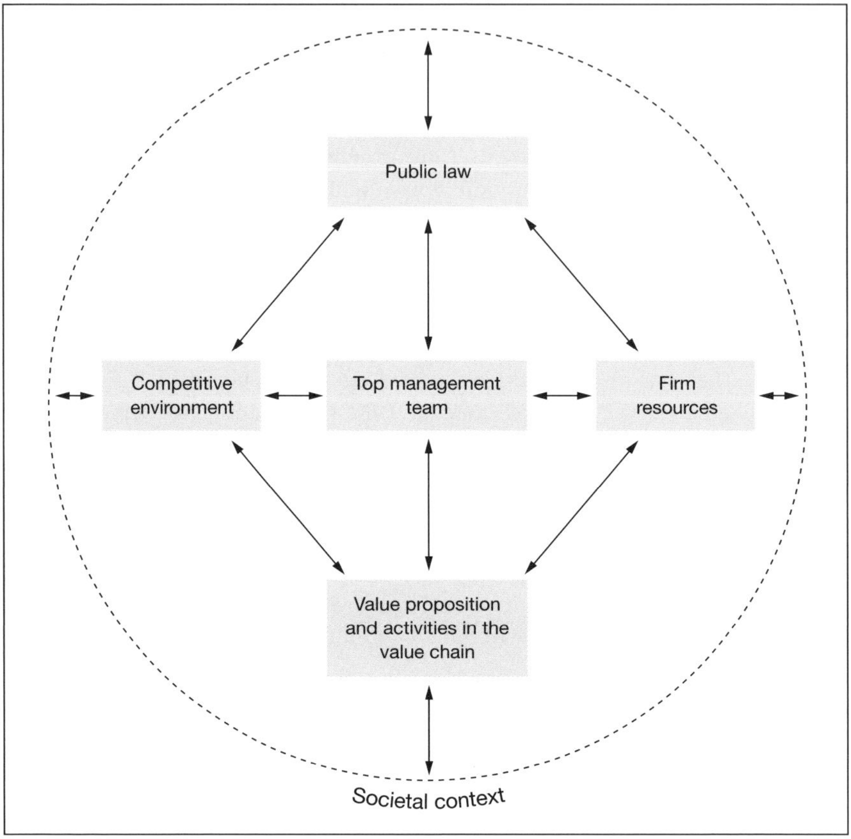

6. Conclusion

Law is more than a force that constrains managers and their firms. Properly harnessed by a legally astute management team advised by strategically astute lawyers, the ability to manage the legal aspects of business actively can be a source of sustained competitive advantage. Legal astuteness requires: a set of value-laden attitudes; a proactive approach; the ability to exercise informed judgement when managing the legal and business aspects of business; context-specific knowledge of the law and the appropriate use of legal tools; and strategically astute lawyers. Legally astute managers can use both the ethical business leader's decision tree and the systems approach to law and strategy to develop and execute an integrated strategy that embeds the top management team in a dynamic societal system that includes not only the firm's resources and competitive environment, but also its value proposition and value chain, public law and the societal context.

Strategy and the leveraging of legal resources

Robert C Bird
University of Connecticut

1. Introduction

Strategy is one of the primary mechanisms by which firms gain a competitive position in the marketplace. Strategy helps to generate superior value that cannot be easily replicated by a competitor.[1] As much as business scholars have investigated the question of strategy, the notion of law as a source of competitive advantage has been underdeveloped – even though chief executives may spend 5% to 25% of their time dealing with legal issues.[2] As "the last great untapped source of competitive advantage",[3] the legal environment of business is a major force that shapes how firms compete in a competitive marketplace.[4]

This chapter looks at how firms can turn legal resources into strategic advantages. Firms use five discrete behaviours to interact with legal resources and the legal environment. Each behaviour is examined, and the limitations and opportunities of each explored. This chapter also shows how more sophisticated legal strategies can yield substantial benefits to the organisation.

2. The strategic legal behaviour of firms

While law–business collaboration has been improving over time, the fields of law and business remain unnecessarily disconnected. Each field may perceive the other as insufficiently knowledgeable about the other's discipline. A manager may consider the legal department as little more than a shield from litigation and an intermediary with regulators that is detached from the process of day-to-day management of the firm. In turn, lawyers may not fully appreciate the business implications of their legal advice or fully engage with non-legal issues. Lawyers may also not fully appreciate what business strategy entails, considering strategy to be simply a means of improving internal processes or increasing output. An overly cautious point of view can lead lawyers easily to dismiss newly proposed strategies since these may seem overly risky to them and they cannot counterbalance this risk against the value that management expects to gain from them. Such situations have created a poor perception in the minds of management. A study of small business owners about the

1 Michael E Porter, 'What is Strategy?', *Harvard Business Review*, Nov–Dec 1996, at 61, 62–64.
2 Paul A Allen, 'Introduction To How To Keep Your Company Out of Court 12' (Paul A Allen ed, 1984); George J Siedel, 'Six Forces and the Legal Environment of Business: The Relative Value of Business Law among Business School Core Courses', 37 *American Business Law Journal* 717, 729 (2000).
3 Larry Downes, 'First, Empower All the Lawyers', *Harvard Business Review*, Dec 2004, at 19, 19.
4 O Lee Reed *et al*, *The Status of Law in Academic Business Study: 1998 Report of the President's Task Force* (1998).

legal function found that the owners described lawyers as "arrogant", "conservative", "authoritative", and "intimidating".[5]

Today, managers across companies view their legal resources and the legal environment with substantially different attitudes. Some managers perceive law as an unnecessary impediment to their achievement of firm goals. Other managers look at the law as a kind of checklist to be satisfied. Still others willingly partner with their legal resources in order to incorporate legal issues into broader business strategies. These attitudes coalesce into five discrete patterns of behaviour. An avoidance approach represents reactions to legal rules that evade legal requirements and detach law from the strategic direction of the firm. Compliance and prevention approaches pursue conformance with legal rules, with prevention doing so through adapting business practices. Advantage and transformation utilise law as a source of competitive advantage and use legal resources to reinforce the firm's long-term strategic goals.

While it may be easy to interpret these strategies as always presenting a choice between better or worse options, the actual environments that firms find themselves in determine which options are ideal for a company. Firms may also have different views on how to deal with legal issues and how that will affect their performance. Some of these differences may lie in regulatory controls that are harsher in one field of business than another, while others may reflect the presence or absence of public scrutiny that influences a firm's motivation to conform to legal rules. Finally, it should be noted that the selection of a strategy does not necessarily mean the formulation of an ethical business practice. For example, a firm that chooses avoidance over compliance may succeed in the short term, but will suffer long-term detriments to the organisation and flout basic ethical standards of what may be expected of a modern organisation.

As with any other plan, a legal strategy cannot remain inflexible. Rather, it must be open to adaptation as the environment changes, new rivals appear or certain facets of the legal environment change or are better understood. The development of a legal strategy over time is likely to be unique for each firm, marked by stops and starts, reassessments and even devolution to a simpler approach. Furthermore, the same strategy may not be viable for each department or division of an enterprise. While an internal audit department may emphasise compliance as its primary goal, a unit whose responsibility is management of intellectual property may place a greater emphasis on innovative legal strategies. Thus, while a firm may have an enterprise-level posture towards the legal environment, there may be multiple approaches to legal strategy occurring concurrently within a single organisation.

3. The five paths of legal strategy

3.1 Stage one: Avoidance

Avoidance is characterised by seeing legal requirements as obstacles to a firm's

5 Milo Geyelin, 'More Law Schools Are Teaching Students Value of Assuming Clients' Point of View', *Wall Street Journal*, September 17 1991, at B1.

development. Firms practising avoidance explore ways of circumventing legal rules. Managers in an avoidance enterprise generally have indifferent or negative attitudes towards the law. The legal environment may be seen as simply a barrier to business and with no real purpose. Managers may not believe that legislators who draft laws understand the competitive position in which they must survive. Laws may seem restrictive for no apparent reason other than to employ lawyers. As a result, legal issues are dealt with only when outside pressures – such as regulation or lawsuits – force the company's hand. Avoidance is generally not a strategy, but a tactic to neutralise fundamental legal obligations and skirt regulatory mandates without incurring regulatory sanction.

A significant rationale for avoidance is the reduction of costs. An aggressive pursuit of such cost reduction can lead to unethical practices and poor treatment of a firm's workforce. This can be particularly acute when regulations are weakly enforced or violations incur low penalties. The past behaviour of the McWane Corporation, an Alabama company operating pipe foundries in the United States and Canada, typifies how an avoidance perspective on law can negatively impact the enterprise.

McWane aggressively reduced its workplace safety budget in order to cut costs.[6] The primary goal of safety managers was not to ensure their fellow workers' safety, but rather to resist supervision and oversight from external regulatory authorities.[7] For example, in one of the numerous fatal injuries suffered at McWane plants during this period an employee died while working at the bottom of an elevator shaft. The company was fined $12,500 by the Occupational Safety and Health Administration (OSHA) – the US federal regulatory agency primarily charged with enforcement of workplace health and safety. However, a manager fought with OSHA to reduce the fine to $4,500.[8] He further commented that the practice at McWane was, "Don't tell anybody anything, especially if they're going to do the testing ... I mean, you don't convict yourself. Let them do it, that's what they get paid for."[9] A former OSHA administrator added, "[McWane] consider[s] OSHA a mosquito. That they'd rather pay the fines than bring their plants into compliance. That they think the law is so ineffective that it's more profitable for them to take the risk by not having safety programs in place than to comply with the law."[10]

This egregious avoidance of legal obligations paid off for McWane as the company remained competitive despite attracting more safety violations than all of its competitors combined. This included injuries to thousands of workers and even amputations in some cases.[11] However, this practice eventually caught up with McWane when it became the target of aggressive enforcement actions by the Department of Justice. Under pressure from government and the media, McWane

6 See 'A Dangerous Business', online interview with Lowell Bergman, http://discuss.washingtonpost.com/zforum/02/r_tv_frontline011003.htm Jan 10, 2003; Sidney A Shapiro and Randy Rabinowitz, 'Voluntary Regulatory Compliance in Theory and Practice: The Case of OSHA', 52 *Administrative Law Review* 97 (2000); 'Frontline: A Dangerous Business' (PBS television broadcast January 9 2003), transcript available at www.pbs.org/wgbh/pages/frontline/shows/workplace/ etc/script.html

7 Frontline, *supra* note 6.

8 *Ibid.*

9 *Ibid.*

10 *Ibid.*

11 *Ibid.*

changed its practices, taking safety issues more seriously and entering into more positive relationships with regulators. A number of managers were fired and workers reported positive changes at their factories. There is now evidence that McWane would no longer be considered an example of an avoidance enterprise.[12]

McWane's conduct was particularly egregious. However, not all avoidance practices are necessarily illegal. For example, firms may utilise regulatory loopholes to avoid paying taxes or shouldering obligations. Even if the spirit of the rule intends regulation, the letter of the rule may have been drafted in such a way that it enables avoiding the obligation. A company may reduce its tax burden by engaging in various activities that only superficially meet the reasons for tax reduction. Another option may involve – with the introduction of a new regulation – delaying implementation as long as possible.

Michael Porter has chosen the term 'operational effectiveness'[13] to describe a firm's ability to outperform its competitors in certain areas. However, operational effectiveness is not the same as strategy. The limitation of operational effectiveness is that it can be easily imitated by rivals. This can occur in the legal discipline, whereby a new interpretation of law enables a relaxation of compliance resources. While such an interpretation can bring value to a firm, it will not be long before other firms learn of the interpretation and apply it to their own enterprises, thus neutralising the advantage. Furthermore, in the case of illegal activity, regulatory authorities may promptly halt the practice and apply sanctions. As such, the optimal route is to implement a practice that competitors cannot easily imitate.

Operational effectiveness may lead to a type of arms race, in which one company creates an advantage that will soon be copied by its competitors. When other competitors increase their operational effectiveness in ways that are observable and applicable to rivals, such rivals will quickly follow. These innovations advance the best practices of the industry, but do not necessarily enable individual organisations to outflank rivals over the long term.

3.2 Stage two: Compliance

Unlike an avoidance firm, which may deliberately ignore legal rules because of a fundamental disregard for the purpose and function of law, a compliance firm will generally pursue adherence to the letter and spirit of legal obligations.[14] A compliance firm may not necessarily embrace regulation, but it should perceive the legal environment as a necessary cost of doing business in a free and fair market. Compliance firms meet the minimum requirements of the law. Much like avoidance, compliance firms envision the legal department's main role as shielding the firm

12 PBS Frontline, 'Frontline: A Dangerous Business Revisited', www.pbs.org/wgbh/pages/frontline/mcwane/

13 Porter, *supra* note 1, at 61–64.

14 The use of the term 'compliance' in this chapter refers to compliance in the general sense of conforming to required government rules. It does not specifically intend to describe only the compliance function in firms as led by a chief compliance officer or other executive. Alternatively, the term 'conformance' could be used to describe this stage, in order to reduce confusion with the current use of 'compliance' as a specific function in the enterprise led by a chief compliance officer. In spite of the possible definitional confusion, an application of the five stages of legal strategy to the compliance function is an intriguing possibility. See Thomas R Fox, 'The Strategic Use of Compliance', *FCPA Compliance and Ethics Blog*, (Nov 21, 2014), https://tfoxlaw.wordpress.com/2014/11/21/the-strategic-use-of-compliance/

from liability. However, unlike avoidance, compliance is seen as necessary and justified. The cost of resources allocated to conform to the law does not generally create incentives to circumvent legal obligations.

Compliance firms rely on legal counsel and legal staff to provide guidance on how to adhere to legal rules. Rather than being called upon only in cases of emergency, legal counsel are steady advisers that maintain management's conservative approach to conforming with the rules of their business environment. There may be a parallel co-existence, but not necessarily a partnership, between managers and lawyers in compliance firms. Managers may delegate the task of establishing codes of conduct to attorneys without close supervision. The legal department, in turn, may present rules that mandate conformance to law that are either excessively legalistic or indifferent to a firm's broader strategic goals. Thus, compliance firms may not view in-house counsel as strategic partners.

A compliance culture may arise from the perception that laws are essentially immutable and inflexible. Such firms may adopt a checklist approach to legal rules and not be exposed to managers who understand the law more dynamically. Managers may also pursue a compliance culture in order to minimise their own exposure to liability. Should a manager find himself in court because of corporate misconduct or criminal activity, the severity of the sentence may be influenced by whether compliance systems had been put in place. This also extends to cases where organisational or employee misconduct may lead to managers becoming liable for failing to impose such a system. Awareness of such implications may make conforming with rules a high priority – a practice that is certainly not harmful to the manager or the firm. However, the compulsion to comply under risk of sanction may obscure value-added opportunities embedded in legal rules, leaving strategic opportunities underutilised because of the hyper-focus on averting sanction.

Firms practising avoidance have an incentive to keep information about themselves closely guarded, in case indications about their behaviour become public. Information about compliance companies, however, is more widely available. Among the latter is Intel, one of the world's leading microprocessor producers. Intel is influential not only because of its influence on the personal computer market, but also because of its impact on smartphones, tablets and a host of other high-end electronics.[15] Intel has long been vulnerable to potential antitrust liability, and in the early 2000s it pursued an active compliance programme with the goal of minimising the kind of antitrust litigation that has plagued firms such as Microsoft and AT&T.

For Intel, this was described as "the world's best antitrust compliance program".[16] It consisted of training all relevant employees in antitrust law and regulations, ranging from the executive level down to a majority of the employees outside of manufacturing. The training programmes covered not only the legally clear rules about such issues as price fixing or exclusive contracts, but also murkier areas such as tied sales and technical cooperation. It should also be noted that this training was

15 David B Yoffie and Mary Kwak, 'Playing by the Rules: How Intel Avoids Antitrust Litigation', *Harvard Business Review*, June 2001, at 119, 119.

16 *Ibid* at 120.

not a one-time deal, but rather was followed up by later programmes providing in-depth information relevant to certain departments, such as informing product groups about intellectual property rights.

Furthermore, the legal department at Intel was given the authority to imitate actual investigations by authorities. Without warning, email, electronic storage and paper files could be seized. Managers would be questioned about their conduct arising from the information seized that potentially showed poor compliance. This high-powered monitoring[17] served to educate managers about the value of rigorously complying with regulations.

As with some avoidance practices, compliance produces operational effectiveness for the firm. However, though initially valuable, such practices can be imitated by competitors. Advantages gained may be neutralised over time. Compliance, however, benefits from a certain 'fit' between the legal and non-legal interests of the enterprise. The actions of attorneys and managers become consistent with one another, increasing the possibility of high-level substantive interaction and collaboration. This is known as a first-order fit: a firm's legal practices are consistent with the overall strategy of the firm.[18] In practice, it means that efforts within the company are consistent and strive towards the same goal rather than interfering with each other. It also allows coordinated strategies to be developed that can be better understood by employees as well as customers.

Although compliance may seem to be a relatively maintenance-free practice, firms must be vigilant to ensure their actions continue to conform to established legal rules. In 2009 the European Commission found that Intel unlawfully excluded competitors from the marketplace by using its dominant position in the market for central processing units.[19] Intel used its 80% market share to offer rebates to original equipment manufacturers on the condition that they agreed to purchase all or nearly all of their central processing units from Intel. Intel also paid a European computer retailer to sell exclusively computers that utilised Intel central processing units. Intel was assessed a fine of more than €1 billion for driving out its rival AMD from the European market in violation of European competition law.[20] The fine is the largest ever levied for a breach of competition law in Europe. Even the most laudatory compliance practices cannot guarantee behaviour that stops substantial regulatory action.

A firm that conforms to legal rules should keep itself relatively free from regulatory scrutiny. This is certainly a laudable and valuable goal, as government sanctions from non-compliance can impose substantial costs and be a public relations problem. From a strategic perspective, the value of conforming with the law without going further can remain transitory. What enables a firm's strategy to have more long-term value is when the legal measures are more and more closely

17 Donald C Langevoort, 'Resetting the Corporate Thermostat: Lessons from the Recent Financial Scandals About Self-Deception, Deceiving Others and the Design of Internal Controls', 93 *Georgetown Law Journal* 285, 315 n106 (2004).

18 Porter, *supra* note 1, at 71.

19 Paul Jones, 'American Antitrust Jurisprudence Applied to *European Commission v Intel*', 7 *Brigham Young University International Law and Management Review* 52, 52–54 (2010).

20 Liam Tung, 'Intel Loses Fight Against €1bn EU Antitrust Fine', June 12 2014, available at www.zdnet.com/article/ intel-loses-fight-against-eur1bn-eu-antitrust-fine/

interlocked with the business practices of the rest of the company. The following stage – prevention – introduces such a practice.

3.3 Stage three: Prevention

Much like compliance firms, prevention companies seek to reduce the risk of legal exposure from their operations. Yet the difference lies in the fact that prevention companies are more likely to rely on legal requirements to reinforce and advance business goals. Compliance is about ensuring that practices conform to established standards. By contrast, prevention focuses on implementing initiatives that reduce the chances of improper conduct happening in the first place. Prevention firms develop business practices to cope with legal problems. Employees in a prevention climate will be empowered to monitor their own conduct and ensure that measures are in place to prevent mistakes.

One example is Home Depot, which during its early years of operation had a decentralised and non-bureaucratic management style.[21] This style may have been useful for a rapidly growing enterprise, but it left the organisation without a legal strategy.[22] Hiring and promotion issues were handled as executives felt intuitively appropriate and primarily targeted males from the home repair field. Benevolent though their practices were intended to be, they were entrenched in an avoidance approach with little concern for legal or diversity issues.

As such, the accusation of gender discrimination in training, hiring, promotion and assignments in a class action suit was a more or less a logical consequence.[23] The female employees of Home Depot advancing the lawsuit argued that the male-dominated corporate culture sidelined women and kept them from being promoted to better positions. Before a trial was to begin, the parties reached a settlement agreement that would ensure personnel decisions were not made subjectively or influenced by stereotypes.[24]

Had Home Depot remained in avoidance mode, it might have tried to exploit loopholes. Had the company chosen compliance, following the consent decree would have been the end of its efforts. Instead, Home Depot chose to implement a preventive measure, namely an automated hiring and promotion system called the job preference process or JPP. With a computer telephone system installed inside the stores, anyone could apply for a position fitting their qualifications or interests, whether employee or outside applicant. The JPP was required to be used during hiring and promotion, and managers had to select at least three candidates. According to one source, "the JPP was equivalent to Home Depot's drug test – the company's only absolute rule: Do this or you are fired."[25]

---

21 Susan Sturm, 'Second Generation Employment Discrimination: A Structural Approach', 101 *Columbia Law Review*, 458, 509 (2001).

22 Ram Charan, 'Home Depot's Blueprint for Cultural Change', *Harvard Business Review*, April 2006, at 60, 60.

23 *Butler v Home Depot, Inc*, case C-94-4335 SI, 1996 WL 421436 (ND Cal January 25 1996).

24 Sturm, *supra* note 21, at 511–12. The full consent decree is presented in *Butler v Home Depot, Inc*, case C-95-2182 ST, 1997 US Dist LEXIS 16296 (ND Cal 1997).

25 Sturm, *supra* note 21, at 516 (citing interview with Fay Wilson, Senior Vice President, Value Initiatives, Home Depot (July 5 2000)).

As a result, the pool of potential candidates grew and the male-dominated bias was minimised. The JPP system also encouraged advancement of candidates who would otherwise have been allocated to lower-skilled positions. For example, a woman applying as a cashier, even though she had 10 years of experience in home repairs, was hired as a building materials sales associate because of the JPP highlighting that experience. The system was so successful at effectively allocating skills to positions that it was eventually used throughout the organisation.

With a first-order fit between legal practice and organisational strategy, prevention companies can run their business smoothly and consistently. As they meet legal requirements from the start, less investment is needed in handling litigation, while regulatory authorities only tangentially impact the firm's operations.

While this seems similar to compliance companies, there is a difference in that prevention firms establish a business advantage by turning their legal resources into a strategic benefit. The prevention measures improve the company performance but, unlike operational effectiveness, other companies cannot easily adapt them for their own use. As such, they form a competitive advantage that moves the company beyond the best practices of the industry, where rivals cannot immediately follow.

Yet any advantage gained is not impervious to imitation. Copying a system such as the JPP – an information system along with a shift in corporate culture towards a systematic and less-biased hiring and promotion process – is hardly impossible. In this case the technology platform at the heart of the JPP may be commercially available and thus presents no barrier to development. A rival could adopt the technology and try to change its own culture, thereby reducing its own employment-related lawsuits.[26] Thus, while a prevention strategy can create competitive value, it remains subject to imitation by determined rivals in the long term.

3.4 Stage four: Advantage

At this stage, legal strategy becomes more mature. Unlike earlier stages, legal resources are seen to be on a par with other disciplines. Instead of serving as a shield or as a means to comply with the law while producing a beneficial side effect, legal resources are leveraged towards a specific business goal. Managers and lawyers are more likely to work together in formulating strategic plans. Attorneys are more likely to be involved in the decision-making process and not just used as a check against possible wrongdoing.

Advantage firms can reframe legal challenges as opportunities. PepsiCo's Frito Lay division became aware of increasing concerns over the supposed unhealthiness of their products, which might have led to liability lawsuits. In close cooperation with in-house attorneys, management sought to turn the potential threat into a new marketing opportunity.[27] By changing its existing products to healthier recipes, as well as removing trans-fats, PepsiCo expanded into a market niche that no other firms had previously exploited.

A firm can also use a legal strategy not only to invigorate its own image as a

---

26 Peter J Sampson, 'Lowe's Minority Workers in New Jersey Sue, Alleging Bias, Abuse, Harassment', *Knight Ridder Tribune Business News*, February 10 2002, at 1.

27 Constance Bagley, *Winning Legally: Using the Law to Create Value, Marshal Resources, and Manage Risk* (Harvard Business School, ed, August 4 2006), at 4.

company, but also to affect the organisation as a whole. In 2004 Google commenced its first initial public offering (IPO) of stock.[28] The traditional path of an IPO is to hold meetings with institutional investors and set share prices so that wealthy or institutional investors can purchase shares below market prices. The result is that larger investors have advantage over smaller ones.

Instead, Google opted to enhance its brand image as an innovative and egalitarian enterprise by selecting the Dutch auction model for its IPO.[29] This model gives computer users the facility to bid for shares online. Not only is it seen as more democratic, but it also reduced the larger investors' advantages in acquiring sub-market-price shares. In essence, any individual had an equal opportunity to invest in the firm or, as stated by a Google executive, "This auction is the perfect IPO expression of Google's own business model. The company's success has derived from its ability to democratize access to information via the Internet, and its auction will likewise open its shares to a wide spectrum of investors."[30] They also opted out of the large-scale advertising schemes and instead chose "the diffusion of buzz through informal user networks".[31] This reinforced its image in that it allowed the financial media to highlight this IPO as a fight of populism against elitism or Silicon Valley versus Wall Street.[32]

Further details of the IPO also heightened Google's populist image. Google set goals based on numbers of interest to mathematicians: Euler's number in dollars ($2,718,281,828) was set as the target amount of money it wanted to raise. A share offering presented 14,159,265 shares – the first eight digits of pi. The founders also insisted on using their first names in their offering documents, rather than utilising a formal address. All of this contributed to increasing its brand equity as an egalitarian company working for the good of its users. Google's chief executive speculated that their efforts may have contributed to the firm's increase in quarterly revenues at the time.

Other firms have captured value through innovations arising from financial regulation.[33] The Sarbanes-Oxley Act of 2002 established requirements in part for maintaining financial controls. Many managers viewed the act as just another obstacle to be avoided or grudgingly complied with. Other firms, however, perceived the act as an opportunity to streamline their information and improve the integration of existing business units. These improvements were also noticed by investor rating services, inducing them to raise their ratings and thus improve the respective firms' access to funding and investors.

The difference between advantage and prevention firms lies in the deeper integration of legal strategies into the functioning of the enterprise. Advantage firms implement a so-called reinforcing fit.[34] This second-order fit means that two activities mutually benefit each other and promote each other's goals. It is similar to the

---

28 John Shinal, 'Google IPO Achieved Its Major Goal', *San Francisco Chronicle*, August 22 2004, at J1.
29 'Google's Dutch Treat', *Wall Street Journal*, May 3, 2004, at A20. See also Victor Fleischer, 'Brand New Deal: The Branding Effect of Corporate Deal Structures', 104 *Michigan Legal Review* 1581, 1595 (2006).
30 Google's Dutch Treat, *supra* note 29.
31 *Ibid* at 1601.
32 Fleischer, *supra* note 29, at 1596.
33 Stephen Wagner and Lee Dittmar, 'The Unexpected Benefits of Sarbanes-Oxley', *Harvard Business Review*, April 2006, at 1, 5–6.
34 Porter, *supra* note 1, at 71–72.

concept of asset–stock interconnectedness, whereby the growth of one sort of asset (eg, research and development or marketing value) can positively affect another type of asset (eg, information technology or corporate culture).[35] The requirements of law and business work harmoniously together to research a result that would not have been possible without this coordination.

3.5 Stage five: Transformation

The fifth stage represents the most advanced form of legal strategy. Transformation is the most likely strategy to implement a competitive advantage that rivals cannot sustainably copy. More than just improvements, legal resources may even lead to changing the company's goals. Rather than simply exploiting the present market, transformation firms may succeed in growing new markets ahead of rivals. A transformation strategy requires sophisticated levels of legal astuteness that work across functional domains.[36] For example, research and development and patent strategy may partner with branding and trademark strategy to produce a more effective rollout of a new product. Lawyers and managers not only work together, but also jointly participate at the highest levels of strategic decision making.

What makes this approach more sustainable in the long term is also what makes implementing transformation so difficult. Transformation demands that a firm change fundamental characteristics, such as its mission or culture. Transformation also requires a firm to shift fundamentally its attitudes towards law and regulation. Managers and executives may have long-standing attitudes that are indifferent to or suspicious of law and lawyers; such attitudes – in part shaped by the media and personal encounters with law – can be very difficult to change in an organisation.

When an organisation is successful in rethinking its attitude on law and legal resources, it can result in a practice that revives the organisation. IBM has long been a leader in the computing industry and was built on a history of innovation. By the 1990s the firm was threatened by foreign competitors and suffering from a stagnant business culture.[37] Some commentators believed that IBM's best days as a major competitor were behind it.

IBM responded to these competitive and cultural pressures by looking closely at its strongest legal assets – a vast library of intellectual property rights that were established through prior innovations in information technology.[38] IBM could have used its expertise with intellectual property in a number of ways. Acting as an avoidance firm, IBM could have copied the patents of rivals and relied on their deep pockets to fight off patent lawsuits and exhaust plaintiffs into settlement. This would have been particularly effective against smaller firms which might not have had the resources to endure costly litigation.

---

35 See Ingemar Dierickx and Karel Cool, 'Asset Stock Accumulation and Sustainability of Competitive Advantage', 35 *Management Science* 1504 (1989).

36 Robert C Bird and David Orozco, 'Finding the Right Corporate Legal Strategy', *MIT Sloan Management Review*, Fall 2014, at 81, 83, 85–86.

37 Gideon Parchomovsky and R Polk Wagner, *Patent Portfolios*, 154 *University of Pennsylvania Law Review* 1, 47 (2005).

38 Kevin G Rivette and David Kline, 'Discovering New Value in Intellectual Property', *Harvard Business Review*, Jan-Feb 2000, at 54, 55–56.

Compliance was another option. IBM could have simply enforced existing patents wherever violators were found. When a violator appeared, it would be sued and prevented from further infringement. A prevention strategy would be to establish proactively a patent monitoring system, whereby employees would actively search for infringement or potential infringement with the goal of resolving disputes before they result in patent litigation. Pursuing the advantage approach would have seen IBM continue to license out its patents in current use and protect them as needed.

Instead, IBM used its legal resources to transform itself back into a dominant competitor. IBM inspected its archive of patents for new revenue streams and energetically licensed them to generate revenue. This programme boosted revenues through patents in the decade from 1990 to 2000 from $30 million to almost $1 billion. IBM also ensured that it would not reach a monopoly position that would invite antitrust investigations. This was achieved by carefully selecting which patent lawsuits to pursue and by releasing a number of its patents into the open-source arena. While IBM had supported open-source in the past, it released some of its patents in order to allow independent software – such as the Linux operating system – to carve out a larger share of the market for itself, thus posing a threat to rivals Microsoft and Sun Microsystems. IBM's licensing programme was so successful that it generated a business of its own, consulting to other firms on how to maximise their own patent portfolios.

4. Conclusion and further directions

How legal resources can be a source of competitive advantage is only scantily understood.[39] Legal strategy needs to be more fully developed in specific domains – such as the negotiation and management of commercial contracts. Legal strategy also has the ability to influence marketing and other business practices.

Those seeking to understand better the potential of legal strategy should also look inwards to the human resources of the enterprise. For example, the chief legal officer (CLO) and his associated legal department has often been viewed as the 'Department of No',[40] which blocks innovative ideas with a reflexive antagonism against any possible legal risk. Such a view neutralises the CLO's potential as both a strategic partner and a positive force on corporate governance. The CLO has no less potential than any other member of the senior management team to both create and protect value for the enterprise. There is much to learn about the CLO's impact on the firm.

While embracing legal strategy can be a substantially positive force for the enterprise, it also has the potential to be misused, and such abuse of legal astuteness compels further analysis. For example, while legal strategy can be used to create new value or open up new markets, it also has the potential to be used for rent-seeking that increases firms' wealth without creating new wealth in society. Furthermore,

---

39 See Robert C Bird, 'The Many Futures of Legal Strategy', 47 *American Business Law Journal* 575, 582–85 (2010).

40 For example, Jennifer Nycz-Conner, 'The Department of No', *Washington Business Journal*, April 14 2008, available at www.bizjournals.com/washington/stories/2008/04/14/smallb1.html?page=all

firms may utilise their new lawyer–manager partnerships selectively to ignore legal rules in order to spur innovation in the short term and mobilise public opinion to get inconvenient laws changed.[41] The ethical and moral implications of legal strategy should not be ignored.

Modern firms consistently pursue competitive advantage; however, such an advantage in legal resources remains largely untapped. The long-standing division between law and business has inhibited close cooperation between lawyers and managers. Increasing that awareness will help to change a firm's corporate culture towards law. This in turn will encourage a proactive view of regulation that encourages development of legal strategies.

This chapter shows that increasing integration of legal resources into a firm's business strategy can yield strategic advantages. Firms in a wide range of industries have used legal resources to capture value and achieve gains over rivals. A firm's legal resources should not stand in the way of a firm's success. Legal assets should not be discounted and managers should perceive lawyers and legal staff as valuable potential partners in strategic decision making.

This chapter is an edited version of an earlier published article: Robert C Bird, 'Pathways of Legal Strategy', 14 Stanford Journal of Law, Business and Finance *1 (2008). The editing assistance of Marc Hertel is gratefully acknowledged.*

41 See 'Shredding the Rules', *The Economist*, May 2 2015, available at www.economist.com/news/business/21650142-striking-number-innovative-companies-have-business-models-flout-law-shredding

The difference between carrying out legal work and adding value

Abhijit Mukhopadhyay
Hinduja Group

---

1. Introduction

The business environment is witnessing rapid change. In the global market there has been a paradigm shift from the West to the East: emerging markets in Asia, Africa and South America are the new kids on the block. Today, the BRIC bloc (Brazil, Russia, India and China) is being expanded to include Mexico, Indonesia, Nigeria and Turkey (known as MINT). In the last three decades the Chinese economy has grown by 10% on average every year, generating a formidable gross domestic product (GDP) of $12 trillion. Although at present China has slowed down to a level of 7%-plus annual growth in terms of GDP, it remains the largest economy in the world. The Indian economy has also grown to $2 trillion GDP, making it the seventh-largest economy in the world. Together, the Chinese, Japanese and Indian economies account for some $21 trillion in GDP. Brazil and Russia were previously growing at a faster rate, but this trend has been halted – albeit for different reasons. If China is known as the manufacturer of the world, India is fast becoming a service sector giant – particularly in the areas of information technology, back office support and innovation/research and development (R&D).

2. The traditional role of the legal department

The traditional role of the legal department depends on the size of the organisation; however, the legal department's basic function is to service the business as and when required. Until recently, the legal department was revered and respected from a distance, and would be contacted only in the event of a crisis. There was little interaction with the business or with the decision-making process, and the department's entire role was confined to giving advice when required. If an organisation is large, its legal functions may be either centralised or decentralised; however, this situation is changing, most likely on account of an increase in global trade and the rise of the new emerging economies.

3. The modern role of the legal department

In the last decade legal departments have witnessed change for a number of reasons. Businesses are now more global than ever, creating an increasingly competitive marketplace; cross-border transactions involving multiple players in different continents are now the norm rather than the exception.

Take the case of India: when the economy was first liberalised two decades ago, few Indian companies had investments abroad and the number of Indian multinationals operating globally was very small. Twenty years later, the situation has changed dramatically, as the structural reforms that began in 1991 have opened up the Indian economy. A relaxation of the rules governing foreign investments by Indian companies, overseas acquisitions and the establishment of companies has allowed Indian companies to go global. As a result of this relaxation, in the last decade 700 Indian companies and more than a dozen banks have invested at least $20 billion in the United Kingdom, generating a combined annual turnover of $22 billion and creating 100,000 jobs. Today, many Indian companies have acquired large enterprises in the United States and Canada, as well as in Europe; many have also commenced operations in the United States and are listed on the New York Stock Exchange or NASDAQ. Many Chinese companies have likewise gone global – particularly in the banking, real estate and oil and gas sectors.

The outcome of all this development is that legal departments – particularly in global corporations – have been forced to transform their role and become more proactive. Simultaneously, the role of the general counsel has undergone a transformation: in today's globalised corporations, it is no longer enough simply to carry out legal work.

4. The new role of the legal department

The role of the legal department is now multifarious. It is no longer enough to give legal advice when required; the department must be actively involved in the decision-making process. General counsel should be 'walking managers', who move around the business in order to understand what is wanted and how they can help. In order to do this, an understanding of the business is crucial. Without an understanding of how the business is structured, how it functions and what its production processes and marketing operations are, it is impossible for a general counsel or legal department to function and provide value-added services.

It is important for the legal department to advise at the initial conception stage of a business proposal, rather than at the end by highlighting the difficulties of doing a deal or completing a transaction. To this end, a solid knowledge of the business is vital, as well as an understanding of organisational needs. Only then can legal knowledge be applied to fulfil the organisation's business aspirations. At the same time, risk assessments of a business or geographical territory are also important, calling for the development of relevant skills in this area. In a cross-border transaction, an understanding of and compliance with local requirements are essential; however, are these skills enough?

5. Other skills

Interpersonal skills are fast becoming an important key consideration because the relationships between the people within an organisation matter. Therefore, acquiring skills in human resources management is vital – particularly in a large transnational organisation with a presence in many countries around the world. Cultural sensitivity is also key to understanding the differences between people in diverse geographical locations. Acquiring this skill is important for becoming not only a successful legal executive within an organisation, but also a successful negotiator in business transactions.

In today's uncertain global geopolitical environment, an understanding of geopolitics is assuming greater significance. A general counsel can add value if he understands global politics – particularly in those countries where his business operates and which have the greatest influence on global politics. Global politics is an integral part of global economics, which can have a significant effect on a business. The imposition of sanctions is common these days; understanding the implications of their expected withdrawal while considering the political situation is fast becoming a necessity.

Legal departments and general counsel need to assist their businesses, help them to grow and make them competitive; this is possible only when the legal department performs a proactive rather than a reactive role. In today's fast-changing economic and political environment, the traditional role of compliance alone may not be enough.

6. Some examples

Today's business environment is dynamic and ever-changing; the opportunities are abundant, but so too are the problems and challenges. It is no longer sufficient to comply with the laws of the land; it is also necessary to assess their implications and advise businesses on how to overcome them. The structuring of a business deal is assuming ever-greater importance; therefore, ongoing value addition by legal departments is vital. Businesses will respond favourably if legal departments contribute in a proactive and positive way to achieve the objectives within the frameworks of law and corporate governance. The general counsel's role has likewise become more complex: he must now ensure compliance with the regulatory requirements of different jurisdictions while at the same time coming up with solutions to business and regulatory challenges. This is when value addition or 'going the extra mile' in line with the business objectives and commercial requirements of the organisation becomes important. Undoubtedly, understanding the business's requirements is key. Alongside this, the legal department must be passionate enough to add value without compromising the regulatory risks and corporate governance norms.

In the role of general counsel of several multinationals and large corporations, the author has experienced many challenges. Whenever these challenges occurred, the organisation looked to the legal department to come up with solutions that would add value. Let us look at some of these challenges.

Many countries are subject to international sanctions – imposed by the United Nations, the United States, the European Union and, in some cases, by several western countries. Approximately 42 countries are currently subject to different sanctions which prohibit individuals and organisations from dealing with or supplying products, goods or services to those countries. However, it is not an option to avoid trade and commerce with these countries for an extended period of time. To add value, legal departments can initiate dialogue with the authorities in order to obtain approval for trade and commerce with the sanctioned countries. This is often a difficult process and presenting the organisation's case before the relevant authorities (eg, the Export Control Organisation in the United Kingdom or the Office of Foreign Assets Control in the United States) can prove challenging. However, in the author's experience, when such matters were taken up with the authorities as a test case and approval was received, the businesses benefited greatly.

The author also has experience of performing proactively when dealing with international litigation and arbitration. In one such instance, despite the commencement of international arbitration with one of the world's largest corporations, the legal department proactively persuaded its external legal advisers and internal management to enter into a settlement dialogue with the opposing party. As a result, not only was the matter settled despite the commencement of arbitration, but costs were also saved. More importantly, good relations between the two parties were maintained, leading to more business between them.

In another cross-border dispute, the legal department – despite internal pressure to commence litigation – opened a channel of negotiations with the party that was in breach of contract. This resulted in the dispute being settled.

In another interesting example, the legal department took a proactive role in order to avoid litigation with a major joint venture partner by preparing grounds for protracted negotiations and dialogue to settle outside the courts.

In another case, commencement of arbitration against a cross-border party was delayed as much as possible to facilitate negotiations. When negotiations failed, litigation was started, but was monitored at every stage to facilitate back-room negotiations while the litigation/arbitration continued.

The author also has experience in the area of risk assessment at the geopolitical level. The country in question was subject to severe sanctions; after assessing the risks, the legal department convinced internal management not to explore business opportunities in the country, despite the presence of many other international organisations there. It was a difficult task to persuade internal management to refrain, for fear of loss of future opportunities when the sanctions were lifted in the future. An understanding of world politics and the geopolitical situation at ground level helped internal management to arrive at a conclusive decision in this regard. The decision was key – particularly for an organisation which has a presence in many jurisdictions around the world. When withdrawing business opportunities, internal discussions took place on how to resume business opportunities once international sanctions were lifted. This was a delicate task to balance. Although, strictly speaking, the legal department may not have had a role to play, the department took proactive steps to become involved in the decision-making process and assisted the business and the organisation in reaching a conclusive decision in the matter. This example illustrates that a legal department can make or break a deal and, to a great extent, it is the desire to add value in the decision-making process that matters.

7. Adding further value

In these changing times, value can be added to a business in some unconventional ways. One is to educate and create awareness of the basic compliance and legal requirements which the business should keep in mind when negotiating deals. In the author's experience, this can be achieved through the circulation of legal publications on relevant and interesting topics. For example, an update on the dos and don't's of executing a contract can benefit anyone who is negotiating legal contracts. In large organisations, contracts are executed on a daily basis and it is neither possible nor desirable for the legal department to look at every single one. Instead, it can generate value by educating the business and the people who will be directly negotiating and signing such contracts.

Legal circulars can also be issued covering other areas, such as changes in law – for example, in the financial sector or concerning IP rights, including patent, copyright, trademark, design and licensing requirements. In many countries there are regulatory requirements concerning the licensing of technology and it can be beneficial for the commercial team to be aware of these requirements when negotiating on licensing opportunities with their counterparts. Pharmaceutical companies place great value on their patents. Obtaining a patent in the pharmaceutical industry or another technology industry is a complex process, which varies from country to country. Legal departments in those businesses can take proactive steps to help the R&D team to keep such regulatory requirements in mind when obtaining patents. Trademarks are another important tool for businesses to market their products. Legal departments can advise – particularly the marketing department – to be aware of the legal requirements for registering trademarks. They can also add value by spotting patent or trademark violations and advise the business on how to deal with them.

In a previous role, the author was part of a legal department which fought a trademark battle for more than three years in a small European country all the way up to the Supreme Court. The main challenge was the non-existence of a developed regulatory procedure to deal with complex trademark violations. The only way to deal with it was to work closely with the businesses to understand the reality on the ground and advise management on how to defend the company's trademark rights. The legal department can also advise the business on the need and possibility to register their trademarks.

In many countries it may not be possible to obtain product patents, with process patents the only option. In this situation, advising the R&D department on how to obtain a process patent – particularly in the pharmaceutical industry – will add significant value. The bottom line is that legal departments should work hand in hand with businesses in order to complement each other. In the author's experience, if the legal department is proactive and displays a desire to add value, it will be highly respected. This is unlikely to happen overnight and constant efforts must be made to communicate with the business at all times. There is no contradiction between the legal department performing a compliance role and also assisting the business to grow within the regulatory framework. In today's ever-changing, globalised world, where cross-border deals are happening all the time, the functions of the legal department are becoming more challenging. Value addition is fast becoming the rule rather than the exception.

8. Cost centre or profit centre?

Often the legal department is viewed as a cost centre rather than a profit centre. The time has come to change this perception. In today's globalised world, networking is crucial. It has many advantages. Knowing people can bring in business; it can also help in negotiations and improve the knowledge base. It can also improve the communication skills of legal professionals and allow them to act as brand ambassadors for their organisations. Value addition through networking is hard to measure, but it can benefit an organisation significantly. For example, networking and dealing with external lawyers can help when it comes to negotiating and fixing fees. Knowledge can be improved by networking and attending seminars and conferences. By accepting free invitations to attend such seminars, an effective general counsel can act as his organisation's goodwill and brand ambassador. Involvement with international bodies such as the International Chamber of Commerce and the International Bar Association can also potentially raise a general counsel's profile, as well as adding value to the functioning of his legal department. If interested in adding value to his role and responsibility, a proactive general counsel can potentially arrange business deals through networking. In the author's experience, networking can also help to resolve issues; for example, in one matter, through networking with relevant officials, the approval process under the applicable laws was expedited. As previously stated, this cannot be measured in value terms; however, in this case the advantages were substantive and beneficial to the business and organisation as a whole.

Value addition can also enhance the profile of the legal department. It may be debated whether the functions of a legal department should extend to different areas or be restricted to the core functions of compliance and advice; however, in the author's experience, going the extra mile by adding value within the basic role of the legal department is always appreciated. Since a general counsel deals with the top management, the board of directors and the chief executive on a regular basis, taking a proactive role which considers the organisation's interests is usually much appreciated and could pave the way for further advancement in the general counsel's career.

The most important role of a general counsel in today's changing environment is the development of a strong commercial sense. He should possess strong persuasive skills in order to help his peers and colleagues to understand the complications and implications of law in their day-to-day functions. Legal departments usually interact with the top management, including the board of directors; thus, there is a consistent demand from members of the legal department to be elevated to board level, where they feel their voices can be better heard. But this is not always the case. Title or position alone does not guarantee respect or importance in an organisational hierarchy; one must rather become an integral part of the decision-making process. However, this cannot be achieved merely by assuming an important position; value must be added to functions so that they become an asset to the organisation. This value addition can be achieved through:

- a deep knowledge of the law;
- an understanding of the business;
- knowledge of the organisation and its people;
- strong interpersonal skills;
- effective networking; and

- an effective application of legal knowledge for the benefit of the business and the organisation, without compromising the core values of the legal department's functions.

As stated above, in today's cross-border business environment, an understanding of world politics in general – and the political situations in those countries in which an organisation operates in particular – is also crucial; without such an understanding, a general counsel and his legal department cannot perform their roles effectively.

9. Dispute prevention and resolution

Dispute prevention is always better than resolution once the dispute has arisen. Resolution can be achieved either through mediation or settlement or through litigation or arbitration. All are costly and can affect the day-to-day running of the business and even relations between partners. Disputes arise for many reasons – for example, because of: bad or imperfect drafting of a legal document; an interpersonal relationship between partners at different levels going sour; or a partner's unreasonable behaviour. Whatever the reason, a dispute is inevitably time consuming and costly; therefore, prevention is always better than cure. As one of its value-added services, the legal department can establish a dispute resolution policy for the benefit of the organisation. There is no hard and fast rule on how this can be developed. It might be based on spotting possible areas of conflict in a transaction and taking preventive measures to address those possibilities in order to avoid disputes. Ultimately, it is the people who matter; therefore, it is important that the policy be developed in advance, in a language that everyone understands. Implementation of such a policy will be beneficial – particularly in a large organisation consisting of multiple players. While working in a large joint venture between a major foreign multinational and a sovereign government, the author experienced protracted disputes over the internal equations between the employees of the joint venture company representing both joint venture partners. Fortunately, the business did not suffer, because of the partners' strong work ethic. Looking back, the dispute arose primarily because of defective drafting in the joint venture agreement; this was followed by difficult relations between the top management personnel representing both joint venture partners. Eventually the dispute was resolved at the political level. To add value, the legal department came up with a reference list of dos and don'ts to prevent future disputes from arising.

Dispute resolution is an area in which the general counsel can play a very constructive role. On a large development project in which the author was involved, cross-border partners agreed to establish a joint venture company, with equal representation on the board of directors; however, the minority shareholder in the project was given veto rights on critical decisions relating to the project. This raised an issue as it was possible that any decision resulting in disagreement could trigger a dispute with no deadlock mechanism to resolve it. Despite the fact that the shareholders' agreement had been signed, the legal department persuaded internal management to open a dialogue with the joint venture partner, even at the risk of creating tension between the parties. The department successfully convinced all partners that it would be in their best interests to create an effective dispute resolution mechanism when deadlock arose. They also successfully argued that, despite the partners having equal representation on the board of directors, the chairman should have the casting vote to break any deadlock for non-veto items. The parties had also previously agreed not to include an exit clause in the shareholders' agreement. However, the general counsel successfully argued for the inclusion of such a clause when looking at future disputes. The project was to run for a long time and the absence of an exit clause and deadlock resolution mechanism would not be in the interests of either party.

Determining how best to structure a deal and creating a corporate governance structure are critical for a joint venture project. In the author's view, this is a potential area in which the legal department in general – and the general counsel in particular – can add value. Value can be added by creating a structure which would trigger minimal or no disputes; and if a dispute should arise, there should be a sound mechanism in place to deal with it.

Disputes are very common in large construction contracts. The International Chamber of Commerce Commission on Arbitration and Alternative Dispute Redressal has established the Dispute Settlement Board – a permanent body which can resolve any dispute that may arise, particularly in large construction projects. Usually when a contract is being negotiated, matters such as dispute resolution are given low priority and often the legal department is asked to do a 'cut and paste' job to avoid time constraints. An effective general counsel always resists this kind of attitude by insisting on a detailed dispute resolution mechanism both at the internal level and at the level of the joint venture partners. When the author was working on a large, technically complex chemical project involving several foreign corporations, the legal department insisted that before formal arbitration or even formal mediation began, a shareholders' committee should be constituted to attempt to resolve any dispute that could not be settled through the multiple levels of dispute resolution process. This value addition was appreciated and a detailed dispute resolution mechanism, other than mediation and arbitration, was included in the joint venture agreement. In order to achieve this, the legal department and general counsel needed in-depth knowledge and experience, and to be sufficiently articulate to obtain internal acceptance and approval so the matter could be taken up appropriately with the joint venture partner. Convincing the partner was critical; any effective general counsel should possess the strong interpersonal skills needed for such a task. In the author's experience, if a general counsel can take a proactive role, he can facilitate the commercial, business and financial teams in negotiating a good agreement. It is always in the organisation's interest for an agreement to be properly negotiated and drafted with clarity, so that future disputes over language can be avoided.

10. General counsel as company secretary

The general counsel often also performs the role of company secretary. This can give him an edge, because as company secretary he has the advantage of frequent interaction with the company directors. In this role he is expected to advise the chairman and the chief executive; and his presence at the board of directors' meetings can allow him to articulate his views on complex legal matters. Knowing the directors of the board individually is always advantageous, because the board as a collective body has the final decisions on most matters.

The role of company secretary is primarily confined to arranging and managing meetings of the board of directors in close coordination with the chairman of the board. However, in the combined role of company secretary and general counsel, the general counsel has the advantage of bringing legal matters to the attention of the board of directors by personally presenting them to the board. Otherwise, the general counsel is not usually expected to attend such meetings unless specifically asked.

At previously stated, it is important to educate the commercial and business functions of an organisation on ever-changing laws and their implications. In the author's experience as a company secretary and general counsel, this combined role can add value by keeping the directors apprised of changing laws and their operational implications. This can help the directors to update their knowledge on a regular basis, ultimately helping them to appreciate business-related issues better. In addition, this can enhance the profiles of the legal and secretarial departments. As company secretary, the author experienced several boardroom battles between the directors and joint venture partners. In this situation the role of company secretary and general counsel becomes critical, because he must be impartial and act with utmost caution so as not to be seen to be taking sides. In this kind of difficult situation, effective board management comes into play and the company secretary and general counsel can contribute significantly to the resolution of many issues.

A general counsel should assume a greater proactive role when dealing with external legal counsel. He should be seen to be proactive enough to get involved in the decision-making process and should work closely with external legal counsel by giving suggestions for their consideration. His knowledge of his organisation and its businesses, as well as his understanding of the law, should work to his advantage. However, this cannot be achieved overnight and a general counsel should constantly strive for excellence in all these areas.

11. Future role

The future role of general counsel and legal departments will remain a challenge. As more companies go global and more cross-border transactions take place, an effective legal department headed by a proactive general counsel will be an asset to any organisation. The general counsel of the future should be:

- an effective compliance officer who introduces and monitors a global compliance system within an organisation;
- an expert in risk assessment and management, particularly in the current changing geopolitical environment;
- an effective negotiator, with good interpersonal and human resources management skills to articulate his views;
- someone who understands the business and how it operates, with solid financial knowledge;
- a keen learner who can constantly upgrade his knowledge and develop skills

not only in the legal function, but also in associated areas; and
- someone who can develop core competencies in certain areas of law.

12. Conclusion

To be a good and effective executive in any discipline, passion is the key. Passion brings proactiveness and proactiveness brings the desire to add value in every aspect of a general counsel's work. In today's complex, globalised, cross-border business environment, there is no other option but to develop these qualities. It is not simply a question of carrying on with the job, but rather a question of survival of the fittest in a highly competitive business environment. This is equally true for legal departments and general counsel.

Managing legal risk: a bridge too far for lawyers?

Peter Kurer
BLR & Partners AG

---

1. Introduction

Legal risk is a rising threat to global companies and it puts the smooth operation of globalisation increasingly in jeopardy. Is the source of this phenomenon simply the normal operation of the law creating certain risks? Or is it a matter which involves many other aspects? Can legal risk be managed by the classical instruments of the legal profession? Or is legal risk management a requirement beyond lawyers?

When the EU Commission brings charges against Google and other tech giants for abuse of market power, at first sight it looks like just another legal case. And, indeed, the lawyers quickly try to gain control of it. However, as a matter of fact, these charges have roots in an ecosystem which goes far beyond the unbiased application of the law and implications which are a far cry from the legal domain. The Google case might be wrapped up in the cloak of antitrust laws – and so might the recent charges against Gazprom or the LIBOR prosecutions against a number of global investment banks. However, are all these cases really about enforcing well-founded principles of competition law? Or is Google, honestly, more about limiting the power of US innovation in a Europe which has become so weak in terms of home-grown technology? Is the case pure protectionism, as President Obama claims? And Gazprom: is this really a legal case or the moving of a pawn in the war over Ukraine? Finally, would the LIBOR case survive a day in a proper court of law or is the collection of heavy fines merely the result of clever manoeuvring of prosecutors and regulators who want to line the pockets of their governments and receive applause over their merciless revenge against the Wall Street masters of the universe who failed so terribly during the financial crisis?

I leave the answers to these questions to the reader since it is difficult to come down with a balanced and neutral view on these matters. The chief executive of the tech giant or bank who sees his company at risk might have different answers to these questions than those of a bureaucrat in Brussels whose livelihood depends on long and procrastinated antitrust cases. Fortunately, however, there is no need to give an answer here since most people will agree on at least two things.

First, legal risk has risen tremendously over the last 20 years or so. Fines have reached astronomical heights and the overall costs spent by companies on lawyers are intolerable. The activities of lawyers have developed to have a scope and depth which is good for the profession but not for society as a whole.

Second, companies do not really have legal risks under control. They themselves are extremely concerned about this. If you survey senior company leaders on their top concerns and uncertainties, legal and related risks regularly top the list. There are a number of such surveys and, without going into details, their empirical results are univocal: a cluster of political, legal, compliance and regulatory risks now outweigh classical entrepreneurial risks such as economic, environmental or technological risks.[1] But there is a paradox, an enigmatic riddle attached to this: while senior leaders perceive these legal and related risks as topping the long list of their concerns, they do not think that they really understand these risks and they do not believe that they know how to manage them.[2] There is a higher confidence about this in the ranks of the legal and compliance specialists than among board members and senior managers, but this is not sufficient comfort: given the seriousness of the situation, boards and senior leaders should be able to understand these risks and control them by themselves.

In my recent book on legal and compliance risks[3] I wrote extensively on this legal risk paradox and presented a number of management tools which allow senior managers to manage legal and related risks with a systematic and process-oriented approach – much as they manage other key processes in large companies, such as strategic business planning, marketing, operations, manufacturing, technology, resourcing, human resources and so on. In many ways, this chapter summarises my arguments in the book; in others, it goes beyond it – in particular when I discuss the limits of lawyers in this area.

2. Some definitional issues

Lawyers are obsessed with definitions. All of us have listened to – or made – tedious and convoluted presentations on legal issues, and more often than not these presentations start with 'definitions'– more so in continental Europe than in the Anglo-Saxon world. In many ways, too much definitional concern stands in the way of really understanding the problems of the world; but some definitional clarity helps from time to time. This is the case in the domain of legal risks, where people have very different and often conflicting views on the nature of the beast. I do not hold a monopoly, but in my book and here I operate within the following definitional framework.

2.1 Legal risk

The financial industry spearheaded the discussions and early definitions of the term 'legal risk'. Often banks and similar institutions define 'legal risk' in a very narrow sense such as: legal risk is the risk that a contract, indenture, security instrument or pledge is invalid and non-enforceable. In this way, they neatly distinguish legal risk from related risks such as liability risk (ie, risk to pay damages for breach of contract or law) and compliance risk (ie, risk of being non-compliant with regulations). There

---

1 Michel Syrett and Marion Devine, *Managing Uncertainty* (London: Economist & Profile Books, 2012) pp13f; Accenture, 'Risk Management for an Era of Greater Uncertainty', *Accenture 2013 global risk management study*, available at www.accenture.com/microsites/risk-management-research/2013/Pages/home.aspx, p9; Berwin Leighton Paisner, 'Legal Risks Benchmarking Survey' (October 11 2013), available at www. blplaw.com/expert-legal-insights/articles/legal-risk-benchmarking-report/, p2.

2 Berwin Leighton Paisner, *supra* note 1, at pp1 and 6.

3 Peter Kurer, *Legal and Compliance Risk* (Oxford: Oxford University Press, 2015).

are two principal reasons for such narrow definitions and neat distinctions. The first is that they allow for clear allocation of responsibility within the organisation and the second is that they create the basis for measuring these and other operational risks in terms of different capital requirements, with a view to underpinning these risks with appropriate regulatory capital.

Although I operated for many years in the world of financial services and was involved in defining these risks in such a way, I do not use these narrow definitions for the purpose of this discussion. Rather, here, the term 'legal risk' represents the risk that a company may pay damages, fines, settlements or similar monetary compensation as a consequence of a legal process or conflicts which are legal in their nature – predominantly or partially at least. The source of such a legal risk might be the violation of a contract, a tort situation or a breach of law. But in many cases, the original cause of the risk might be of a different nature than legal and might evolve into legal risk only by consequence. Take, for example, the 2010 oil spill disaster in the Gulf of Mexico, which will end up costing BP more than $50 billion and which arguably is the biggest legal risk ever affecting a major global company (perhaps together with the interrelated demises of Enron and Arthur Andersen). The root of the Gulf of Mexico disaster was not breach of a legal rule, but a technical and process failure. Furthermore, many of the serious trading issues emanating from the big investment banks are rooted in human conduct issues, but, nonetheless, they became serious legal risks. Thus, I do not distinguish between whether a legal risk was a legal breach from the outset and whether it was rooted in an operational or human factor failure and only later developed into a legal issue. The key thing is that an event has a legal cost attached to it and therefore these risks should be identified, assessed and measured as legal risks, even if the legal quality arises only as a consequence.

2.2 Compliance risk

A risk class which is closely associated with legal risk is compliance risk. In many ways compliance risks are nothing more than redefined legal risks, but in others they go beyond them and – in particular – are managed in a different way. I usually do not distinguish too sharply between the two risks (and regulatory risk for that matter) and often use the terms 'legal risk' and 'compliance risk' almost interchangeably. Nonetheless, it is necessary to note a few important qualifications. First, in one way compliance risks are more narrow than legal risks because legal risks dwell in an unlimited space (ie, may emanate from any legal or contractual rule), while compliance risks mean a limited universe of clearly defined risks such as specific regulations for the financial industry or pharmaceutical companies, or specific laws such as antitrust laws or anti-bribery laws. Secondly, and reversely, compliance risks go beyond legal risks in the sense that they might involve the breach of rules which are not strictly speaking 'legal'– such as codes of conduct, ethical requirements or even certain contractual obligations. Thirdly, compliance risks are often managed (or better controlled) by lawyers, but more recently a second important profession has been created to manage these risks: the compliance officer or compliance manager. Finally, these compliance officers have a mission to manage and control legal risks in a very different way from that undertaken by lawyers. Lawyers advise on applicable rules, represent clients, write contracts and manage legal cases, such as litigation or contract negotiation. By contrast, compliance officers watch over – and control – adherence to legal, regulatory and ethical rules. They run processes and technologies which are designed to improve the compliant behaviour of an organisation. The activities of lawyers and compliance officers will often overlap or operate alongside each other, but in many ways they are also different: lawyers manage rules, whereas compliance officers nudge people and organisations into complying with rules.

2.3 Legal risk management

There is also some lack of clarity when it comes to the term 'legal risk management'. Many people – in particular lawyers – want to give this activity a relatively narrow scope. They basically mean by legal risk management (or control) the activities of identifying, assessing and measuring legal risk, which is at the heart of every risk control concept. These are very important activities. They aim to know: what risks affect an organisation (identification); how threatening they are for the organisation in terms of frequency and impact (assessment); and what the likely monetary or other value fallout would be if they materialised (measurement). However, legal risk management goes far beyond this: it has a strategic element; it has an operational level which encompasses a whole organisation; it has to do with resourcing (ie, what experts are used); it involves technology; and it has an important behavioural aspect. If defined in this way, managing legal risk surpasses the activities of lawyers or the efforts of compliance officers. It is a comprehensive and integrated activity which aims to reduce legal and related risks for the company, and which involves the board, line management, lawyers, compliance officers, a number of control and communication functions, and ultimately every employee. From this point of view, a well-executed legal risk strategy becomes a central management tool, a principal operation resource and a distinctive capability of an organisation.

2.4 Legal risk in the modern world

There is a third way in which legal risk transcends the legal space as such: at its core, law is a rationalistic concept – at least so we learn at law school. It embodies a notion that there are rules and that these rules serve to allow people to live in peace with each other and regulate their conflicts in an orderly way. In this traditional view, laws should apply in an equal way to everyone and no one should be above the law; everyone should have access to courts and there should be due process, fair trial and sanctions which correspond to the gravity of the crime. In the real world – and in particular in the world of global business – this is not the way it works.

When a legal issue of some importance becomes apparent and this issue involves a well-known company or brand, the chances are that this will quickly evolve into a public scandal. The news about the alleged perpetration will spread around the globe within an hour; it will be commented on aggressively in the blogosphere and social media; and then the traditional media will move in and condemn on the basis of limited factual knowledge. In a next step, non-governmental organisations and parts of the public will cry foul and shame, and press the case. This will cause the politicians to become active and ask for remedy. Finally, the regulators and prosecutors will take control and put pressure on the company. Often – and increasingly often – this process leads to amazingly quick solutions in terms of a deferred prosecution agreement, a consent order or a corporate integrity agreement (or whatever other instrument has been invented by regulators and prosecutors around the globe to bring companies to their knees without needing to go through a fully fledged investigation, an orderly prosecution, a fair trial or proper hearing).

In the ideal world of lawyers there is a rational process between crime and punishment. In the real world of big companies, the road between crime and punishment is built of media hype, scandal, public emotions, political indignation and the deeds of clever politicians, regulators and prosecutors who know how to channel public anger into a situation where big companies roll over quickly since they can no longer stand the pressure on their reputation, customer relationships and share price. Although in the classical legal space the alleged culprit could appeal against any court decision, this new world knows no form of appeal.

Figure 1: A roadmap to legal risk management

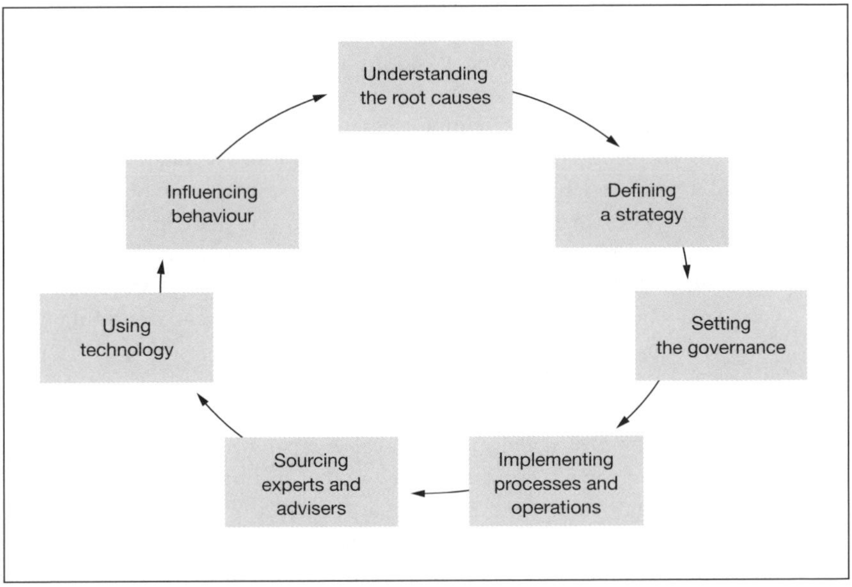

3. A roadmap to legal risk management

In my book I presented a number of interconnected tools for managing legal and compliance risks.[4] The top element of these tools is a strategic approach to the challenges of legal and compliance threats which – as we have seen in the preceding section – go beyond the law and the activities of lawyers in many ways. I have called

4 Peter Kurer, *Legal and Compliance Risk* (Oxford: Oxford University Press, 2015).

this top element the roadmap to legal risk management. The term 'roadmap' suggests that companies should take a strategic and organised approach to coming to grips with these risks; and they should do so from the very top of their organisations. In other words, management of these matters should not be left in the hands of experts alone. Figure 1 depicts the roadmap.

The key idea is that a company should go – and should go repeatedly – through a process which consists of seven steps.

3.1 Understanding the root causes

It starts with understanding the root causes of legal risks. I recently talked to a well-versed lawyer who educated me that legal risk has increased because there are more and more new laws and rules. Yes, I said, but is this an answer? This answer is as good as stating that the staggering increase in the world's population is due to the fact that more and more babies are being born. As a matter of fact, as in the case of population increase, there are huge sociological, technological and economic shifts behind the astonishing rise of legal risk in recent decades. In simple terms, the main root cause of the rise of legal risk for global companies lies in globalisation – or, rather, the technological changes and inventions which have enabled and driven globalisation in its latest stages. First came the reduction in transportation and communication costs by the invention of container shipping and satellite transmission, then the internet, the World Wide Web, Windows and the exponential growth of computing power enabling 'big data' and the Cloud, and the concept of remote computing and control. These and other technologies, which did not exist when my generation went to university, have created a world that Tom Friedman ably called 'the Flat World'.[5] Nowadays, big companies do not trade only with remote places (which they have done since ancient times); they invent in one place and produce in another (low-cost) country. The new emerging global company works and operates everywhere. Elements of a value chain can now be cut into pieces and produced and managed wherever it is appropriate; trading books wander around the world, from Asia to Europe, and from there to the United States, without ever seeing a sunset; executives spend 300 days a year on an aeroplane.

There is a very simple problem attached to all of this: many legal systems will govern any kind of activity of a global company in parallel. We call this 'legal pluralism' and some observers rightly say that this has gone far beyond a battle of different legal rules and reached a situation which one might call legal postmodernism – describing a world where the rational concept of law is deconstructed much like a building made by Richard Gehry or a novel written by Alain Robbe-Grillet.[6] This is a world where the law has become an amorphous and entropic system, where one is often hit by its force by pure happenstance. The operation of this chaos is reinforced – and multiplied – by a number of other factors, such as complete transparency created by many of the above innovations and social media, an increased risk sensitivity and aversion of the public, and cultural clashes

---

5 Thomas L Friedman, *The World is Flat* (New York: Farrar, Straus and Giroux, 2005).
6 Sionaidh Douglas-Scott, *Law after Modernity* (Oxford and Portland: Hart Publishing, 2013).

which become ever more apparent in a society where many people now criss-cross continents and migrate around the globe, and where others yearn for the riches that they see on the web or Google but that are out of their reach. Anyone who does not develop a deep understanding of these technological and global forces at work, and does not know how they will affect their own entrepreneurial activities, will never be able to manage legal risk from a strategic point of view.

3.2 Defining a strategy

The second step of the roadmap consists in defining a strategy. This is a task for the highest bodies within a company – that is, the board and the chief executive. In my experience, boards and senior management tend to leave these things to experts who are more than happy to take care of the space. All of us remember those advertisements by consultancy and accounting firms which sold "peace of mind". They showed a chief executive fishing or engaging in another relaxing activity while it was suggested that the consulting or accounting firm would industriously take care of the company's problems. Interestingly, these kinds of advertisement seem to have disappeared since the financial crisis. However, the attitude is still there in many places: boards administer the big picture and work on the opportunity side of business, while risks are better left to experts at lower echelons. But this is simply a fallacy and a trap. As a matter of fact, a board which identifies the main legal risks facing the company – and understands the main external and internal drivers behind them – can do more for reducing these risks than a whole armada of lawyers and other experts. It can decide:

- not to go into a jurisdiction which is rife with corruption;
- to withdraw a product which is prone to fail;
- to stop a business activity where people must cut corners to be successful;
- to create a culture which helps to be compliant; and
- to build an open information space where misdeeds or impending misdeeds are quickly identified and corrected.

3.3 Setting the governance

There is another element of legal risk management where the activity and personal involvement of the board and top leadership are demanded: setting the governance. An integrated and strategic approach to managing legal risk requires that a clear risk framework be defined. The framework will establish the following key elements of risk management:

- approach and culture of the company in relation to legal and compliance matters;
- role of the individual employee;
- definition of legal and compliance risks;
- responsibility of line management;
- function of supervisors;
- role of the different control and support functions, such as the legal department, the compliance department, operational risk managers, internal controllers etc;

- reporting lines;
- coordination and convergence of risk activities;
- board oversight;
- risk identification and assessment;
- role of technology; and
- handling of special situations (eg, whistle-blowing, investigations, self-reporting and disclosure).

Such a framework will then be written down in specific policies and rules, such as a legal risk policy, a compliance risk policy, operational frameworks for the legal and compliance departments, and so on.

3.4 Implementing processes and operations

The first three activities in the integrated approach to legal risk management centre around strategy and governance, and will mainly be in the hands of the board and top management. Once strategy and governance are clear, they have to be executed. Steps four to seven in the tool are devoted to this. Execution starts with proper organisation, which is always the key element of any good governance implementation. This means setting up and implementing appropriate processes and operations, such as a legal department, a compliance process, a compliance department, internal control and internal audit.

3.5 Sourcing experts and advisers

The second operational step consists in sourcing experts and advisers. Managing legal risk requires many internal experts and outside advisers, such as:

- in-house lawyers;
- compliance officers;
- outside counsel;
- risk managers;
- internal controllers;
- internal and external auditors;
- communication specialists;
- legal project managers;
- specialised consultants; and
- forensic accountants.

Getting the right mix of people and watching over them with a view to them working efficiently as a team is a key ingredient of legal risk management.

3.6 Using the technology

Technology is becoming ever more important in legal, compliance and risk management activities.[7] Among others, technology can and should now be used in the following areas:

---

7 Richard Susskind, *Tomorrow's Lawyers* (Oxford: Oxford University Press, 2013).

- information gathering and analytics;
- document and data handling, including automatic production of complex legal documents;
- operational management systems;
- products with embedded legal risk control;
- mobile computing and communication;
- e-learning;
- e-training;
- e-billing; and
- reporting.

We have all witnessed significant technological development in our generation. I grew up in a world of fully mechanical cars, where radio and television were the only electronic media, the ticker-tape machine was the exclusive transmitter of instant written communication, papers and libraries were the main source of information and the sextant and compass were the principal instruments of navigation. This world is largely gone. I now drive a fully electronic car which comes ever closer to a self-driving vehicle, all my research and communication is electronic and I visit libraries mainly for nostalgic reasons. But all this is not the end of it. Right now, we are in the midst of another technological revolution which will bring exponentially more innovations of this kind. The advent of big data, artificial intelligence, robotics, mini-drones and the Cloud will multiply the opportunities for making legal risk management efforts more efficient, more automatic and less dependent on human interference. This reduces costs, increases efficiency and impact, and, not least, mitigates liability issues, since a tested and regularly audited automatic process is a better defence in case of a compliance breach than a process which depends largely on human behaviour. Despite all this good news, the sober reality is that lawyers and legal risk managers do not yet use these technologies to their full extent. Traditional behaviour and resistance to something that will ultimately make many professionals redundant stand as a roadblock to development.

3.7 Influencing behaviour

The last – but in many ways the most important – element is influencing behaviour. Failure in human conduct can lead to disasters and huge legal consequences. This was sadly obvious when Capitano Schettino drove the Costa Concordia into Isola Del Giglio or when the suicidal Germanwings pilot killed himself and all his passengers who had entrusted their lives to him. It was also visible with the famous rogue traders Nick Leeson of Barings, Jérôme Kerviel of Société Générale and Kweku Adoboli of UBS. However, there are often less apparent human failure issues behind many other legal risk incidents, such as when a trader cuts corners, a manager abuses information, an engineer does not complete a checklist or a lawyer is sloppy in document assembly. A company has to work – and has to work hard – to reduce such failures by influencing human conduct. This has become drastically apparent in the wake of the dot.com crisis and the financial crisis, where bad conduct created disasters.

The issue is, however, that we know relatively little about human behaviour.

Regulators, politicians, compliance officers and the media all now ask for a proper tone from the top, as demonstrated by ethical value building and company culture, to fill this gap. But all these concepts are very general and give little guidance on the day-to-day management of human conduct. Fortunately, there is now increasing enlightenment in this area through the work of some eminent behavioural economists and psychologists, such as Dan Ariely, Ernst Fehr, Gerd Gigerenzer, Jonathan Haidt, Daniel Kahneman, Cass Sunstein, Richard H Thaler and others. These scientists conduct empirical research into such key questions as:

- How do people decide?
- How can I design a proper decision architecture?
- How can I nudge people in the right direction?
- Under what conditions will employees develop deviant behaviour?
- How can I mould staff into self-correcting improper conduct?
- How does a righteous mind operate?
- How can I make reliable compliance surveys which work better than whistle-blowing?

Any manager and legal risk expert who wants to be serious about compliance should know about the results of this research.

4. The role of lawyers

Traditionally, lawyers believe they are the key agents in managing legal risk. Through the course of this chapter I might have sufficiently irritated the lawyers among my readers that they ask: what role is left for us after all we have heard about the importance of the board, senior managers, compliance officers, controllers and auditors, technology and behavioural economy?

My principal argument in this chapter is that legal risk management goes far beyond what lawyers are doing and it should be a broader process than simply running a legal department and compliance operation and retaining proper outside counsel. But this does not mean that lawyers do not play an important part in this management process of legal risk control. In many ways, lawyers, alongside compliance officers, still play the most important role in legal risk management. They are the many foot soldiers whom every company needs in order to win the daily war. However, beyond this, they could play a bigger role. In this section I shall discuss the foot soldier; in the next, a possibly bigger role.

This brings me back to the legal risk framework which I discussed in the preceding section. Figure 2 shows the position of the main agents in the management of legal risk.

The lawyers and compliance managers sit between the board and line managers, who have primary responsibility for managing legal risk on the one hand and the pure control functions on the other. Lawyers and compliance officers carry the main burden for implementing and executing the legal risk strategy in the day-to-day operations of the company. They perform the myriad tasks which are needed to add flesh to the bones, such as:

- finding the applicable rule;

Figure 2: Building blocks of legal risk management

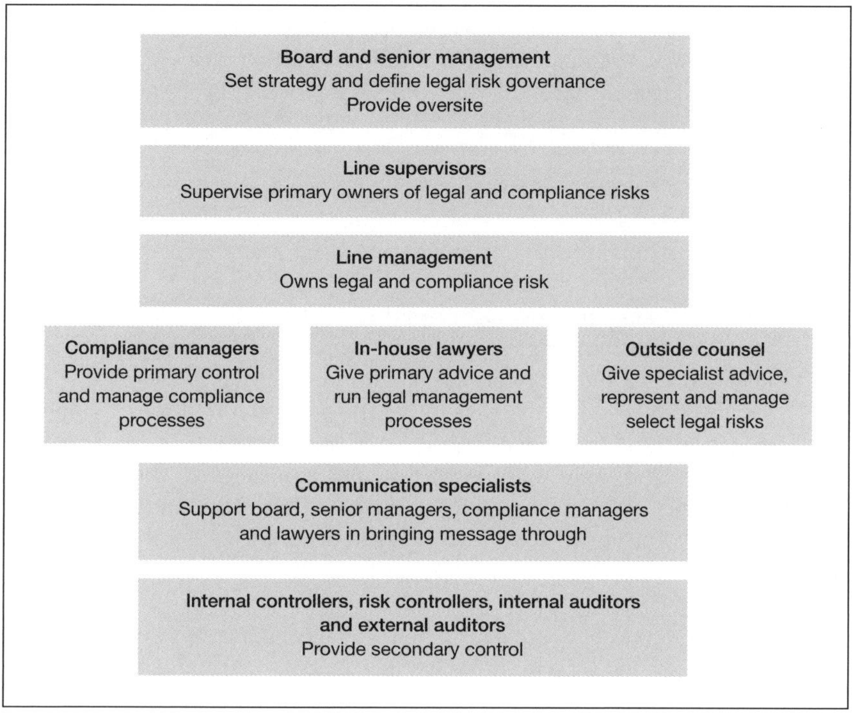

- writing legal documents and policies;
- representing the company in court;
- identifying and assessing legal risks;
- training and educating employees on compliance matters;
- monitoring sensitive transactions; and
- approving new businesses.

Without lawyers and compliance officers, in reality there simply is no legal risk management.

To describe what this means in more detail, we have to look at what lawyers do. Generally and analytically, there are seven functions which a lawyer may perform; among them I distinguish between more classical activities (ie, tasks that have been associated with lawyers since ancient times) and more modern capacities (ie, skills that lawyers have had to develop more recently due to the rise of complex economies and big corporations). These seven functions are described in outline next.

4.1 Rule discovery and advice

The traditional core competence of lawyers lies in knowing the law. They either know the applicable law or they master the techniques to locate and understand the relevant legal, regulatory or contractual rule. I call this skill 'rule discovery and advice'.

4.2 Representation

Lawyers have always gone beyond this. Their second core competency is advocating: they speak on behalf of clients in court and other forums, and in the context of negotiations. You might also call this representation. The key in this capacity is to find and argue the facts and rules which support the client's case.

4.3 Drafting

Drafting is the third competency which the legal profession has mastered. Because lawyers know the rules, they have also acquired the skill to write them, and so they draft contracts, statutes, regulations, policies and many other legal or contractual documents.

4.4 Case and transaction management

In the modern business environment, complex advocacy situations – such as big litigation cases and complex negotiations over legal documentation – as they arise (eg, in M&A transactions) have forced the profession to develop highly specialised management skills beyond their classical mission of rule discovery, advocacy and drafting. Thus, case and transaction management has become a fourth core competency of the legal profession where it excels, although these activities require rather more managerial skills than pure legal knowledge.

4.5 Control

With the advent of ever-bigger in-house legal departments, lawyers had to develop a number of other capacities. The first is the notion of control. Control is an activity which is neither advice nor management, although it contains elements of both. Control means that a process is established to support and supplement a management process in view of technical requirements and with the purpose of bringing it into line with such technical requirements. Thus, we speak of strategic control, financial control, quality control and now legal and compliance control. Control in the legal and compliance area can take many forms. It starts with giving advice and goes on to making advice mandatory for management in certain situations and to demanding pre-approval for certain business activities or transactions, and will lead at the other end of the spectrum to activities such as surveillance, data mining, employee scrubbing or monitoring, as it is mainly provided by compliance departments.

4.6 Legal process management

The second skill set which became necessary with the growth of in-house legal departments and the increasing complexity of legal tasks is legal process management. Here, the lawyer performs the same tasks as any other manager: operating platforms, leading people, sourcing support, coordinating with other functions and so on.

4.7 Risk identification and reporting

Finally, there is now a requirement for lawyers to perform the core technical functions of legal risk control – that is, risk identification and reporting. Here, lawyers help to identify, assess and measure risks. And they will report on this and feed their data and knowledge into the enterprise risk management and risk convergence functions of the company.

The modern profession is split into two camps: the in-house lawyers and the outside counsel. I do not think that these two camps perform the same function in the context of legal risk and on the above continuum, and I do not think they should perform the same functions. There are overlaps and often a blurring of the lines; however, in general an outside counsel should not act as a manager of the legal process of a company or operate as a controller; and I do not think that an in-house lawyer should behave like a legal counsel who happens to work in-house rather than in a law firm. I see the activities of an outside counsel more as those of a highly specialised expert who provides advice and other services in the more classical areas of lawyering (functions 4.1 to 4.4 of the above list), and I see the activities of the in-house counsel as more centred around the more recently developed capacities of the profession (functions 4.5 to 4.7).

In the real world, you will see very different patterns of how companies allocate legal tasks along the above continuum of seven functions. There are companies which provide almost all services in-house and there are others which limit themselves to coordinating the activities of many outside law firms, almost as if they were building a virtual in-house department.[8] It all depends on what the business is and how it can operate most efficiently.

5. Conclusion: cracking the legal risk paradox

My argument here started with the empirical observation that companies nowadays perceive legal risks to be among the top threat to their operations, but at the same time they are not sure whether they have sufficient knowledge to get the challenge under control. I have presented a roadmap and framework which might help business leaders to crack this paradox and to achieve apprehensions and capacity to eliminate them more in line. This is not an easy task, and since the dramatic rise of legal risk is a relatively recent event, companies still have to go quite a stretch to reach the same level of comfort as they have developed in other areas, such as financial control or operational quality.

Implementing such a theoretical roadmap and framework in the real life of a company is a difficult task. It needs analytical skills and determination to implement it. Many companies simply add more and more new resources to cope with the huge challenge. They create new support and control functions without establishing proper coordination and convergence. In all risk areas, including legal risk, we see mushrooming bureaucracies which often compete against each other to attract the attention of top management. I do not see this as an appropriate solution. The future lies in efficient legal risk functions which use technology and behavioural approaches cleverly, are outspoken on the main risks which a company faces and are determined to manage these key risks in a systematic and prophylactic way rather than simply acting as ambulances.

---

8 Mari Sako, *General Counsel with Power?* (Oxford: Saïd Business School/University of Oxford, 2011), available at http://eureka.bodleian.ox.ac.uk/4560/1/General_Counsel_with_Power.pdf, pp6ff.

Lawyers could play an important – if not key – role in this. They sometimes do; but many could do much more. In-house departments could establish dedicated legal risk identification and assessment units, play a role in the business planning process, relentlessly drive the use of technology and draw upon the knowledge of behavioural economists and psychologists. Law firms could give advice beyond their classical domains and offer consultancy in areas such as strategic legal risk management, identification of risks and use of technology. More often than not, they leave all this to the accountancy firms or specialised consultancies. Some pioneering law firms such as Allen & Overy have gone down the route of adding alternative services, but most law firms remain within their traditional confines. This is a dangerous avenue which could lead to a situation where service providers other than law firms achieve the upper hand in the area of legal risk. Law firms should never forget that the biggest legal service provider is no longer Baker & McKenzie but Thomson Reuters. Maybe this will serve as a warning that if the profession does not quickly adapt to modern times, the best days of law firms could be behind us.

Corporate governance issues

Bruno Cova
Paul Hastings

1. Introduction

In this chapter I argue that corporate governance in the 21st century will increasingly become a key proving ground for general counsel[1] (more so than for any other corporate officer). I will examine why this is the case and address some of the issues that are likely to become of greater relevance. My views on the role and relevance of corporate governance for a general counsel are coloured by three perspectives.

The first perspective is that of senior corporate counsel. My four in-house roles were: general counsel of the Exploration & Production Division of Eni; chief compliance officer (CCO) at the European Bank for Reconstruction and Development; group general counsel at Fiat; and acting general counsel at Parmalat following the discovery of large-scale fraud. In each role I dealt with a range of corporate governance issues that included the banal functioning of corporate bodies, dealing with major crises[2] and reforming corporate governance and internal controls.[3] During my time as general counsel I also sat as a director on the board of listed and non-listed companies in jurisdictions including Italy, Belgium, the Netherlands, the United States and the United Kingdom.

The second perspective is that of a private practice lawyer who regularly advises boards of directors, general counsel, company secretaries and CCOs on corporate governance issues. My advice can cover corporate governance reforms or providing specific evaluations,[4] and usually involves major legal risks.[5] As an outside counsel I have seen and addressed a broad range of issues affecting companies operating in varied industries and under multiple legal systems, with diverse shareholder and governance structures and a range of internal dynamics.

---

1 Throughout this chapter, references to 'general counsel' and 'the legal function' should be read as references also to the chief compliance officer and the compliance function, and to the corporate secretary and his team.

2 For example, the arrest of my company's chairman in the context of the 'clean hands' investigations at Eni in 1993; the industrial and financial crisis and near-insolvency of Fiat in 2001–2003; severe tensions between the board and the company's main shareholder at Fiat in 2001; and of course investigating the €14.3 billion Parmalat fraud and restructuring the company in 2004–2005.

3 For example, the introduction and implementation of anti-bribery policies at Eni Exploration & Production following Eni's privatisation; a complete review of Fiat's corporate governance to take into account the Enron lessons; and the introduction of group-wide compliance policies at Fiat following the introduction of corporate criminal liability in Italy.

4 For example, advising on whether a director can be regarded as independent, or whether a certain transaction should be treated as a transaction with a related party.

5 For example, advice in connection with internal or regulatory investigations, or within the context of the takeover of a listed company or a proxy fight.

The third perspective comes from advising on changes to Italy's code of corporate governance for listed companies. I am one of three specialists[6] selected by the Corporate Governance Committee of Borsa Italiana to advise on reforms. Over the years of this project I have closely observed and studied market trends affecting corporate governance and upcoming regulatory reforms and international best practices in this arena, with a particular focus on the dynamics of internal controls and risk management.

2. External factors driving role of general counsel in corporate governance

Over the centuries more and more of the world's economic development, balance of power, scientific progress and social welfare has come to depend on the success of corporations. Therefore, it is no surprise that society at large has a keen interest and stake in how corporations operate and are governed. Popular attention to corporate behaviour has naturally increased in conjunction with the growth of companies and their power.

Three specific developments over the last 20 years have propelled the general counsel and his team to a prominent position in corporate governance. These developments are outlined next.

2.1 Continued growth of legal risk

The rate of change in business has accelerated, thus creating a constant flow of previously unknown challenges. Globalisation has multiplied the number and complexity of applicable legal standards and the risk of multi-jurisdictional enforcement actions; while regulatory and enforcement agencies have become more assertive, have seen their powers and their resources enhanced, and are increasingly adept at dealing with complexities and cooperating across borders.

2.2 Increasingly pervasive regulation

Several countries have passed legislation[7] *de facto* mandating companies to introduce internal controls to prevent wrongdoing, often to comply with international treaties (eg, the 1997 Organisation for Economic Cooperation and Development Convention on Combating Bribery of Foreign Officials or the recent comprehensive reforms of banking law in the European Union). Some of the new rules attribute specific roles to lawyers in the prevention of wrongdoing (eg, Section 307 of the US Sarbanes-Oxley Act or the tasks attributed by banking regulations to compliance officers in financial institutions).

2.3 Rise in legal risk awareness

Largely as a consequence of major governance failures, boards of directors are

---

6 The other two are: Pier Gaetano Marchetti, professor of company and securities law at the Bocconi University in Milan, and a leading notary public; and Angelo Provasoli, former dean of the Bocconi University in Milan and professor of economics at Italian universities, and a prominent specialist in accountancy and company valuations.

7 Such as the UK Bribery Act and Law 231/2001 on the criminal liability of corporations in Italy.

increasingly being asked – by statutes, by voluntary codes of corporate governance or simply by market expectations – to identify, control and manage risks, with an emphasis on legal risk. Public and media attention on the behaviour of corporations has increased, and the effects of such attention have been enhanced by the growth and immediacy of social media.

These changes have produced an environment in which legal risk has arguably become the most important short-term risk for any company, and the only risk that can transform the outlook of a corporation overnight.

Failure of internal control and legal risks can:

- bring a company to its dissolution, as was famously the case for Arthur Andersen in the wake of the Enron debacle;
- cause changes in ownership (eg, at Parmalat, AIG, Citibank, Royal Bank of Scotland and various other banks during the financial crisis of 2008–2009) or senior management (eg, at UBS, Marsh McLennan, Barclays Bank, Saipem and Siemens); and
- produce changes in strategy, such as the shedding or dramatic downsizing of the investment banking business at several international banks in the last decade.

Often, legal (including regulatory) risks are a consequence and can become the – or one of the – most important multipliers of other kinds of risk, such as: accounting (eg, at Enron, Parmalat and Monte dei Paschi di Siena); product liability (eg, at Ford and Firestone, and General Motors); environmental (eg, at BP in connection with the 2010 Deep Horizon oil spill in the Gulf of Mexico); and protection of customers', third parties' or employees' personal data (eg, at News Corporation, Deutsche Telekom and Telecom Italia).

3. Ensuring general counsel's effective corporate governance role

To assess the role of a general counsel in corporate governance, one must start with a thorough understanding of the responsibilities of those bodies that, under company law, govern the corporation on behalf of its shareholders.

A corporation's governance structure can vary depending on:

- the governance systems permitted by local legislation (eg, one-tier and two-tier boards, or the presence of a board of statutory auditors);
- the type of company (eg, Ltd or plc);
- whether the company is private or has its shares or other financial instruments listed on a stock exchange;
- the preferences of the shareholders; and
- whether the entity operates in a regulated market (eg, in the banking or insurance sector).

To avoid being dispersive in looking at all the various options, this chapter will generally consider a listed company with a one-tier board of directors, with part of its members sitting on various committees, including an audit committee tasked with supervising the company's internal controls and risk management system.

While directors' duties can vary from one jurisdiction to another, they generally encompass providing strategic direction and ensuring that the company operates in the best interests of all of its shareholders and stakeholders. In this respect, directors must focus on ensuring that the company operates in compliance with applicable laws and its by-laws, and properly addresses legal risks.

Therefore, the board has a keen interest in ensuring the effectiveness of the various corporate functions – in particular, those which have a role in ensuring effective risk management and internal controls, such as the audit, risk control, legal and compliance functions.

The ability of a general counsel to contribute on governance issues depends on a number of factors, starting with the personal skills of the individual, but also including whether the general counsel is put in a position to make that contribution. Some of these factors are described in sections 3.1 to 3.7 below. The responsibility for ensuring that a general counsel is well placed to contribute on governance issues lies with the board of directors and the company's management.

The board's interest in ensuring that it can benefit from the general counsel's contribution must lead it to address the role of the general counsel and the legal function within the company and the group. In 2004–2005 when I was chief legal adviser to the commissioner appointed by the Italian government to investigate the Parmalat fraud and restructure the company, as a former general counsel I studied with interest the reasons why such a large-scale fraud could be perpetrated over a period of 15 years without the company's legal department taking any action to prevent or stop it. The reasons were as follows:

- The listed parent company did not have a legal department, as all the company lawyers were in the operating companies;
- The main operating company's general counsel reported to the chief financial officer (CFO) and had no contact with the board of directors or the board of statutory auditors (a body with duties similar to those of an audit committee) or the external auditors of the company or its parent;
- The various legal departments in the foreign operating companies did not report to the main operating company's general counsel; and
- The general counsel had no control over outside legal spending – and 100% of the fraudulent transactions were in fact performed with the (generally unwitting) assistance of outside lawyers under the direction of the chief executive officer (CEO) and CFO.

Parmalat's board of directors was clearly oblivious to the need to enlist the legal department as an agent of good corporate governance.

3.1 Reporting lines

Ideally, the general counsel should directly report to the company's CEO, as this will ensure that the general counsel has a direct line to the company's leader and is perceived within the corporation as an influential executive who is a member of the company's top management. Reporting to the CEO also sends a clear signal inside and outside the company that abiding by the law, strong enforcement of the company's legal and contractual rights, and legal risk management are important features of the company's attitude to doing business.

Other reporting lines (eg, to the chief operating officer (COO) or the CFO, or even to the chief human resources officer) are possible, but clearly not ideal in terms of corporate governance. A board should be sceptical of such arrangements and satisfy itself that they do not interfere with a general counsel's ability to do his job in a way that is consistent with the company's objectives and internal control requirements.

When the general counsel is also company secretary, it is not uncommon for him to report to the company's chairman, or to have a dual reporting to the chairman as company secretary, and to the CEO as general counsel.

In some corporations the general counsel reports directly to the board. This solution emphasises the general counsel's independence from management and stresses his role as part of the company's internal control system, but is often impractical and diminishes a general counsel's ability to be perceived as a member of the company's executive team. The general counsel does, however, need to have open communications with the board and its committees, but this can be achieved outside a direct reporting arrangement.

Reporting lines are as important between the general counsel of the parent company and the heads of legal services in its subsidiaries as they are between the general counsel and the CEO and the board. In fact, it is often the case that legal risks originate in a subsidiary, not at parent company level. My own empirical experience confirms this observation. In 2004–2005 when I investigated Europe's largest financial fraud at Parmalat I found that practically all of the fraudulent transactions had occurred at the level of the company's subsidiaries. When I assist clients in investigating wrongdoing, it is almost invariably found to have been generated in or involved a subsidiary, often based in a foreign jurisdiction.

All heads of legal services in the company's subsidiaries should therefore report to the general counsel – either directly or through other members of the legal function. If the reporting is only functional (in corporate jargon: dotted line), then it should consist of at least three elements:

- the head of legal cannot be appointed or removed without the general counsel's consent;
- his fixed and variable salary should be determined by or in consultation with the general counsel; and
- the budget and resources of his legal department should be determined in consultation with the general counsel.

The general counsel would thus have the 'carrots and sticks' to ensure the subsidiary's head of legal's loyalty to the corporation.

3.2 Sitting on the board

Some general counsel sit on the company board. This is clearly a negative in terms of corporate governance, as it makes the general counsel his own client and blurs the lines of what should be the clearly defined tasks of a general counsel.

However, the general counsel could take a directorship in a subsidiary. This is something I did when I was a general counsel and it greatly helped me to understand the dynamics of a board of directors. However, I would urge caution in accepting a directorship in a subsidiary, as this may lead to awkward conflict of interest situations. I have seen such situations develop when the parent company is in financial distress and is trying to obtain financial resources from its subsidiaries; when the subsidiary becomes involved in wrongdoing; or when there is tension between a general counsel's confidentiality obligations to the parent company and his duty as a director to report information of material importance to the subsidiary. The problem is obviously compounded if there are other shareholders in the subsidiary.

3.3 One salary, but many roles

The three most senior legal or quasi-legal roles in a corporation are those of general counsel, company secretary and CCO. Each corporation seems to have its own recipe for whether these roles should all be covered by one individual or by separate individuals, or combined in pairs, or covered by different individuals reporting to the general counsel. This disparity of views is quite appropriate given the different requirements of each corporation, which may vary over the years.

Certain regulators have recently started to take the view that the CCO should not be the general counsel or report to him. In deciding whether a general counsel should also be given the role of company secretary and/or CCO, in addition to giving due consideration to any industry sector regulation, the board should carefully assess whether a multiplicity of roles might hinder the individual's ability to act with a sufficient degree of independence in each role. In the event that the three roles are kept separate, the board should satisfy itself that adequate cooperation protocols exist to allow each officer to benefit from the others' input when relevant.

3.4 Attending board meetings

Even when the general counsel is not the secretary of the board, he should be invited to attend all board meetings, as well as the meetings of certain board committees, such as the audit committee. Such participation is necessary to ensure that the general counsel is aware of any issue discussed by the board that may have an impact on the company's legal risk. The general counsel's presence will also allow the board to seek his view on any corporate governance or legal risk issue.

In the same vein, the board should verify whether the general counsel or a member of the legal department should be given the opportunity to sit on those company's internal committees where legal risk issues may arise, such as the executive committee or the investment committee.

3.5 Access to adequate resources

Since the emergence of the financial crisis in 2007–2008, the growing demands on legal departments have coincided with an overall reduction of the resources made available to them, often resulting in increased exposure to legal risks which cannot be adequately managed. The board should assess whether the legal and compliance functions have an adequate level of resources to fulfil the tasks attributed to them in the context of the internal controls and risk management system of the corporation.

3.6 Outside counsel

The vast majority of corporations source their legal requirements through a combination of internal and external legal services. The general counsel should have ultimate responsibility for all legal matters, including those handled by outside counsel, which are an integral part of the company's legal risk management system. The board should ensure that the general counsel are responsible for the selection and management of outside counsel.

This approach is also beneficial to outside counsel, who will deal with a company officer who is ideally suited to providing clear instructions and all necessary information, and who can ensure that external advice is appropriately disseminated within the company and its functions.

3.7 Choice of general counsel and control of financial incentives

Considering the importance of corporate governance and legal risk to a corporation, directors should take an interest in who the general counsel is and the way in which his performance is rewarded and incentivised.

Directors are generally involved in the selection of the head of the internal audit function and they should be involved in the choice of the company's general counsel. As a matter of fact, choosing the right general counsel is usually more complex than choosing the internal auditor, because the corporate governance and legal-risk profile of a company can change considerably over the years and often require *ad hoc* professional figures. For example, years ago the vast majority of general counsel had a transactional background, while these days litigation or regulatory experience have become far more relevant.

To avoid the risk of perverse incentives, a general counsel's compensation and the criteria for determining its variable elements should be set by or in consultation with the board of directors.

A board of directors' interest in the general counsel should also extend to his removal. Directors should make clear to management that they will interview a general counsel if he is removed or leaves the company for no obvious reasons, or if his responsibilities are changed.

4. The Mad Hatter: coping with unique and multiple roles

No other officer in a corporation can wear as many hats as a general counsel. He:

- provides legal advice to the board of directors and senior management, and – through the legal department – advises senior and mid-level management;
- leads and administers the legal department;
- is a member of the company's senior executive team; and
- procures and manages outside legal services.

Often, the general counsel is also the company secretary and occasionally the CCO. In some cases he is also given additional responsibilities, such as administering the company's real estate or IP assets, or leading the government relations or security functions.

While all general counsel and legal functions play a role in corporate governance, the boundaries of the role change from one organisation to another, as well as over the years. There is no one recipe that works for all companies or for the same company at all times. The reason is clear: companies are different and change over time. For instance, the corporate governance role of the legal department in a listed and/or regulated company will be different from that in a portfolio company of a private equity fund, and its involvement in corporate governance issues will change considerably depending on whether the situation is a proxy fight or takeover battle, or a regulatory investigation.

As a senior officer of his company, the general counsel has a broad range of relationships with parties inside and outside the company. Some of these relationships are clear and no different from those of a similarly senior officer – for example, the general counsel is the boss of his team, a colleague and a peer of other senior managers; he is a service provider to senior management; and he is the client of external providers of legal and other services.

However, other relationships are unique to the role of general counsel. He is probably one of only a handful of senior company officers with direct access to the board (the others usually being the CFO and the head of internal audit). Even so, although the roles of the CFO and the head of internal audit (of listed companies) are regulated in many countries, the general counsel's role in relation to the board, the company or the markets is typically not regulated by the law, the company's by-laws or voluntary codes of corporate governance (other than – and to a limited extent – in connection with the general counsel's tasks as company secretary). The interaction between the general counsel, the board, the company and the markets is largely left to each company's own intended regulation.

However, in some jurisdictions the general counsel does have certain specific legal obligations, such as under rules attributing specific roles to lawyers in the prevention of wrongdoing (eg, Section 307 of the US Sarbanes-Oxley Act), or may have their role as CCO defined by industry regulators (eg, in the banking sector).

By the nature of his job (and in some cases to abide by applicable codes of conduct for members of the bar or of the in-house profession), the general counsel must act in what is in his own interpretation the best interest of the corporation, rather than in what the CEO or even the board believes is its best interest. This issue becomes particularly acute when there is the possibility of conflicts of interest or wrongdoing having occurred or potentially occurring.

5. Playing multiple roles

General counsel will increasingly play a major role in the corporate governance of their companies. What kind of corporate governance role is attributed to them is defined by a number of company-specific factors:

- the applicable legal regime (eg, whether the company is listed or operates in a regulated sector and the extent to which local law regulates the role of the general counsel, the CCO or the company secretary);

- organisational issues (eg, the attributions of the legal department and its organisation; whether the compliance function is part of the legal department or a separate unit; the internal reporting lines; and whether the general counsel also acts as company secretary);
- soft issues (eg, the attitude of the CEO to legal matters, the personality and credibility of the general counsel, and the attention paid by the board of directors to governance issues); and
- factual circumstances (eg, the ownership structure of the company or the presence of activist shareholders).

Therefore, the actual responsibilities of a general counsel and the legal department in the context of a company's corporate governance can vary considerably. Some of these responsibilities are outlined in sections 5.1 to 5.5 below.

5.1 Designing internal controls and risk management tools

The general counsel assists senior management and the board of directors in the design and adoption of the corporation's internal control and risk management system. Directors have an obligation (usually directly or indirectly enshrined in law and/or mandated by applicable codes of corporate governance)[8] to act in an informed manner and protect the company's assets. The internal control and risk management system is the organisational tool usually adopted to achieve the desired result. Legal departments play a key role in supporting senior management in designing such a system, usually taking primary responsibility for the development and implementation of policies to protect the company's assets (eg, its intellectual property, its contractual rights and the operation of its procurement function) and to ensure compliance with the law (eg, in the areas of antitrust, bribery, transactions with related parties, insider trading and the protection of whistle-blowers). Moreover, legal departments often support other corporate functions in the development and implementation of additional relevant policies (eg, on disclosure or financial reporting).

5.2 Legal risk assessment

The focus on risks has become an integral part of many corporate governance systems[9] and – as stated above – legal risks are among the main risks faced by

---

8 See, for example, Article 7.P.1 of the Code of Corporate Governance for Italian listed companies: "Each issuer shall adopt an internal control and risk management system consisting of policies, procedures and organisational structures aimed at identifying, measuring, managing and monitoring the main risks. Such a system shall be integral to the organisational and corporate governance framework adopted by the issuer and shall take into consideration the reference model and the best practices that are applied both at national and international level."

9 See for example Article 1.C.1 of the Code of Corporate Governance for Italian listed companies: "The Board of Directors shall:... b) define the risk profile, both as to nature and level of risks, in a manner consistent with the issuer's strategic objectives; c) evaluate the adequacy of the organisational, administrative and accounting structure of the issuer as well as of its strategically significant subsidiaries in particular with regard to the internal control system and risk management"; also Article 7.P.2 of the code: "An effective internal control and risk management system contributes to the management of the company in a manner consistent with the objectives defined by the Board of Directors, promoting an informed decision-making process. It contributes to ensuring the safeguarding of corporate assets, the efficiency and effectiveness of management procedures, the reliability of financial information and the compliance with laws and regulations, including the by-laws and internal procedures."

corporations. For example, of the largest 40 Italian listed companies, 20 (a staggering 50% of them) have been or are subject to criminal or regulatory enforcement actions, often resulting in major financial, reputational and strategic impact. The general counsel and the legal department usually assist senior management and the board of directors in their assessment of legal risks or support – where present – the risk function in assessing legal risks. A legal department will typically be involved in the mapping and measurement of legal risks, whether as part of a periodic risk assessment or within the context of specific transactions (eg, a joint venture or the acquisition of assets or other companies) or developments in the company's strategy (eg, entry in new markets).

5.3 Advice on corporate governance matters

The general counsel advises senior management and the board of directors on specific corporate governance issues, ranging from normal occurrences (eg, the evaluation of the independence of directors or related party transactions) to extraordinary circumstances (eg, a hostile takeover of the company) and major crises (eg, criminal or regulatory investigations). The latter are areas in which the general counsel is often put to the test, as we will see later.

5.4 Ensuring the functioning of the board and its committees

When the general counsel is also the company secretary, he will be responsible for the minutes of board of directors' meetings and will generally assist the company's chairman in managing his responsibilities – such as convening board meetings or providing timely information to the directors. Likewise, the general counsel will often be given the responsibility of supporting the activities of certain committees of the board. In connection with these duties the general counsel can play a very useful role in ensuring the effective functioning of the board of directors and resolving occasional conflicts that may arise.

5.5 Dealing with regulators

In listed companies the general counsel is often the primary liaison between the company and the stock exchange regulator. He also often has primary responsibility for the interaction with other regulators, such as antitrust authorities or industry supervisors (eg, in the banking and insurance sectors). The general counsel also often plays a role in the corporation's efforts to influence future legislation and regulation – either directly or through industry associations.

The legal department's involvement in corporate governance can have a significant impact on how a corporate counsel's performance is viewed by the company. For example, they can demonstrate their ability to factor legal risk into the enterprise strategy and they can raise senior management's awareness of the many ways that the legal function contributes value to the company. At the same time, the legal function's involvement in governance helps the company to ensure that it has effective internal controls and a correct assessment of legal risks, and that its board of directors functions well.

6. Corporate governance issues for general counsel

The majority of a general counsel's corporate governance responsibilities are discharged as routine matters that usually do not pose particular challenges to a well-qualified professional and his team. Given the importance of a general counsel's contribution to corporate governance in particularly demanding situations, I will turn to certain specific challenges that a company lawyer may face.

6.1 Addressing and solving conflicts on the board

The board is, by definition, a difficult constituency to deal with. It is there to support the CEO, but also to check up on him. It can consist of people with different interpretations of their role or with different agendas (eg, directors elected by activist shareholders). It is invariably made up of clever people with strong personalities. The general counsel (particularly when wearing the hat of company secretary) can and often does play a useful role in the resolution of conflicts arising on the board.

His role in these circumstances is primarily to ensure that the law and the company's code of conduct and governance rules are observed, and that the company accurately reports what must be reported to the markets and the regulators. Often, his role is extended to dissecting and rationalising disputed matter, and providing advice on how to resolve a dispute.

When a conflict arises between the CEO (usually the general counsel's boss) and the board, the situation is particularly complex. Some of these conflicts may occur because the board is dissatisfied with the CEO's strategy or work, or because of inadequate communication or lack of trust. Other – and more complex from a general counsel's perspective – conflicts may occur because of possible violations of the CEO's duties (eg, violations of the law, the company's by-laws or its policies; the CEO's failure to report fully to the board; or the CEO's disregard for the board's instructions).

These situations test a general counsel's ability to be an effective custodian of the legality of the company's actions, as well as an agent on whom the board can rely to ensure effective corporate governance. A general counsel's ability to deal effectively with these situations will depend on a combination of professional skills and courage, and on the mechanics of the company's governance. As discussed in section 3 of this chapter, it is up to the board to ensure that the general counsel is put in the position when necessary to stand up effectively to the CEO and other senior managers, and adopt the necessary measures.

6.2 Counselling individual board members

Directors are often concerned about their personal liability. In the United States, long-serving directors of listed companies can almost take it for granted that sooner or later they will be subject to legal action by an aggressive plaintiff. Personal legal exposure has also become more common in other jurisdictions, such as my own country, Italy.[10]

---

10 High-profile criminal cases include those against (mostly executive) directors at: Enel; Eni; Fondiaria-Sai; Intesa SanPaolo; Mediobanca; Monte dei Paschi di Siena; Saipem; Unipol; Telecom Italia; and of course Parmalat. Damages claims have been brought or settled before court against former directors of Cape Live, Generali, Seat Pagine Gialle, Telecom Italia and Fondiaria-Sai.

Particularly when litigation is of a criminal nature, even the potential for it is extremely upsetting to board members because of the associated negative publicity which – in addition to soiling a reputation they have built over often remarkable careers – can hinder their ability to serve in other capacities.

Directors concerned about their personal position will be tempted to turn to the general counsel for advice. Counselling them creates a conflict of interest for the general counsel, who should therefore avoid providing personal advice to directors. If the issue of concern is company-related, the company could always make outside counsel available to the relevant director.

6.3 Reacting to disclosure of confidential information

Another difficult situation for a general counsel is when there is suspicion that one or more directors are leaking confidential information to the press or other parties, such as competitors or companies attempting to take over the corporation.

Leaking information is clearly a violation of a director's duty of confidentiality to the company and may amount to market abuse or insider trading. The general counsel will have played a role in devising the company policies aimed at ensuring the confidentiality of the information made available to the board and will have to assess whether further measures are warranted in the circumstances. He will also have to advise on what steps should be taken to identify the culprit – either through internal investigations or by seeking the cooperation of the relevant public authorities – and on what measures should be taken when the source of the leak is identified.

6.4 Assessing his own independence

Particularly in the context of corporate governance, a general counsel is expected to act with independence. Having spent half of my career as an in-house counsel and half as a private practitioner, I believe that in-house counsel lawyers are not less independent *per se* than outside counsel, and independence should be tested in relation to a particular set of circumstances. In my opinion there are plenty (actually the majority) of situations where a general counsel will be more independent than a private practitioner, and others where only the latter will be the sufficiently independent resource available to the company.[11]

The following factors can often compromise the independence of corporate counsel:

- the employment relationship with a single client, which calls into question the feasibility of withdrawing from representation if professional rules so require;[12]
- the fact that corporate counsel are members of the senior management team, which creates bonds of personal loyalty; and

---

11 Various rules of the bar and codes of conduct for company lawyers address the issue of independence and can provide useful guidance when assessing independence in connection with specific cases.

12 A principle that as a general counsel I have always preached to members of my legal department, and has served me well, is that of 'employability' (ie, always remaining appealing to alternative employers). Having alternatives is a great stimulant of one's courage to do the right thing.

- the inherent conflict that a general counsel may face when called to question matters on which he has advised.[13]

Private practitioners are not strangers to these factors. They may be fearful of losing an important client; they have long-term relationships with, and may be loyal to, certain members of the company's management team; and they may be reluctant to revisit positions on which they have advised. However, the same factors that are considered to raise questions about a general counsel's independence may also constitute an advantage. It can be argued that a general counsel's knowledge of the company, its management and the situation at hand, as well as his commitment to the company, can make the company lawyer the best resource for independently assessing the relevant corporate governance issue.

In my view the concept of independence varies, usually depending on facts related to the specific issue to be addressed. The company lawyer's independence may need to be evaluated in relation to the following:

- a shareholder or group of shareholders (eg, in the context of related party transactions or proxy fights);
- the CEO or other senior managers (eg, if wrongdoing is alleged against the CEO or a senior manager); or
- the lawyer himself (eg, a matter in which the lawyer's advice is questioned).

In my career I have seen situations when company lawyers have shown superb independence and impeccably served their corporation, and when their lack of independence has severely damaged their company.

General counsel should objectively evaluate whether they are sufficiently independent to address a specific corporate governance issue and, when in doubt, seek outside advice or openly discuss the issue with the board or the audit committee. In doing so, general counsel should consider the issues' possible future ramifications, to ensure that their independence will survive the test of expected future developments.

6.5 Exercising great caution in the context of internal investigations

The biggest test of a general counsel's independence is often an internal investigation – particularly when it deals with alleged wrongdoing by the CEO or senior managers within the context of criminal or regulatory investigations. Such investigations are a common graveyard for legal and managerial careers.

These situations demonstrate the friction between being a member of the senior management team and a loyal professional friend of the CEO and other senior managers, and the duties of the general counsel to his corporation. Mistakes are easily made and can have dire consequences for the company and the general counsel's own credibility. The most common mistake is that of confusing one's duty to the corporation with one's loyalty to the CEO and the senior management team.

13 This is one of the reasons why regulators, such as the Bank of Italy, have ruled out the possibility of the compliance function being part of the legal department.

In these circumstances the board and the general counsel should each take steps to ensure the independence of the investigation.

The board should carefully scrutinise the way in which the investigation is conducted and take the appropriate corporate governance measures to ensure that it receives an unadulterated flow of information, the investigation and the defence of the company are not conducted in a manner that is inappropriately influenced by the CEO, and disclosure by the company is coherent with the facts. In many cases this can involve the board itself, or a committee of the board, taking direct responsibility for the investigation – often hiring an independent outside counsel.

The general counsel should carefully reflect on his responsibilities to the company and define an action plan that satisfies the independence requirements of effective corporate governance. This can involve painful choices, such as: delegating the investigation work to an independent outside counsel; having the board of directors appoint an independent legal adviser; or 'shutting out' the CEO or the relevant senior managers from information on the investigation.

Failure to govern the investigation properly or allowing the CEO or senior managers to influence the investigation, the company's defence strategy and/or disclosure can have unpleasant consequences for the company. The board and the general counsel may be accused of allowing or enabling tampering with evidence, obstructing the course of justice or providing misleading disclosure to the markets or regulators.

6.6 Being honest about one's own conflicts of interest

Whether in the context of regulatory investigations or otherwise, the general counsel may be asked to review transactions on which he advised. His independence may be viewed as compromised when reviewing his own work or the work of his legal department.

In this case, the general counsel should take all appropriate measures to ensure that the review can be conducted without being improperly influenced. These measures will typically involve having the review conducted by company lawyers (or outside counsel) who were not involved in advising on the original transaction.[14]

With a view to ensuring its own ability to act on the basis of independent advice, the board should be mindful of the risks associated with these kinds of conflict of interest and satisfy itself that the measures adopted are adequate.

6.7 Dealing with other lawyers on the board

The presence of other lawyers on the board is generally frowned upon by general counsel, who are concerned about lawyer-directors interfering with their work. If the lawyer-director is a non-independent member of the board, there is also the risk of him being or trying to become an outside counsel to the company, which would put the general counsel in a difficult situation.

---

14 In a case I advised on a few years ago, and which involved some banks accused of fraud, I observed with interest how the banks who retained the same outside counsel who had advised them on the original transaction were unsurprisingly told that all was well, while the banks who hired independent counsel were in fact alerted to possible weaknesses in their case. The court found the banks guilty, which must have been a surprise to the banks that kept their original advisers.

Given the growing role of regulatory and legal matters, there is a trend of appointing lawyers to the board. Although their legal background is valuable to the company, they should be careful not to interfere with the general counsel, let alone provide legal advice to the board. The general counsel should openly discuss the situation with the lawyer-director and, if necessary, enlist the chairman's or the CEO's support in dealing with the circumstance, with a view to ensuring that there is no confusion of roles.

7. Corporate governance involves personal risks and opportunities

A normal state of affairs is a temporary condition for most corporations. With ever-increasing frequency, unexpected events call a company's corporate governance into question. These events can include: a dispute between shareholders or at board level; change of control; a major transaction; or a criminal or regulatory investigation. In these situations the career of the general counsel can be made or destroyed, and he is put to a major test.

There are plenty of excellent articles describing the skills that a company lawyer should have to handle these situations and providing advice to general counsel.[15] These articles are usually written by, or based on stories of, general counsel who got it right, and they provide useful suggestions. Other enlightening articles could be written by those general counsel who got it wrong. Not surprisingly, failure is not advertised by its protagonists and the literature of blunders is often written in the form of criminal indictments or enforcement actions.

The importance of legal issues has simultaneously enhanced the role of the legal function and created greater risks for company lawyers – occasionally taking the form of criminal or other enforcement action. A phenomenon traditionally associated with the United States (eg, the enforcement actions against the former general counsel of Rite Aid or Tyco), it has spread to Europe (eg, the investigation involving the former general counsel of News International). In Italy, where enforcement actions against company lawyers were previously unheard of, in the last few years a dozen corporate counsel have been subject to criminal and/or regulatory investigations – generally in connection with alleged violations of securities and company law.

From a corporate governance standpoint, a general counsel's role is beneficial not only to his company, but also indirectly to society, by helping to steer the policies of the corporation and its reactions in socially desirable directions – that is, in directions that maximise the business's chances of success, protect the company's assets, diminish the opportunities for wrongdoing and generally make the corporation act as a 'good citizen'.

In the current environment of high legal risks and heightened enforcement and public attention, a company lawyer's active role in corporate governance can often result in his biggest contribution to his corporation's well-being and to society in general, as nobody within a corporation is as well equipped as a general counsel to support the board and senior management on governance matters.

---

15 For a recent excellent example, see "On Being GC During a Major Government Investigation" by E Leigh Dance, Corporate Counsel, September 4 2013.

When a crisis erupts, corporate governance is also a corporate counsel's most testing proving ground, riddled with difficult choices and obstacles, and challenges to a general counsel's independence. Corporate governance is the battleground on which legal careers are launched and can end in ruin; nonetheless, it is a battleground which is here to stay and will likely become more important in defining the role of the corporate counsel.

New competencies expected of today's general counsel

E Leigh Dance
ELD International LLC

1. Introduction

In working with senior in-house counsel around the world, and particularly in the West, one immediately notices the breadth of new demands on corporate legal and compliance leaders. Internal and external factors are driving the change. Expectations of today's general counsel are fundamentally expanding and thus elevating the position. These expectations necessitate possession of new competencies. Broad legal knowledge is assumed, and it is far from enough to succeed as a legal executive in a 21st-century corporate organisation.

While legal and compliance leaders appreciate their increasingly important seat at the executive table, they also recognise the many potential landmines. The general counsel's profile has definitely risen, as well as his risk exposure. Demands from the company and government regulators in the global economy translate to the need for more work, broader skills and greater finesse. While some general counsel admirably meet the challenge, many legal chiefs in companies worldwide lack important new competencies that may soon be needed for their work.

These competencies surely were not included in job descriptions in the past – and many are not specifically articulated today – but they are a prerequisite to high performance and meeting stakeholder expectations. The requirements are equally important for those reporting to the legal chief. Today's demands mean that new skills are needed throughout the legal and compliance function, and rise in importance as the general counsel progresses in his career.

This chapter aims to provide practical guidance on professional development for senior corporate counsel and compliance professionals, as well as for those who select and work with them. The chapter has four parts as set out in sections 3–6 following:

- Background on the demands on general counsel and drivers of new competency requirements;
- A list of competencies the author and general counsel colleagues find most important today;
- Descriptions of how the competencies are used in practical day-to-day work as well as special circumstances; and
- Professional development to gain new competencies.

General counsel with whom the author's consultancy works internationally, as well as the corporate executives, investors and directors that are their stakeholders, appreciate discussing what the changing expectations mean for their work. In the 2015 benchmarking study of the Global Counsel Leaders Circle, corporate legal and compliance chiefs of international companies listed as the key expectations of their internal clients those areas shown in Figure 1.

Figure 1: Most important expectations of general counsel

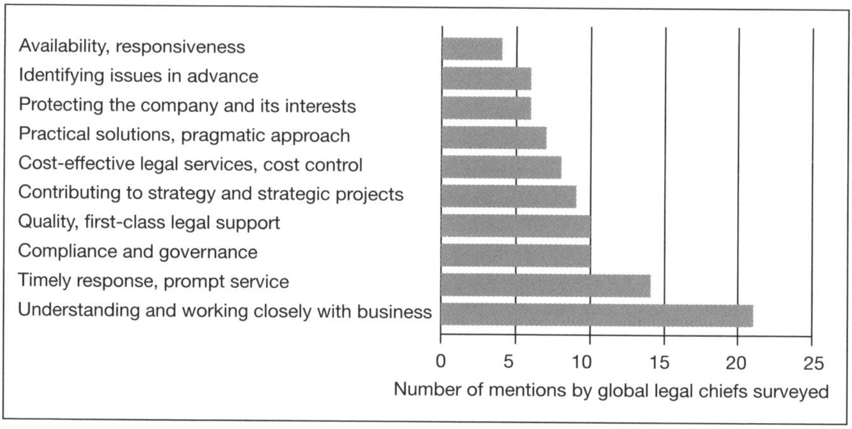

© 2015, Leigh Dance, Global Counsel Leaders Circle[1]

To fulfil these expectations requires a combination of competencies, including:

- legal knowledge and skills;
- business knowledge and understanding;
- management and interpersonal skills; and
- maintaining a network of peers and influencers.

These are the basic competencies that have likely existed for general counsel for more than a decade, though varying by geography. So what is new? Today, technical legal abilities are nearly overshadowed by the other competencies – the need for which has become far more pronounced. We should add that the general counsel of listed companies tend to require a somewhat different set of competencies than legal chiefs with companies that are privately held.

The diagram shown in Figure 2, from Egon Zehnder, provides a helpful view of how the general counsel's performance may be evaluated in relation to a defined set of competencies.

2. General counsel core competencies

As defined by the advisers who prepared the chart in Figure 1, core competencies are:

- strong functional competence;
- results orientation;

1 See www.gcleaderscircle.org/wp-content/uploads/2014/07/Target-Topic-GCLC-GC-Corporate-Governance-final-draft-8-July.pdf.

- leadership and management strength;
- influencing and partnering skills; and
- strategic orientation.

Figure 2: Logic of the competency scales

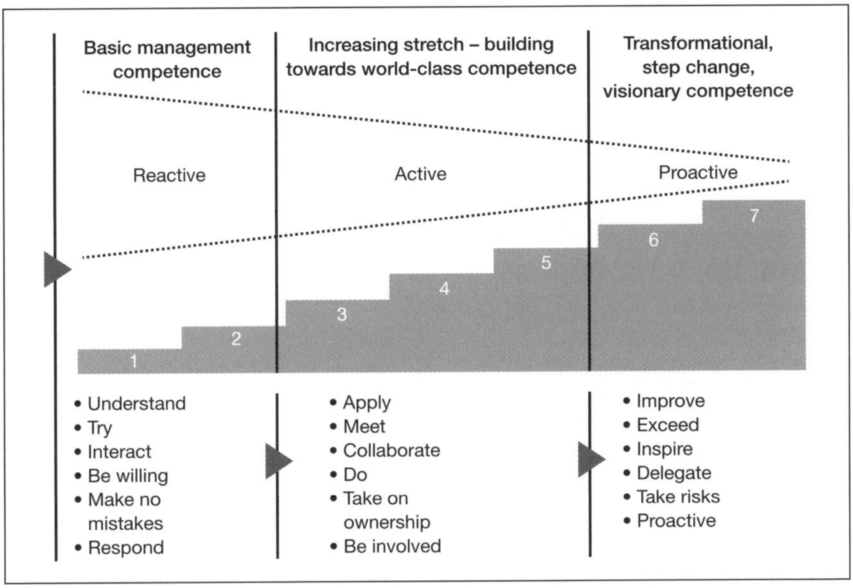

© Egon Zehnder 2015

3. New demands of the general counsel

In the words of Bruno Cova, former general counsel of Fiat and other global organisations:

> *General Counsel typically have multiple responsibilities … They directly provide legal advice to the Board of Directors and senior management and, through the legal department, advise senior and mid-level management; they administer the legal department; they procure and manage outside legal services; they participate in the senior executive team. These roles intersect and are beneficial to the company, and more generally, to society.*

The range of activities of the general counsel described above combine with broad global economic trends to drive the evolution in competencies required of general counsel today. The trends include:

- Rise of legal risk: every major corporate risk today and every major crisis presents potentially serious legal issues. Legal risks or legal consequences of other corporate risks can severely damage or destroy companies in a short time.
- Proliferation of global regulation: more than 40 countries have anti-bribery laws; more than 45 have data privacy and protection laws, etc.
- Increased enforcement actions by regulators.
- Increased shareholder activism in listed companies (particularly in the United States).

- More common crises: in an interconnected global economy this is due to public interest in private sector activity and fast information flows – the internet and social media.
- Paramount strategic importance of compliance to the company: due to negative impact of compliance issues (reputational damage, financial performance, enforcement actions, disputes, etc).
- The rise in priority of control as compared to growth among many Western companies today.
- Prominence of social activism in mainstream media, with continued focus on the activities of companies and banks, and event-related spotlights on other sectors.
- Mistrust of business: stemming from the financial services crisis and highly publicised frauds (Societe Generale, Parmalat, etc).

Many of these driving factors mean that the primary role of the general counsel in larger international companies revolves around the protection of reputation. In these organisations the general counsel is responsible for a suite of linked functions, including legal.

In the corporate governance area, corporate board members increasingly turn to the general counsel to help them navigate the tricky waters, since traditional shareholder activists as well as financial (hedge fund) activists make them feel wary.

A senior counsel with a global technology services company said: "Risk management has become a much greater focus and is top-of-mind for the audit committee and Boards generally. The focus has moved beyond the hot topics such as anti-corruption, and the interest is more broadly in compliance. General Counsels are the primary line to the audit committee regarding identification and disclosure of these issues."

These demands require the general counsel to compare, evaluate and convey the potential magnitude of various risks for non-legal executives and concisely communicate relevant information and analysis. For this reason it is increasingly important for general counsel and the senior legal team to cultivate good working relationships with finance, treasury, corporate communications and investor relations, among other corporate functions.

In a recent white paper on the elevated general counsel role,[2] one corporate legal chief commented: "GCs today need to be able to provide strategic business input and be commercial in doing so; an increased proportion of time is spent on business strategy and advice relative to pure legal advice." Another legal executive concludes: "The General Counsel job is evolving into a business role requiring leadership and management skills and a specialized expertise in legal and compliance matters."

According to Jorg Thierfelder, an Egon Zehnder partner in Germany who focuses on senior in-house counsel search: "Besides offering legal expertise and advising on

2 Global Counsel Leaders Circle, Target Topic July 2014, "Sea Change: How Corporate Governance Demands Are Elevating the General Counsel's Job".

risk exposure, liability, compliance, and governance, General Counsels take a broader view that encompasses the company's reputation and integrity."

The same global business, regulatory and media trends that drive the new demands that we reviewed above elevate the general counsel to a far more important role. This requires having the presence to be effective when in the spotlight and the ability to advocate credibly for the corporation. The general counsel needs to have the stature, composure and understanding of the business to help protect the company's reputation and make a bigger contribution to its future.

John Stout, who advises companies globally on corporate governance for Fredrikson & Byron, and sits on the Governing Council of the ABA Business Law Section and is a leader of its Sustainability Committee, comments: "Given what the Board needs from the legal chief today, this executive must have a very broad vision, a deep skill set and be a superb communicator. It's a very challenging job, with many stakeholders in and outside of the company whose concerns must be balanced and whose demands increasingly require the legal chief's attention. It's no surprise, given their multi-faceted role, that chief legal officers are increasingly considered as CEO candidates."

Many companies do not yet utilise their general counsel in the various ways described here, but the trends suggest that more will want to do so – particularly with the rising calibre of incumbent legal chiefs. In the United States and increasingly in other jurisdictions, the corporate chairman and board of directors have authority regarding hiring and firing of the legal chief, as well as approving compensation and bonuses.

Not surprisingly, many general counsel lack some of the skills that they are increasingly expected to have. If the general counsel has not encountered a demanding situation or complex crisis, no one may actually know which competencies he truly has.

One thing is clear: each person in a global company who heads legal or aspires to head legal must regularly consider the skills that need improvement and address how to improve competencies that will be necessary in the future. Those who can demonstrate their abilities will weather storms far more easily – to the benefit of their employer – and be in very high demand.

Important management, interpersonal and networking competencies are often referred to as 'non-field-dependent skills' or 'soft skills'. They are not always learned as an in-house lawyer and certainly are not taught in classical legal education. This is likely to change in the future.

Many general counsel and their direct reports have found it important to develop and maintain a close network of peers, providers and other 'influencers' with whom they can exchange approaches, discuss challenges and seek advice or a fresh perspective. These networks can be helpful in identifying gaps in experiences and skills of one's legal team, and are also invaluable in particularly challenging times such as a crisis or regulatory inquiry.

4. Competencies required of general counsel

With input from legal chiefs and those who select them, as well as the top executives they work with, the following list of key competencies required of the general counsel in the 21st century has been compiled. Listed in alphabetical order, not all of these competencies are necessary all the time, but most are needed sooner or later. The importance of the competency varies based on the company's particular situation and can quickly change as events transpire.

Thus we have:

- advocacy aptitude and experience;
- business acumen;
- calm temperament;
- communication skills;
- corporate governance understanding;
- crisis management ability;
- decision-making skills;
- foresight and identification of trends;
- independence;
- integrity and good ethics;
- judgement;
- leadership;
- legal know-how;
- management skills (including an ability to involve and coordinate internal and external resources, as well as delegate and supervise);
- media awareness;
- negotiation skills;
- problem-solving ability; and
- time management skills.

Joost Maes, managing partner at Egon Zehnder in Brussels, describes the needed qualities over and above the various competencies above. He says: "There are four essential elements for today's General Counsel to gain the trust that is required to effectively respond to multiple stakeholder interests. These elements are: curiosity, insight, engagement and determination. In other words, leadership is more than ever about character and values. Leaders today must be deeply motivated by the opportunity to be of service and make lasting improvements. Being guided by a clear purpose enables leaders to be resilient in the face of extraordinary volatility and change. General Counsels in today's corporate world have to be those leaders."

5. New general counsel competencies in action

It can be helpful to have examples of the above competencies in action, to demonstrate how they might be used in responding to challenges and fulfilling the in-house lawyer's practical responsibilities. Examples and views from some individuals in the general counsel role are provided below.

5.1 Advocacy aptitude and experience

Advocacy requires a good understanding of laws, regulations and enforcement practices for the business in the jurisdictions where it operates, as well as ongoing interaction with appropriate regulatory officials. As advocate for the company, the general counsel must have a broad strategic vision and recognise concerns of diverse stakeholders and interest groups.

Marsh & McLennan Companies' executive vice president and general counsel Peter Beshar commented: "More often today, General Counsels play the role of public advocate for the company, rather than other corporate executives. To advocate effectively, the General Counsel must be out in front on issues and build and maintain diverse networks of influence."

5.2 Business acumen

Each corporate legal function will have varying definitions of expectations for business acumen based on the corporate culture, history and regulatory situation, but a thorough understanding of the business and its structure is always important. Relationships with key functions such as finance and human resources are part of this. In-house lawyers should be financially literate; they should be comfortable reading balance sheets and other financial statements, and fully understand the key performance metrics used company-wide.

5.3 Calm temperament

One senior counsel explains it: "The GC has to be the cool head in the room, especially in tough situations." General counsel today need to juggle many competing priorities as they demonstrate good reasoning and help to calm others when a crisis may be brewing.

5.4 Communication skills

One of the most important emerging skills for in-house legal professionals is the ability to communicate clearly and succinctly with business vocabulary, using consistent terms and avoiding legal jargon – both in written and oral communications. Equally important skills are: strong presentation skills; understanding when and how to communicate in writing and when to use other channels (effectively emails); and how to be a good listener and succinctly provide advice.

According to Tom Sabatino, general counsel and chief administrative officer of Hertz, stakeholders and business partners "want to understand the real-world issues and get practical advice. If you try to impress them with your brilliant legal mind, they will feel either that you are trying to talk down to them or are hiding something behind the legal 'mumbo jumbo'."

Bill Mordan, general counsel of Shire, has said: "GCs must continue to distill complex risk and legal matters in concrete, cogent and concise language that stakeholders can appreciate. This is more important than ever, because business, regulation and legal risk are more complex than ever, and directors cannot appreciate the connections and the challenges without clear explanations."

5.5 Corporate governance understanding

Corporate governance expert Bruno Cova has said: "A General Counsel's active role in corporate governance can often result in her biggest contribution to the corporation's and to its many stakeholders' well-being ... When a crisis erupts, corporate governance is both an opportunity to shine and the in-house lawyer's most testing proving ground."

In-house lawyers at middle and higher levels must have a deep understanding of the corporate governance structure, processes and policies. For listed companies this includes an understanding of governance rules by the various stock exchanges. All legal chiefs and their direct reports must have a thorough knowledge of the organisation's directors and the committees of the board, and have a clear sense of board of directors' expectations.

5.6 Crisis management ability

A general counsel cannot perform his job without the ability to reduce and avoid many potential crises, and deal with many others to help contain, resolve or address them. The company relies on senior corporate counsel to help move forward from a crisis and lessen the long-term negative impact. In laying the groundwork to deal with a crisis, each in-house legal leader needs a methodology that works for his professional style or industry. This can be learned from peers and perfected with experience.

5.7 Decision-making skills

General counsel are increasingly generalists who must gain comfort from the many shades of grey in making decisions about business risks with legal implications. Alexia Henriksen, global general counsel of Volvo Financial Services, calls it "comfort with ambiguity". No single in-house lawyer will be expert in all areas of the law, yet senior counsel often advise across legal practice areas (obtaining appropriate expertise when needed) and among varying legal systems (by jurisdiction). Research continually shows that internal business clients expect general counsel to gather and distil information quickly from a range of sources and propose a position or recommended actions, supported by thoughtful advice, without complete information.

5.8 Foresight and identification of trends

Michael Going, global compliance officer of CNH Industrial, describes this competency as the ability "to follow world developments, anticipate what could be the operational impact on your business, and take preparatory steps to respond". An example for international corporate counsel is anticipating potential sanctions and understanding what steps will be necessary to implement the sanctions.

Another example is recognising and getting ahead of disputes or regulatory investigations that are likely to jump national borders and be repeated in other jurisdictions.

5.9 Independence

Many situations that in-house lawyers face will test their independence. There is often friction in the roles of being a member of the senior managerial team and a loyal professional friend of other executives, and fulfilling the duties the general counsel has to his organisation. Mistakes can have dire consequences for the company and the general counsel's own credibility. Informal and formal training with case examples will help to ensure that in-house counsel anticipate necessary steps to ensure independence.

5.10 Integrity and good ethics

General counsel must obviously be a champion for integrity and good ethics. Business conduct and ethics programmes offered by many legal and compliance functions will provide case examples and role plays that can clarify appropriate conduct in sensitive situations.

5.11 Judgement

Some in-house lawyers describe good judgement as expertise with the 'sniff test': they recognise if something doesn't 'smell right' and then ask more questions and look deeper. Boards of directors increasingly want legal and compliance leaders they can call on to evaluate effectively the implications of a situation. It is both experience and good judgement they are looking for. Demonstrating one's own judgement capability is difficult; often, the best indication is how others describe the senior counsel's approach and the results.

5.12 Legal know-how

Legal know-how is specific to the job, the business, the industry and the jurisdiction. Sometimes the legal know-how required in a position changes because of product developments or market expansion. It is then important to clarify what know-how and skills are required for each in-house role, and this process often leads to continuing education.

5.13 Management skills

Corporate counsel today typically manage a changing mix of people, providers, processes and projects – including third parties. Management skills required include the ability to involve and coordinate internal and external resources, as well as delegate and supervise. Counsel need adequate management skills to deliver legal services in a timely way. Corporations often have management training courses which can be useful to in-house counsel.

5.14 Media awareness

The evolution of media and the internet, increased transparency and new distribution channels for information combine to make media awareness an important competence for today's general counsel. As information flows become harder to control and news travels far more quickly, corporate counsel must have a thorough understanding of social media and search engines, and be in close contact with their company's media relations professionals. In addition to the external communications aspect, tech-savvy in-house counsel recognise that social media provides options for in-house legal teams to communicate effectively internally as well.

5.15 Negotiation skills

Strong negotiation skills are a key competency in improving internal business relationships. In-house lawyers at every level must listen well and demonstrate empathy and understanding. They must be equally adept at the art of persuasion in order to effectively influence internal business clients to take their advice, or to make headway with government regulators. Negotiation skills are also central to corporate counsel when resolving disputes and moving good commercial transactions forward. As a Canadian lawyer said: "When you encourage the parties to reach their own agreement that they're happy with, there is often more satisfaction in the outcome."

5.16 Problem-solving ability

Internal business clients often say they do not want a large amount of legal analysis; they want their adviser to take a position and suggest the best approach. Corporate counsel are more effective when they can offer a position and a solution that they believe strikes the right balance of risk and reward.

5.17 Time management skills

It is not uncommon to hear general counsel lamenting the constant pressure to do more with less. Time management skills are essential and include: prioritising; differentiating between mission-critical, urgent and important; running a productive meeting; utilising tools that increase efficiency; and meeting deadlines. There are many web-based workshops that provide the basics of good time management. In-house counsel are generally behind the curve in adapting new technologies that can save them time.

6. Approaches to developing new competencies

Learning and developing new skills while in-house has become essential for motivation and retention – particularly since progression in the typically flat structure of a legal department can be slow. In-house counsel learn on the job and through informal and formal professional development.

Continuing legal education requirements are one motivator for general counsel to gain new competencies – but unfortunately many of the new areas of competency are not covered adequately in continuing legal education. Gaining new competencies can be far more effective when the legal function designs its own professional development curriculum which has various approaches to gaining skills. A tailored professional development curriculum can change as the company changes. A curriculum improves the level of engagement of talented corporate counsel at the same time as it improves their ability to serve the business effectively.

"We provide ongoing in-house education, often developed by our senior in-house lawyers in response to what they find may be needed. They are typically short-term training workshops that we organize ourselves", said Gloria Dagnini, general counsel for corporate activities and legal coordination at Eni, a Europe 100 oil and gas company. Eni also rewards talented counsel by funding postgraduate education outside the company. In the past they have had two corporate counsel each year in part-time Masters programmes at Bocconi University.

Tim Glassett, once general counsel of Hilton Hotels and now legal adviser to several organisations, recommends that a professional education programme begin with an assessment to identify where there are particular needs and determine which of the competencies to prioritise. The assessment should review the legal department's vision, mission and goals, and then consider opportunities, gaps and weaknesses in the in-house team's legal skills, leadership competency and business knowledge. "You need to ask yourself what would be the right curriculum and what are your mission-critical subjects? It's not merely a list of courses – you need an inventory of teaching tools that includes situational on-the-job learning", Glassett says.

Some legal functions such as those at energy company Eni and information company Thomson Reuters make a significant effort to integrate individual lawyer performance plans and professional development. They want to recognise and leverage specialist legal expertise at the same time as they value generalists and legal managers. Often legal department leaders work with individual in-house lawyers to mobilise their talent by gaining competencies, which also helps with succession planning.

Planning and preparation helps to insure that your legal function's professional education opportunities are not just dull continuing legal education materials, but align closely with the company's growth strategy and the legal department's objectives. Many professional development initiatives have a cost, and since budgets are tight in most corporate legal departments, corporate counsel must carefully select their investments.

Marsh & McLennan Companies' legal department created a professional development fund, to which in-house lawyers may apply for funding for development opportunities they choose. According to Marsh & McLennan Companies' group general counsel Peter Beshar, applying corporate counsel must give a business case for the cost/benefit of a particular course or development opportunity. "We've awarded development funds to individual counsel for initiatives including a Columbia University course on Financial Accounting for the Nonfinancial Executive, a Wharton conference on building high-performance teams, and a Harvard Law School Executive Education program", he said.

Education in some of the competency areas can often be acquired at no expense. Many corporate counsel now require continuing legal education as a value-added service provided by their preferred law firms. The corporate communications function may offer presentation skills training as well as 'concise writing' training.

Business knowledge can often be improved with workshops provided internally, again at no expense. Many legal departments invite guest speakers from various parts of their organisation, including finance and information technology. The human resources group can help to administer a client satisfaction survey, where internal clients can evaluate the competencies of general counsel so that areas for improvement can be highlighted.

This is common practice for Accenture, British Telecom, Cisco, Coca-Cola, Heinz, Eni, Thomson Reuters and many other companies, and helps to connect the legal professional development curriculum to the business. For example, key executives may present at monthly programmes for corporate counsel, to explain their strategic objectives and the vocabulary and measures they use to evaluate performance. Presentations to provide orientation to new directors and executives can be very informative for corporate counsel. Since speaking the language of business is one of the ways the legal team becomes more closely integrated with the business, listening to and discussing strategic priorities is also valuable.

The days of the general counsel waiting to be called out of his office to issue the stamp of approval on a contract or agreement are long over, and have been for many years. The elevation of general counsel today is also illustrated by the interest of corporate boards in selecting the general counsel and by the number of senior partners in major global law firms who leave their partnership to become an in-house legal chief. In-house legal leaders need to continually improve their skills in order to meet today's and tomorrow's demands.

General counsel as innovation agent: the end of the 'Department of No'

Paul Lippe
OnRamp Systems

1. Introduction

An analysis of the role of general counsel as an agent on innovation requires us to consider five topics:

- What is innovation and how does it trade off with risk?
- How have things changed in companies in ways that affect the general counsel?
- What is the role of the general counsel and how does it differ from a law firm lawyer?
- How can general counsel innovate in the work of their legal teams?
- How can general counsel foster innovation in their companies?

Before we do, let us reflect on two iconic general counsel stories of the last generation.

In 1992, when I became general counsel of a public software company in Silicon Valley, a friend and peer was hired as the 'contract manager' for another recently public Silicon Valley company (today in the Fortune 50). The reason he was hired as contract manager and not general counsel was that a member of the board had declared (around 1988). "The day we hire a lawyer is the day I quit the board." Why?

Think back to the culture of Silicon Valley at that time. In those pre-internet days, most companies were led by executives who had moved westwards from East Coast companies – very often IBM, AT&T, Xerox or Kodak. Those four companies had all been dominant players in their spheres and had been subject to antitrust enforcement which led to powerful and risk-averse legal cultures. IBM in particular was known for its extremely powerful legal department, intensely scrutinising all actions that might possibly lead to vulnerability in IBM's long-running antitrust case.

Most IBA readers are familiar with Harvard Business School Professor Clayton Christensen's twin notions of Innovator's Dilemma and Disruptive Innovation. Long before Christensen came along, savvy companies recognised the risk of disruption and the tendency of law and lawyers to be a source of organisational friction, increasing vulnerability to disruption.

The counter-example comes from Enron, which went bankrupt in 2001 (and took down Arthur Andersen with it) because of the accounting fallout from its special-purpose entities (SPEs) – set up to hide expenses and create false profits, including absurd personal profits for the Enron executives who owned them. These

SPEs were signed off on by Enron's accountants and lawyers, even though they did not pass the 'sniff test' once they came to light. The Enron debacle gave rise to the question "Where were the lawyers?", implying that Enron's lawyers had lost their independence and failed to prevent catastrophe. Enron led to the Sarbanes-Oxley Act and the elevation of the role of general counsel.

So which is it: are lawyers a source of friction bringing innovative companies to their knees, or are they essential guardians of corporate integrity and preventers of catastrophic failures? Take a look at the recent article from McKinsey on "the eight essentials of innovation" before you decide. According to McKinsey, "Virulent antibodies undermine innovation at many large companies. Cautious governance processes make it easy for stifling bureaucracies in marketing, legal, IT, and other functions to find reasons to halt or slow approvals."[1]

In his companion piece (see next chapter), Kent Walker, general counsel of Google, describes how the general counsel of an innovative company approaches these issues in 2015.

2. What is innovation and how does it trade off with risk?

Innovation is certainly a hot theme in the world of 2015. From Christensen to UK Prime Minister David Cameron, everyone in public life and business (except, generally, lawyers) is talking about innovation. The dictionary defines innovation as "1. the introduction of something new. 2. a new idea, method, or device."

Note that an innovation is not necessarily better (although obviously it aspires to be), but simply new. This presents a particular challenge for lawyers, because while people who create innovations want them to be better, the fact of their betterness is not implicit, but can only be seen over time through use. Any innovation contains the possibility that it will in fact make things worse, even in the medium or long term (if it lasts that long), and almost any innovation is going to make some things worse in the short term. For a scientist or engineer, that paradox defines the scientific method of experimentation and empirical observation, and represents 'a feature, not a bug'; for lawyers, that paradox means risk, and risk is to be avoided. But such a narrow definition of 'risk aversion' means that lawyers will always be the enemies of innovation – what some clients would call the 'Department of No'.

Let us explore for a moment the case of Uber. Uber is a new car service, accessed via a phone app, which allows users to simply summon a ride wherever they are, automatically charging the expense. Uber drivers are not employees of Uber; they are usually not licensed taxi drivers in their locale; and they own (or perhaps lease) their own cars. Uber collects rider feedback on drivers and makes that available to riders as the primary means of ensuring quality, and also collects feedback on riders and makes that available to drivers. Similar services such as Lyft have come along in Uber's wake. Uber almost certainly violates the taxi regulations of many – if not most – municipalities, and has faced legal challenges in many places. At one level Uber is just a slightly different model for a car service; at another level, in a world of 'sharing

1 Available at www.mckinsey.com/insights/innovation/the_eight_essentials_of_innovation?cid=other-eml-nsl-mip-mck-oth-1505&_tmc=MQ3j5mYxRRX9D2SK7WcfBwYuSJbKxb0Zibdno3pPWn8

economy' and soon 'driverless cars', it may represent a fundamental shift in the transportation system infrastructure, where many individuals do not own cars but simply summon them on demand. Uber has attracted massive investment and valuation ($50 billion). Uber is a start-up – in part because one cannot imagine an existing company taking on the risk of introducing a service like Uber, including the legal risk and uncertainty.

According to Christensen, every established company now faces some form of disruptive competition in the vein of Uber, but the role of lawyers in established companies is frequently to impede innovation because of perceived risk, increasing their vulnerability to disruption. Perhaps that is prudent, but often it is not. As discussed below, we must do a much better job of differentiating between true legal misconduct, uncertainty and business risk. But just as importantly, as McKinsey describes, innovation is a process, not so different from compliance or managing risk. Rare indeed is a creative genius like Steve Jobs, but most organisations can still innovate by following the eight-step process that McKinsey describes. But while innovation does not require genius, it does require an open frame of mind, which some lawyers lack.

There cannot be a risk-free economic system. When folks talk about 'risk' today they are often talking about three very different things. One is the core financial notion of 'risk', a probabilistic (as best one can assess) determination of a future adverse event and its likely cost. Companies manage a portfolio of risks; performance is a function of how those risks all balance out in the end, not a 'zero risk' scorecard. But as large institutions find themselves under intense regulatory scrutiny, a second definition of 'risk' can also come to mean simply personal accountability for one decision out of many that turns out less well than hoped. To the extent that the new regulatory tone suggests no risk is acceptable and any failure will be judged in hindsight, companies become more bureaucratic and risk averse. Although the goals of most regulators are nominally progressive, the unintended consequence of this risk aversion is likely to be quite regressive and ultimately exacerbates the very large risk of disruption. The third definition of 'risk' – an action that clearly violates a legal rule – is quite a different notion of risk.

Peter Kurer's chapter herein on managing legal risk does a great job of describing the changing risk environment for corporations and the challenges for general counsel in responding to it.[2]

3. How have things changed in companies in ways that affect the general counsel?

While most business school professors have a reasonably current and deep understanding of how business organisations operate, almost no one in a law school has ever worked in a business and most have little curiosity or empathy about them. So for most law schools, their understanding of the organisational norms of most companies is perhaps 50 years out of date and does not reflect the changing

2 See also Peter Kurer, *Legal and Compliance Risk* (Oxford: Oxford University Press, 2015) for more granular definitions of types of risk.

dynamics that most impact law and innovation. It is rare in my experience that a conversation with a law faculty does not quickly reference the most egregious examples of client behaviour – the Ford Pinto, Enron or BP's Deepwater Horizon – without any understanding of what those examples actually entailed beyond a general view of corporate misconduct that should have been prevented by the innate ethical superiority of lawyers.

3.1 Transparency

The single biggest factor that has changed in the world of business (and the world at large) is transparency. Much more information is much more widely available. Most litigation and enforcement actions against companies (eg, Barclays' LIBOR, Merck's Vioxx) have come about because information systems (email, text, chat) capture comments that would have faded into the aether in a less digital world.

But what most litigation and enforcement actions reveal is that most companies are relatively less transparent to themselves – the bad actions are not obvious when occurring, only in hindsight, because companies are drowning in data.

In law school we were taught the three-defences approach to the Kettle Case – "I never had the kettle, the kettle was broken when I got it, the kettle wasn't broken when I returned it"; but in a transparent world, someone will show up with a mobile phone video or a text about the kettle, so if you argue things that are shown to be false, you lose all credibility. It is much better to provide the context in which all the facts (including the bad ones) can be understood, than try to suppress or fantasise away the adverse data.

3.2 Legal complexity

To be a global, multi-business-line business is to be complex. For example, banks are subject to many regulators, which have strong local incentives (including funding their operations through fines and advancing to higher elective office) to create complexity and inconsistency.[3] At the same time, many of the new forms of regulation such as anti-bribery or data privacy rules are not just constraints on behaviour, but prescribe complex and affirmative duties that must be followed by companies and passed along to their suppliers and other counter-parties, and are often not consistent across jurisdictions. Contrary to what most law professors believe, the practical reality is that if someone in a large organisation suggests that an action is likely to cause a legal problem, there is enormous organisational weight against that action.

3.3 Distributed authority and management by compensation

The traditional corporate model was based on the Union Army in the US Civil War and the railroads that were managed by people who came out of it. Authority was largely centralised at the top. Information flowed up from employees and

3 According to Philip R Wood, the "disproportionate increase in size and complexity of the legal regime makes the law inaccessible and therefore directly causes unwarranted legal risk". 'International Legal Risk for Banks and Corporates', Allen & Overy Global Law Intelligence Unit, vol 1, 33 (April 2014), available at www.allenovery.com/SiteCollectionDocuments/GLIU_-_International_legal_risk_volume_1.pdf.

instructions flowed down from managers. Typically there were multiple layers of interchange both ways, with filtering taking place at every level. When Bill Gates started using email to communicate directly with all Microsoft employees in the late 1980s, and when employees started using email and the web to communicate with each other and outsiders, that command-and-control model changed. Direction from the top went out to everyone simultaneously, regardless of status in the hierarchy and largely unfiltered. Information flowed up unfiltered. And any external (or internal) communication via the web or email was *de facto* an official communication from the company, even if it came from someone who was not 'authorised'. Now with 'big data', everyone in the organisation has potential access to tremendous data and insights, and rarely are they filtered up in a predictable way. At the same time, companies are run by corporate-wide, horizontal, end-to-end processes, and individuals are measured (and paid) by specific objectives aligned with company-wide objectives. Rarely will a corporate decision be clearly made by the chief executive officer (CEO), and rare indeed is a CEO who would make an explicitly ethically questionable decision following contrary advice from a lawyer.

3.4 Disruptive competition

Long before Christensen codified these terms, managers in Silicon Valley woke up every morning afraid of a new, lower-cost, more technology-enabled competitor.[4] But now, for perhaps the first time, global enterprises face three classes of disruptive competitors:

- greenfield, lower-cost disruptive start-ups like Uber;
- lower-cost (most often based in Asia) medium-sized and large companies, typically with some form of government backing and preferred treatment in their home market; and
- huge, cash-rich, ubiquitous, customer-connected, established companies like Google and Apple, with tremendous capacity to cross-subsidise new business models in wholly new markets like finance or health.

According to a recent report from Accenture, "Digital disruption has the potential to shrink the role and relevance of today's banks ... To make the impact positive, banks ... need to shake themselves out of institutional complacency and recognize that merely navigating waves of regulation ... won't protect them from obsolescence."[5] With the further professionalisation of capital in private equity and venture capital firms, together with the short-term focus of most public investors, it is as likely as not that a start-up will have a lower cost of capital and equivalent access to capital as an established company, and therefore greater ability to take financial risk.

To confront an intensive, costly and friction-creating regulatory regime at the same time as facing new disruptive competitors is not a comfortable place to be; many companies lost out on market opportunities when they faced the twin challenges of antitrust regulatory enforcement and new, lower-cost competitors.

---

4 See Intel CEO Andy Grove's "Only The Paranoid Survive".
5 See www.accenture.com/us-en/Pages/insight-future-fintech-banking.aspx

4. What is the role of a general counsel and how does it differ from a law firm lawyer?

When the first wave of general counsel of the 1970s and 1980s were asked to define their job, they would frequently say something like, "We're just like a law firm, only we just have one client." Today, if you ask a sophisticated general counsel like FMC Technology's Jeff Carr, they would say something like, "We're just like the rest of the business, only we have legal training and we focus more on risk and long-term returns." Although we often hear of companies hiring prominent lawyers with government or law firm experience and trumpeting their credentials, as often as not we see that followed by continuing risk-based losses for the company and the general counsel's departure within two or three years. Any general counsel who does not understand that his role is very different from a firm or government lawyer's is unlikely to be successful.

The simple comparison in Table 1 shows the most common elements of the dichotomy.

Table 1: Differences between general counsel and law firm lawyer

	Firm lawyer	General counsel
Time orientation	Reactive	Strategic
Cost orientation	More spend = more quality	Save money
Specialisation	Highly specialised	Generalist
Problem orientation	One matter at a time	All matters, all times, all connected
Source of authority	Expertise, ability to compel CEO, board	Relationships, ability to persuade at all levels
Source of pride	Ethics	Effectiveness
Locus of production	Individual	Team
Information	Scarce	Abundant
On stones	Leave no stone unturned	Look under the right stone
Primary knowledge	The law	The business
Temperament	Adversarial	Collaborative

continued on next page

	Firm lawyer	General counsel
Self-image	Expert	Learner
Commercial success	Assumed	Always at risk
Likes	Complexity	Simple

Jeff Carr gives an excellent summary of the four things lawyers do:

- advocacy – representing the client's interests in relationship to external parties, most commonly litigation;
- counselling – advising the client on actions that favour long-term over short-term interests;
- content – providing information about legal issues; and
- process – moving information from one place to another to create legal work product, typically either generating or analysing contracts, or working through discovery-based work in litigation or investigation.

We could go one step further and define the classes of activity in which the nature of the lawyers' role will vary:

- Create legally defined assets such as patents, leases or securities.
- Manage legally mediated conflicts.
- Shape the competitive battlefield.
- Influence corporate governance and incentives and constraints, including managing tensions between the 'agents' of the enterprise and the interests of the firm.
- Provide information that leads to appropriate classification decisions.

4.1 Create legally defined assets

This is the most straightforward task of lawyers and generally falls within Carr's 'process' category. Although this can sometimes involve government processes (eg, filing a patent), in general these activities are fundamentally commercial and lawyers should pursue them with commercial principles of simplicity, speed, alignment and efficient hand-offs. Some of the savviest general counsel – like Cisco's Mark Chandler – say that sales contracting is their most important function because it drives the business; Jeff Carr takes that one step further and shifts contracting responsibility more clearly to business owners, subject to predefined legal guidelines. Very little of the activity in this arena is truly about legal risk (eg, making a concession in an indemnification clause is simply a form of pricing concession). Lawyers should be concerned that information and incentives are aligned throughout the organisation (engineers should not be paid for lousy patents, salespeople should not throw lousy deals 'over the wall' to legal that are likely to result in poor revenue recognition) and should focus on using technology to streamline these processes.

4.2 Manage legally mediated conflicts

If the company is subject to (i) litigation from another non-governmental party but under the supervision of a court, or (ii) investigation by a government entity, the general counsel has to balance his strong sense of advocacy with a strict adherence to the formalisms of the processes. The sort of information stacking that would be acceptable when dealing with commercial counterparties can be catastrophic when managing a judicially overseen process, because the company could be subject to severe sanctions (eg, not being allowed to present a defence) for withholding or misrepresenting information. Because of the new reality of transparency described above, companies are extremely vulnerable in these types of matter and the lawyers' instinct to frame things for their client may work to their disadvantage as transparency causes new facts to emerge.

4.3 Shape the competitive battlefield

Perhaps the most interesting role for the general counsel is to help shape the overall environment for the company's success. This is a mix of law and regulation, partnering with other companies, and protecting and enhancing reputation. IBM's efforts to partner with hundreds of companies to create a Watson ecosystem represent the most interesting recent example; Apple's efforts to partner with Hollywood for iTunes or Uber's battles with local taxi regulation are other examples. To shape the competitive battlefield, general counsel must take a long-term view and integrate the perspectives of many stakeholders, again resisting lawyers' tendency to seek maximum short-term tactical advantage. In 2015 IBM's general counsel was talking about Watson passing the bar exam, but in 2012 the same general counsel coordinated a letter to the American Bar Association objecting to possible rule changes that would allow for non-lawyer-owned firms. Not a few sceptics noted the apparent inconsistency.[6] A more expansive, long-term, win–win view of dealing with different stakeholders – although not the tactical lawyer's first instinct – is needed here.

4.4 Influence corporate governance and incentives and constraints

In the world that was, the primary notion of a general counsel (or any lawyer's role) was to 'advise' the CEO and then the CEO would integrate that advice into decisions (commands and constraints) that were imposed on the rest of the organisation. In today's world, CEOs seek to distribute decision-making as much as possible. The legal department will generally have decision-making, not advisory responsibility for any decision that has significant legal content, and it will be exceptionally rare for a businessperson explicitly to overrule (as opposed to challenge or escalate) a cautionary judgement from legal. The higher-value role of the general counsel is around design – to make sure that the incentives, constraints and information for individual decision-makers reflect an appropriate mix of legal/ethical and risk-managing considerations. Where corporations seek to drive decision-making to where the work is being done, the general counsel must ensure the right tools are available there as well (broadly now referred to as the 'compliance' function, although in my view it is

---

6 http://prismlegal.com/meet-new-lawyer-ibm-watson/

a mistake to separate it from the general counsel's role). As Ronald Coase – and many others in his wake – illustrated, the 'firm' is not one thing, and there are many principal–agent tensions between individual managers and the enterprise as a whole. Most legal problems arise not because of a deliberate and unethical decision by the firm as a whole, but because of locally-optimising or incompetent decisions by individual managers, driven by company-wide incentives and management systems. A primary role of the general counsel is to ensure optimum levels of alignment and transparency, even while recognising that while everyone calls for transparency, usually they are much more eager to see it applied to others than themselves.

4.5 Provide information that leads to appropriate classification decisions

This is the most fraught area. In addition to developing, making and selling its products or services, the core process of a company is coming up with financial statements that provide transparency and perhaps insight to investors, and feedback to the firm. Those financial statements (like Enron's) are derived from an infinite number of discrete judgements, including legal judgements, which have inherent subjectivity. The problem in Enron was that the Enron lawyers acted as 'zealous advocates' for the accounting treatment that the CEO and chief financial officer wanted, not stewards of Enron's long-term interests in providing accurate information. Similarly, the financial crisis was driven in part by rating agencies (eg, Moody's) providing AAA ratings to credits that later proved to be far less than AAA – again influenced by inputs from lawyers.

Outside lawyers now will often perceive that they were engaged to be advocates for the firm's position, so it falls to the in-house lawyers to understand the business well enough to provide a true picture to whomever (eg, the audit firm) is making the classification.

5. How can general counsel innovate in the work of their legal teams?

5.1 Be specific about the nature of activity and the role of lawyers

As described above, lawyers perform a range of roles in the enterprise – the notion that they all involve the same precise theoretical law school mix of zealous advocacy, independent ethical judgement and reactive issue-spotting is a generation out of date.

5.2 Start with design

Along with Christensen's Innovators Dilemma and Disruptive Innovation, the hottest idea in the business world is around 'design'. Crystallised by Steve Jobs' iPhone and other innovations at Apple and Jobs' admiration for design,[7] and scaled by George Kembel at Stanford's d-school or Institute for Design (and copied at Harvard's i-Lab),[8] design thinking means starting with the most desired result and working through to the simplest, most elegant way of achieving it. For more than a generation, businesses have been driven by differently labelled end-to-end thinking

---

7 See www.newyorker.com/magazine/2015/02/23/shape-things-come

8 See http://dschool.stanford.edu/our-team/

processes – TQM, Six Sigma, Lean, Agile and others – but design is the most appropriate for lawyers, because its primary goal is not cost reduction but effectiveness, and it works on a single matter rather than requiring scale and repetition. When I was in law school, I took a trial advocacy workshop from Irving Younger, perhaps the premier trial lawyer of his day. Younger taught our class that the way to prepare for a closing argument was not to review all the testimony of the case the night before closing argument, but to begin writing the closing argument from the moment you got the case and make sure every aspect of the trial worked to support your closing argument. So lawyers were inculcated in design thinking long before the term was codified.[9]

5.3 Support innovation; accept feedback

General counsel should actively encourage innovation among their teams, which includes a recognition that some innovations will be unsuccessful. General counsel should make sure their teams are aware of innovative practices inside their companies and at other legal departments, constantly exploring which approaches are working elsewhere and could be applied in their world. Legal teams should actively try to redesign one to two processes a year and take very seriously their internal client complaints about excess friction (bad design). This TED talk (from TED Conferences, LLC) provides an example of an extraordinary redesign, where the people who brought us the 'captcha' (the text box that allows a website to confirm whether you are a person or a robot) was redesigned to also enable 'crowd-sourcing' of translation and ultimately learning of different languages.[10] Innovative approaches typically begin by acknowledging problems with the status quo (always hard for lawyers) and developing ways to measure performance that can lead to significant improvements.

5.4 Avoid waste

The primary conversation for the legal function since the 2008 financial crisis has been around cost reduction. On the whole, we think this is overdone, but general counsel should still be on the alert to avoid waste and inefficiency. Legal services is a corporate function, so any waste in legal undermines the company's internal credibility; legal also has an enforcement role, so whenever clients come into contact with the legal department and it is being unfocused and inefficient, it undermines the credibility of the legal function. When working with outside firms, those providing legal services should be sure to define the 'search space' for the firm's activities – clearly defining goals and scope, according to design principles. Most law firm inefficiency comes from lack of focus: it is better to pay for 10 hours of an expensive partner's time to get to the right answer rather than 100 hours of associate time to thrash out an issue whose resolution does not matter anyway.

5.5 Create and manage the legal work product in a modern way

Paper and ink was certainly the pre-eminent technology for two millennia, but today

---

9 See www.abajournal.com/legalrebels/article/legal_by_design

10 See www.ted.com/talks/luis_von_ahn_massive_scale_online_collaboration?language=en

digitally stored and managed information is much easier to access, understand and manipulate. One lesson of the financial crisis was that many risks were undetected for lack of systematised management of key legal information, so sorting through problems was quite cumbersome.

To manage risk and enable innovation, we need to deliver legal work in a different way: systematically and by being information-centric. Great lawyers design systems that balance risk and improve transparency; mediocre lawyers play whack-a-mole, reacting to problems by creating fear and friction. Similarly, clever lawyers help clients to shape (or perhaps distort, as did Moody's AAA ratings on certain collateralised debt obligations) external perception of risk; great lawyers help clients to price internal risk correctly.

To paraphrase Professor Larry Lessig of Harvard Law School, "contracts want to be code", to be readily translated into business-value-like risk, asset value, optionality and cash flows. Across the set of all agreements to which an entity is a party (and third party), it is now possible to describe the expected revenue or liability flowing from those agreements, improving profitability and reducing costs. Legal staff should ensure that the work product is transparent and ties in with other systems.

6. How can general counsel foster innovation in their companies?

6.1 Drive accountability

As previously discussed, companies have to innovate and take risks to survive. So lawyers should help to create compensation and governance systems that reward appropriate behaviours and align individual incentives with the company's longer-term interests. The general counsel should make sure that decision-making processes are transparent (without being unduly bureaucratic). Most legal problems arise from incompetence, not malevolence.

6.2 Avoid creating unneeded friction

If the legal department becomes the 'Department of No', it will not reduce risk, it will simply cause businesspeople to avoid it, increasing the aggregate risk for the company. The legal department has to be an attractive place for businesspeople to engage, where their problems can be creatively solved. When legal says no, the reason should be compelling and credible to non-legal stakeholders and mindful of other companies' practices.

6.3 Distinguish clearly between business risk and legal/ethical/reputational risk

Building a new solar cell plant based on uncertain technology or going long on the RMB is a risk; secretly dumping toxic chemicals into a river above a city is another risk, but the latter is illegal, unethical, a reputational catastrophe and just plain stupid, whereas the former is what a business may choose to do. Legal staff should be clear whether their 'risk' advice is around business risk or a truly illegal or unethical act. Some businesses are inherently risky – every drug that a pharmaceutical company introduces will have adverse consequences, so legal's job is to ensure proper documentation of risk and a credible assessment of comparative risk, as well as accurate submissions to assessment agencies (eg, the US Food and Drug Administration). In a transparent world, imagining that adverse facts will not eventually become public knowledge is foolhardy.

6.4 Maintain an effective network

The most important aspect of any legal department discussion with management is knowing how a peer company handled a similar situation. General counsel should maintain strong networks with their peers (especially those companies with common board members) so they can be prepared to answer the objection, "Well I'm on the board of Acme, and they were OK with XYZ, so why are you objecting to XYZ????"

Other general counsel are also the best source for ideas about innovative practices for the legal department.

6.5 Understand the business

It goes without saying that general counsel must have a deep understanding of their business so that they can provide context-specific insight. References to 'widgets' or hypotheticals are forbidden. Acting as devil's advocate and questioning all initiatives equally is nearly as useless, since it abdicates responsibility for true judgement, differentiating risks and focus on real hotspots, and forces innovators to run a bureaucratic gauntlet instead of providing helpful assistance. All descriptions of choices must be fact based and specific to the organisation. While most risk is hard to quantify, legal staff should be prepared to provide relative risk ratings. As Kurer points out, legal risk is now indistinguishable from PR risk, so lawyers cannot imagine that they are reducing risk just by following tactical, legal approaches that once disclosed will make their company look obtuse, self-serving or defensive. An effective general counsel must understand the commercial and social value of the business, and be able to align and advocate corporate actions in ways that lead to public acceptance.[11] We like to say that law is now 'embedded' in the business, being so complex and pervasive as to be part of every decision, not a discrete event that can be channelled to legal experts. So legal decision-making cannot be readily separated from overall business decision-making.

7. Conclusion

Some general counsel view risk management and compliance as being at odds with innovation – in 2015, that view is well out of date. Effectively managing innovation and effectively managing risk are two complementary outcomes of competence, rooted in understanding the business and managing appropriate processes. Savvy general counsel know how to integrate innovation with their job, both in how their team does its work and how they enable innovation across the company.

---

11 In the Deepwater Horizon disaster it appears that BP's lawyers did an effective job of shifting the nominal legal risk to subcontractors Transocean and Halliburton, but that did not prevent BP from 'holding the bag' for more than $40 billion when catastrophic failure hit. BP's lawyers would have been much more valuable if they had advised the CEO that instead of going sailing and being quoted as saying "I want my life back", he and the executive team should have been on the beaches of Louisiana cleaning up oil with cotton swabs.

Lawyers at the revolution

Kent Walker
Google

1. Introduction

An explosion of innovation is changing the way we live and work. Blogs, wikis, social networks, video sharing, mobile networks and the internet itself let people participate and work with each other in dramatic new ways. Within this new environment, lawyers play a critical role in promoting innovation.[1] In the face of change, the lawyer's role is not about protecting the status quo, but about helping innovators to make sense of the constraints and opportunities of current and future legal regimes to maximise the benefits of new technology for everyone.

2. The new New World

2.1 Present at the creation

"You and I, dear friend, have been sent into life at a time when the greatest lawgivers of antiquity would have wished to live", John Adams wrote to Abigail in 1776. It was an amazing time. And what kid growing up has not dreamed of being present at the creation of a world-shaping event like the American Revolution?

2.2 Trumpets and fireworks

But of course we are in the midst of a revolution – the Information Revolution – that is just as real and, arguably, even more important for the lives of people around the world. It may seem like hubris to think that our times are as important as something like the founding of a nation; popular culture conditions us to think of revolutions as all trumpets and fireworks, as moments when slowly building events reach a crescendo. Even scholarly works of history can reinforce this sense of high drama by telescoping events to form a ready narrative.

2.3 The subtle power of the everyday

And yet, maybe that is exactly where we are. Sometimes we swim in the ocean we swim in and do not recognise it as an ocean. The everyday challenges we face have a subtle power and lay the foundations for great changes. As I tell my team, the people sewing the sails and hauling the rigging of ships exploring the New World doubtless focused on the bad food and the blisters, but they were taking part in a revolution.

---

1 This chapter is based on a speech given at *The Economist*'s Third Annual General Counsel West Coast Roundtable, "Outstanding leadership in a rapidly evolving business environment".

2.4 **Newcomen's engine**

Earlier this year, I took my kids to see Thomas Newcomen's steam engine – there is a replica at the Science Museum in London – a huge thing of steel and brick. I told my kids that this was the most important and coolest thing they would see in England and they immediately told me what a dork I was. Newcomen was solving an ordinary problem – water leaking into a coal pit in Wales – but his solution, an external combustion steam engine, led to the internal combustion engine and unleashed the Industrial Revolution.

2.5 **Weber's electric current**

Max Weber wrote of the electric current of history passing through different places at different times. Usually, it is through the political and financial capitals of the world; sometimes it is a coal pit in Wales. But in the past few years, there is an argument that that current has passed through Silicon Valley and its cousins around the world – or at least that Silicon Valley is 'ground zero' for the disruptive technological and informational changes we are seeing. These changes are the 21st-century version of Newcomen's steam engine or Gutenberg's press – and the long-term implications are just as hard to judge.

2.6 **Accelerating technology, accelerating progress**

We talk about an information revolution, but it is really a technology and telecommunications revolution. Technological change is the bedrock of progress. If you glance at a graph of *per capita* welfare, it is clear that the world existed for millennia in a Malthusian universe in which short bursts of progress were quickly swamped and the average standard of living plateaued for centuries. That changed dramatically in the 18th century and the accelerating pace of technological change has driven not only new economies, but new social structures as well.

2.7 **Faster and faster**

We have seen stunning developments within a couple of decades: leaps of advancement in integrated circuits and personal computers; the rise of networking software and tools; the popularisation of the internet browser; the emergence of online marketplaces and user-generated content; and the rise of mobile computing. And each technology shift comes faster: if you look at telephones, radio, television, personal computers, the internet and cell phones, it took less and less time for each to reach broad adoption.

2.8 **The Cloud – substance and process**

Now we have the network, the Cloud – interconnectedness and infinite access to information – and, with Web 2.0, the ability to create information – giving everyone his own printing press. What are the implications of that change – and the globalisation that it drives – for the law and lawyers? In this chapter I discuss the rising field of information law, how we as lawyers should think of our role in that field and how these same technologies will change how all of us will work in years to come – lawyering in the Cloud.

3. The rise of information law

3.1 Horses for courses

Just as new technologies drive new economic and social structures, new economic and social structures drive the development of the law. It is not an accident that the law of property and trusts and estates flowered in the feudal era of the 14th century, where control and inheritance of real property was the central economic question, and that we still talk about Queen Ann's Rule and use terms drawn from Norman French to describe property rights. Nor is it an accident that the law of contract really developed in the 17th and 18th centuries with the influx of masterless men into the cities, where relationships were governed by contract more than feudal status.

3.2 Information law

Similarly, we are now seeing a dramatic rise in importance in certain areas of law most affected by and affecting the widespread flow of information. Global content laws, privacy, intellectual property, competition, jurisdiction and regulatory laws – a constellation I dub 'information law' – are all rising in prominence with critical decisions reinterpreting long-held principles in light of new circumstances.

3.3 The sometimes provocative role of law and lawyers

Let me start with a few examples of the important, and sometimes provocative, ways that laws have shaped the Information Revolution. Most revolutions may come out of the barrel of a gun, but in the Information Revolution – like the American Revolution – lawyers have played their part. Most would agree that the internet has been a huge benefit to people everywhere. But it has also been a disruptive force to many industries and those industries have sometimes tried to claim that important internet developments were illegal. But lawyers have generally been successful in showing that the traditional first principles of information laws support innovation and benefits for consumers.

(a) eBay in France

eBay, a former employer, had to consult five French law firms before finding one that would argue that it was legal to operate in France in the face of Napoleonic Code sections limiting auction houses to those given charters by Bonaparte. Today, more than 10 million people in France use eBay's services.

(b) Browsers and search engines

In the mid-1990s, when I was at Netscape, some argued that the very act of using an internet browser to copy and view someone else's content violated copyright law. Similarly, some have challenged the operation of search engines by questioning whether they have the right to crawl the web to build useful indexes of content. But courts have regularly resisted attempts to expand IP law to block new and useful innovations, harking back to core principles of fair use and fair dealing.

(c) ***Safe harbours***

The platforms that permit unprecedented creation of user-generated content would not exist without new laws around the world that support the democratisation of speech. Laws such as the Digital Millennium Copyright Act or the Communications Decency Act in the United States or the E-commerce Directive in Europe have created safe harbours for the new services and platforms that opened the way to widespread sharing of even controversial views and information, which otherwise might have been shut for fear of threats over defamation and copyright infringement.

3.4 Fear of the new

In hindsight, many legal concerns with new technology seem reactionary, but they are very real at the time. People fear the new. It disrupts the settled order. But it is also the essence of capitalism, which Joseph Schumpeter called "a gale of creative destruction", sweeping away the outmoded guilds and orders of the past. However, yesterday's guilds and orders are today's vested interests, which benefit from the current ways of doing business and sometimes seek to entrench through legislation rules that protect the status quo at the expense of users.

3.5 The law of the horse?

The well-respected jurist Frank Easterbrook wrote an article almost 20 years ago called "The Law of the Horse", arguing that we did not need new laws for the internet any more than Europe needed new laws for the horse when it came from the New World – rather, it fitted into existing legal categories. In other words, this is just old wine in new bottles. To some degree it is a question of granularity – if your bottles are big enough, if all law involves either things that people do with each other either voluntarily (contract law) or involuntarily (tort law), Easterbrook may be right. However, there is an advantage to thinking more granularly through unique new problems informed by new circumstances. The last 10 years have shown a steady rise in the importance and growth of information law – in response to new technologies, new business models and new social developments. Here are some examples.

(a) ***Global content***

Globalisation – Tom Friedman's flattening world – brings us closer than ever before. There are now billions of internet users in the world today, growing at a rate of several hundreds of millions a year. But that closeness highlights some of the differences: we have one internet but more than 200 countries. The globalisation of content poses serious challenges to local culture and laws. Different cultures have very different understandings of the balance between free expression and social order. For example:

- We wrestle with issues in Turkey when people post material criticising Ataturk, the founder of the modern Turkish state and a symbol of Turkish secularism, and in Thailand when people post material critical of the king, who is a demigod in Thai Buddhism and widely beloved by his people.
- In the United States many people are sensitive to displays of nudity, but easily accept pictures of people brandishing firearms. In the United Kingdom the reverse is generally true.

- We understand German sensitivities around expressions of Nazism. But what about religious criticism and debate between Hindus and Muslims in India, which have experienced massive riots and violence over religion within the last 60 years?
- And what about the case of China's authoritarian regime, with a mix of situations ranging from investigations of common crimes to suppression of dissent (or, as the Chinese government sees it, threats to public order)?

Before the internet, these differences in how each country views freedom of speech would have been interesting only to a scholar. The theoretical question "Are France and Germany's definitions of illegal Nazi speech the same or different?" had little practical application because the speech was local and, for the most part, locally confined. In contrast, most internet communication is, by default, global. When an Australian talks about Nazis on a Canadian discussion site, those words are, by default, available to people in Germany and France. "Are France and Germany's definitions of illegal Nazi speech the same or different?" is now a real question that may have practical ramifications.

So in this interconnected world, what is the benchmark for how much democracy, how much transparency and what kinds of speech-limiting law are okay? Expression that is tolerated in some countries is highly offensive and possibly even dangerous in others. There is a clash between the spread of universal information and local cultures and laws. How do we balance our commitment to free expression with corporate social responsibility (and keeping our employees safe)?

(b) Privacy

In the modern world of information, more facts about all of us are available more readily and more permanently. More information gathering, better search tools and strong public disclosure laws challenge older ideas of 'privacy by obscurity'; and yet it is precisely the innovative use of personalisation and customisation that makes many new technologies both useful and fun.

With the technological landscape of privacy changing, it is more important than ever to return to bedrock principles of privacy law to understand how those principles should be interpreted in light of technological change. And yet, here again, cultures differ.

The United States takes a sectoral approach to privacy, with specific laws privileging financial and medical records, children's information and, oddly, video rentals. Americans are concerned about government misuse of information and more accepting of private-sector uses where there is consumer benefit. In Europe, on the other hand, privacy is seen as an inalienable human right. Many are comfortable with government access to information (street cameras etc), but uncomfortable with the potential for private-sector abuses. And the Asia-Pacific Economic Cooperation forum takes yet a third view, focusing on a sliding scale of protection based on the potential for harm to the data subject.

These varying standards are tricky for all multinational corporations and there have been various efforts to harmonise them or create recognised safe harbours for transfer. The inconsistent rules are particularly difficult for those of us in the information industries, where data flows freely through the Cloud.

(c) Competition law

When it comes to competition law, different regions again have very different standards – from the approach of Europe that traditionally focused more on the protection of competitors and the market ecosystem, to the recent approach of many regulators in the United States, which are focused on consumer welfare, and the evolving approaches of many countries in the developing world that are just starting to wrestle with these issues.

Layered on top of those differences are new law-and-economic theories of special factors – network effects, lock-in, path dependency – that apply differently to the many different settings and markets in the new economy. The challenge for lawyers is to work through these concerns while keeping traditional notions of consumer benefit as our North Star.

(d) Intellectual property

Likewise, when it comes to the law of intellectual property (IP), the field perhaps at the core of information law, technological change can challenge some existing notions but does not change the bedrock principles of law.

For IP law, those bedrock principles are explicitly set forth in Article I, Section 8, of the US Constitution: the whole system of IP law exists to protect creativity and innovation, but for the benefit of the whole of society. As Article I, Section 8, says – and it is the only grant of powers modified by a purpose clause – the purpose of these limited monopolies is to encourage "the progress of science and the useful arts". In this spirit, Google is committed to a balanced approach to IP protection that furthers the interests of both creators and the public at large.

The Laffer curve of intellectual property, often mentioned during the Reagan era, shows how a zero tax rate generates no revenues and a 100% tax rate generates no revenues. There is an analogue in IP law – creating the IP monopolies of copyright, patent and trademark supports innovation in some areas, but also creates vested interests with an incentive to push for a one-way ratchet expanding the scope of those government-granted monopolies. And making those monopolies too broad shuts out competitive innovation at the margin.

With regard to specific aspects of IP law, the following comments are relevant:

- *Patents:* Our patent law system was designed to fuel innovation, but I fear in some sectors it is falling short. Twenty-year cycles are not suited to the fast-paced technological world. Our system is overwhelmed with bad patents that we lack the tools, expertise and incentives to detect. We should push to protect what is truly innovative by increasing the number and quality of patent reviewers and pushing for uniformity in the process of review. But we also need reforms to avoid abuses that actually punish innovative companies through arbitrary jurisdictions, unreasonable damage awards and weak but irreversible patents.
- *Copyright*: Likewise, we build a solid foundation for creativity by getting

copyright law right. In describing the balance of effective copyright law, the British Lord Ellenborough wrote in 1803, as later quoted by the US Supreme Court: "While I shall think myself bound to secure every man in the enjoyment of his copy-right, one must not put manacles upon science." The digital era creates the potential for wider misuse of copyrighted goods; but in trying to stop that possibility, we face the offsetting risk of overextending the practical enforcement of copyrights. Fair and beneficial uses of copyrighted material that were never stopped before (eg, indexing a book) are being challenged to no one's benefit. The aggressive enforcement of digital rights management schemes has restricted the use of copyrighted material, sometimes in unreasonable ways. In adhering to copyright law's historical balance, we find a reasonable middle ground for enforcement that also promotes creative fair uses while protecting incentives to create copyrighted work.

- *Trademarks:* Trademark law does not get as much press as patent and copyright law, but it likewise plays a role in encouraging the development of quality goods and protecting consumers. But we have all too often seen systems designed to protect consumers get hijacked and used to protect incumbents. In Europe, a trademark is almost a moral right, protecting the investments of luxury goods makers; in the United States there has been a greater focus on helping consumers identify the source of goods. In the era of an internet that allows for more information, wider choices and better comparison shopping, the goal should be helping consumers get what they want. When a grocery store puts a less expensive item next to a popular item, the consumer has a choice. This is how new brands gain market share and consumers benefit, and thus far it has been the approach that most courts have taken.

(e) ***Jurisdiction***

The internet has breathed new life into the musty old jurisprudential questions of jurisdiction – which are now suddenly critical to questions of how and whether one country should be able to regulate the content of a global internet. What are minimum contacts in the Information Age: a website, a local domain, people in a country, data flowing through a country, business contacts, etc? We have no clear – let alone universally accepted – answers.

(f) ***Regulatory law***

From time out of mind, regulation and regulators have been subject to capture by special interests that have twisted legal rules originally designed to serve the public interest into barriers to entry against new competitors. Where one industry can entrench itself by co-opting the legislative or regulatory process, the public suffers. The internet – and the free flow of information and access that it permits – has challenged a number of these limits around the world, reducing entry barriers and eroding information monopolies. I have mentioned the old French rules against competition for auctions. In the United States, we have seen the Federal Trade Commission repeatedly take action against legislative and bureaucratic barriers to ecommerce, the Department of Justice recently move to stop discrimination against online real estate brokers, and the Supreme Court rule that laws against the interstate sale of wine (chiefly through ecommerce) unconstitutionally discriminated against interstate commerce.

I expect that all of these areas of law – information law – will continue to expand and be special areas of legal focus for years to come, paralleling the evolution of the Information Age economy.

4. The role of lawyers in a world of innovation

4.1 Lawyers as innovation facilitators

So how do we navigate these technological developments, steering by the stars of traditional legal precedents? Many of our rules are often framed for very different situations and the laws of different countries and regions clash. These are situations where a deep understanding of precedent and first principle, and the courage to weather pressure and uncertainty while these issues are resolved, are key attributes of good legal counsel. We as lawyers – as much as the policy wonks or the moral philosophers – have a role to play. We are sometimes criticised for being agents of the status quo, but understanding and applying the spirit of the law to new technological innovation can be affirmative as well as defensive: we can push for improved approaches to problems, to approach new issues from new perspectives, to maximise the benefit of technology for everyone.

4.2 Helping with the transition

For 150 years the reporters of *The Economist* have pledged themselves to take part in "a severe contest between intelligence, which presses forward, and an unworthy, timid ignorance, obstructing our progress." Like the press, lawyers can be agents of progress – not just papering the deals and prosecuting the patents, but helping to imagine and bring about the new businesses that bring the benefits of innovation to everyone. As lawyers, we have our roots in precedents, the experience of history, but our default position should not be to slow down the pace of growth. Concerns about technological change are real and understandable. Radio had a hard time adapting to television and print is having varying success on the web. The success of YouTube took many people by surprise. New technologies can disrupt business models. And the problem is that if you are in the old technology and the old business model, there is a natural need and desire to hang on. If the old business does not find creative solutions to adapt to the changing environment, it is in trouble. Lawyers, at our best, can facilitate a transition from one system to the next, helping companies find a productive approach to the new economy.

4.3 Officers of the court

We are both advocates for our clients and officers of the court. As I have argued, our collective goal as lawyers should be to promote social benefit for people around the world. When I was a federal prosecutor, we were inspired by the saying "the government wins when justice triumphs". The obligation in the private sector is just as strong; it is the commitment to the right thing for society that animates both the commitment to compliance and the commitment to the end user – people and society writ large. I think that that is the key to being on the right side of history.

4.4 Our mission

For lawyers at Google, we look back to our mission statement: "organising the world's information and making it universally accessible and useful". What you need to believe is simply this: on the whole, information is good. Information is power. Information increases the pie and ultimately transforms peoples' lives. Different companies, and different lawyers, will have different areas of emphasis and different ways of achieving those goals.

4.5 Respect for law

As lawyers in a democracy, we look to the law as the distillation and codification of the ethics of a community. No one argues that a person, or a company, should violate the laws outside the rare circumstances where the laws themselves violate international standards of human rights. And yet the rapid evolution of technology and disputes over how to apply legal precedent pose fundamental questions for lawyers. At Google, we work in an industry that changes quickly. But we also work in an era where many of the laws and policies governing information have their roots in the world of 300 years ago. We constantly ask ourselves: are we being true to the spirit of those legal roots? Are we being bold enough in supporting innovation? Or are we letting the law be bent to prohibit innovation, to create structures that will make it harder and harder to make substantive progress? Where is the right balance of compliance, accommodation and support for innovation?

5. Lawyering in the Cloud

5.1 What does it mean in practice?

How does all of this affect the way legal departments practise now and in the future? The participatory aspect of the modern internet has eroded the hierarchies of information control. Applications in the network cloud – blogs, wikis, video sharing, mobile networks and the internet itself – let people work with each other in dramatic new ways. Collaboration and universal access to information are each becoming both easy and essential in the business world.

5.2 Collaborative lawyering

It is far easier to organise and access information that our friends and colleagues create. At Google, we constantly use videoconferencing to hold meetings between colleagues in various parts of the world. We use programs such as Google Docs so that team members can simultaneously edit the same document no matter where they are in the world. Small, distributed teams become both possible and often the most efficient way to accomplish a task. Organisational design changes: less hub-and-spoke, more a fishnet of nodes, distributed intelligence. Everyone is smarter than anyone. It has always been true – but now we can put it into practice.

5.3 The death of command and control

How do lawyers practise in a world that is less about hierarchy, or command-and-control, and more about an all-volunteer army where there is a lateralisation of decision-making power and numerous people have the ability to veto new initiatives? What used to be management becomes facilitation, what was direction becomes persuasion. Focusing on collaboration and teamwork can be hard for lawyers; we were the guys in the library on Saturday night while the MBA students were networking at a party. Compounding this change is the generational shift – people are used to being persuaded, not just being told. As a result, we have to change not just how we practise, but how we counsel our clients.

5.4 Working and playing – the collaborative norms of the next generation

These tools are not just at work any more. With social networking and new technologies, there are lower barriers to entry and higher expectations of shared communication. Just look at your kids' Facebook pages, with 'personal' conversations played out in public. There is less control over the voices in the space and new voices are being heard for the first time – everyone has his own printing press. People used to be told what news mattered; now they can decide what news matters to them. Search engines can give you information as to what people are thinking more quickly, and then you can decide what your own view is.

5.5 What happens to gatekeepers when the gates come tumbling down?

It is possible to find information on almost any subject by simply typing a few keywords into a computer or a hand-held device. So the generations of lawyers and business people coming up are not looking to you for answers – they are just as likely to be able to find the right answers on a law blog as you are. Lawyers had been the gatekeepers of information; increasingly, we need to become the interpreters and the counsellors based on information that everyone knows – valued for our judgement as much as for our specialised skills.

5.6 Insight over expertise

I would argue that we as lawyers tend to overvalue content and information and even knowledge, and undervalue the service of making good advice readily accessible and useful. Contrary to most management gurus, who preach that the answer is "more communication" – no matter what the question – I suspect that the answer is better communication: fewer meetings and emails, more insight.

5.7 Re-engineering the profession

It is no secret that the legal profession is not geared for change. Our own professional regulation blocks inventive activities that might transform legal markets. If Larry Page and Sergey Brin had had to get degrees in library science before they could embark on "making the world's information more accessible and useful", they probably would have thrown in the towel. The result of too much regulation, too many barriers to entry, is the risk of a homogeneous pool of lawyers, thinking of problems in pre-identified and filtered legal categories, and having a harder time thinking outside of the notorious box.

5.8 Bimodal lawyering

It may surprise you to learn that the average salary for lawyers in the United States went down in recent years. You would not know it, because the prices we see in corporate America go nowhere but up. But that just says that we are seeing a dramatically bimodal distribution. Top lawyers – lawyers who offer good advice and analysis – are paid more. Like investment bankers, there is a huge premium at the top and there is even an argument that the best lawyers are underpaid for the value they deliver. But bankers are paid only if successful. Lawyers are generally paid by the hour and it is often hard to tell whether a given lawyer is good or not, so we may start to see an increasing tendency for companies to look more widely for great legal services rather than sticking with the well-known, but increasingly expensive, brand-name law firms. And at the same time, the lawyers who do not evolve face a tougher and tougher world, where globalisation facilitates outsourcing and automation of commodity work. Mere information – how to draw up a will, handle a basic divorce, how to incorporate a company – is standardised and easily available in books and online. The high-end value of information analysis is where the big marginal returns are for lawyers in future.

5.9 New beginnings

We all need to think critically about the role of lawyers in the decades to come. We have the opportunity to be part of shepherding in the technologies that will change the way we interact, work and live. If we promote legal frameworks that promote innovation and creativity, and legal practice that promotes collaboration and judgement, we can help to ensure that that change benefits people around the world.

5.10 New generations of creators

By the time they have completed high school, the vast majority of kids in the developed world have authored work online – whether it be a YouTube video or a blog or a MySpace page. Think about that. This wave of technological innovation has the potential to make my kids and your kids and, ultimately, kids in the developing world not merely passive consumers of entertainers, but a generation of creators – of authors and artists, scientists and educators.

5.11 And back to Adams

So let me close where I began. John Adams said that he studied politics and war so that his sons might study mathematics and commerce, and their children might study painting and poetry, music and art. We practise as lawyers in the hope of building a world where it is easier for our children to thrive as authors, artists and inventors. Affirmative lawyering – lawyering in a time of change, lawyering for innovation and lawyering in defence of time-honoured principles but with an eye to the potential of the future – can help bring that world closer.

The case of PGGM: the transformational legal department

Max Hübner
PGGM NV

1. Introduction

The Financial Times regularly makes awards to those who have made a particular contribution to the legal community by introducing sweeping, innovative change. In 2013 PGGM was ranked most innovative in operational change in-house for "encouraging high performance from the team through smart management, cutting costs and making the legal department one of the most respected in the company". In this chapter I describe how this occurred at PGGM and give some pointers to how transformational change in providing legal services can be achieved.

2. A few preliminary remarks

There is no need to address the changes and forces of discontinuity that occur in the field of legal services. There are many things that have created or will potentially create a discontinuity; we are all familiar with them and aware of their impact on law firms and legal departments. Let me take you on a journey about transformational change and how I have proactively managed my legal teams over the last two decades. During the past 20 years I have often failed, never given up and finally succeeded in changing the play in the middle of the game. Thus, let me challenge you. Let me – I am known for this – irritate you. Let me indulge you. Please allow yourself the opportunity to understand how to turn those stumbling blocks into stepping stones to transform your legal department. That is, if you want to make a future difference in delivering in-house legal services starting today. I will address the importance of integrated quality when I made that difference. I will reflect on how to achieve better results with lower headcounts and at the same time reduce costs. I will start with a few preliminary remarks. First, on how we can wish for change and at the same time cannot neglect the craftsmanship of the legal professional. Secondly, on challenges that general counsel face, but do not need to fear. Finally, I share an observation on how to overcome conventional wisdom.

2.1 Change is more than wishful thinking

When it comes to change, I am the first to confess that there really is nothing new under the sun. Change has always been, is and will always be a product of wishful thinking. We, as an executive, want to change. We want to improve the way we deliver legal services to our companies. That is why we think wishfully about change – the wish being 'executive' and the thinking being 'professional'. This is not an easy exercise, as you will discover throughout this chapter. We have to bear in mind that in the field of professional services (whether legal or not), it is possible to distinguish between a professional world and an executive (or managerial) world. Professionals are to be found in a world of legal excellence, where they strive to reach the highest legal standard. Meanwhile executives wander around in their world where earnings before interest, taxes and amortisation is king.

At the same time we can recognise a double interplay between the wish and the thinking. This double interplay was introduced by Willem Riphagen as a pattern of a scientific model of the techniques to be applied in international law.[1] I redesigned the Riphagen model and applied it as a legislator for the Dutch government when negotiating and drafting treaties.[2] The model clarifies the interaction between parties when dealing with complex matters that need to be addressed and written down. It also applies to the interaction between professionals and executives. The professional is not willing to give up on legal excellence when the need for change occurs. The executive will sell his soul for the company's profitability, so why not legal excellence? They interact with each other in their own play, so there are two games played at the same time. That is the double interplay.

Today I use the model to stipulate the importance of an understanding to be able to establish transformational change. In the world of legal services, the double interplay is that between 'ought' and 'be' and between 'executive' and 'professional'. In this interplay the 'ought' corresponds to the 'managerial wish' part and the 'be' corresponds to the 'professional thinking' part of the wishful thinking of change in professional services organisations. The interplay is one of the more important elements in transformation. When you are able to recognise this interplay, you are likely to be successful. That is, if you do not want to reach the perfect balance. In my humble opinion, managers in search of change too often strive to make the wish and thinking compatible. They try to separate 'ought' and 'be' and at the same time 'executive' and 'professional'. I made that mistake for the first time 15 years ago. One of my friendly professionals asked me if I really believed that the gap between the executive and professional could be fully bridged – in other words, that a perfect balance could be attained between wish and thinking. The answer was, is and always will be: no. When on the quest for delivering outstanding legal services, one can only approach such a balance as is the case with the 'more for less' challenge.

2.2 The 'less for better' experience

Many might still believe that general counsel and law firms are facing a never-ending 'more for less' challenge. I believe they are wrong. Professor Richard Susskind described this particular challenge for the first time in 2008.[3] In his bestselling and much quoted book, Susskind questioned the future of law firms. It is a fact that they are still around. Recently he offered lawyers an introduction to their future.[4] The

---

1 Willem Riphagen, 'Techniques of international law (Volume 246)', *Collected Courses of the Hague Academy of International Law*, Brill/Nijhoff, Leiden/Boston, 1994.

2 Max Hübner, 'The United Nations and International Law Enforcement, applied techniques of International Law', Open University Utrecht, 1996.

3 Richard Susskind, *The End of Lawyers? Rethinking the Nature of Legal Services*, Oxford, 2008.

lesson learned? One can rethink the nature of legal services, question the end of lawyers and predict their future, but those who deliver legal services are the only ones able to reinvent those services. I started to reinvent legal services in 1998, although at the time I did not know that this was the case. Ten years later Susskind more or less helped me to put things in place. I learned that for a number of years more innovative trailblazers had already been making their way out there in the so-called future of legal services. And there are more to come.

General counsel naturally face pressure on costs. This is not unique. Every executive has to deal with budget constraints. But it does not necessarily mean that they will be looking for more services or (worse) value for less money. Since the early 1980s I have witnessed an ongoing increase in legislation and regulation, but I have never felt the pressure to reduce the headcount in my legal department or legal spend. Why? I chose to shape the future of my legal departments. As a result they proved to deliver better legal services and at the same spent less time and thus money on delivering them. Legal counsel on my past and present teams share the very important 'less for better' value. Not a stumbling block or burden, but a personal value that appeals to high-quality standards from a professional point of view and at the same time takes into account the need to be penny-wise not legal-foolish. What about the legal fools likely to be left behind in this decade? Here is a mirror.

2.3 Conventional wisdom

The concept of 'conventional wisdom' was first presented by John Kenneth Galbraith in 1958,[5] although some argue that it originated in the 19th century. Over and over, despite the fact that the opposite is all around us today, it is stated that the majority of legal services can only be delivered in person. From a historical point of view it does not surprise me. Conventional lawyers and thus legal counsel have their roots in the 7th century, when the practice of law became a real profession due to the knowledge, skills and expertise needed. We can agree that law firms and legal departments once were – and most still are – professional services organisations. David Maister compares them to a medieval artisan's shop – a shop in which we can find lawyers who are apprentices (trainees), journeymen (more experienced associates) and master craftsmen (senior partners).[6] As in those early days, there is still a leveraging system in place to maximise revenues. Classical law firms do not want to sell products; they provide high-quality legal services by giving bespoke advice (trustworthy relations need 'face time'). The same applies for too many legal departments. They want the same prestige as their law firms – except that these legal departments do not maximise revenues but, acting as ancient artisans, increase costs.

Since 2000, when the 'more for less' challenge started to become apparent, some general counsel introduced new concepts to reach an innovative level of executing the legal profession. For example, I unbundled the legal activities at a governmental legal department. I subsequently standardised and outsourced parts of the legal tasks.

---

4 Richard Susskind, *Tomorrow's Lawyers, An Introduction to Your Future*, Oxford, 2013.
5 John Kenneth Galbraith, *The Affluent Society*, Boston, 1958.
6 David Meister, *Managing the Professional Service Firm*, Simon and Schuster, New York, 1993.

It was not difficult, only awkward – that is, from a legal professional's point of view. Today, many law firms are still unwilling to unbundle, standardise or 'mass produce' their services because their revenues come from billing hours with – so they state – clients who have different needs and demands. More important is the fact that many general counsel too are still stuck to their conventional wisdom and therefore accept the ancient business model of delivering legal services.

I believe that, despite some brave attempts, the medieval organisational structure and its impossibility to alter is one of the most persistent conventional wisdoms in the field of legal services. Many general counsel hang on to this wisdom when they should know better. Too few general counsel have an appetite for unbundling their legal services. In my experience standardised contracting (commoditisation) can be easily embedded in the business, with no legal counsel involved. I admit that the legal professionals had to overcome their fears when 'giving away' those well-caressed contracts to the sales barbarians. At first, the barbarians were reluctant to use those wicked things called contracts without any legal aid, but with a little help they finally succeeded. So it surprises me that many legal departments still hang on to the artisan's shop and thus the conventional wisdom for delivering legal services.

But the thing with conventional wisdom is that it is not necessarily true. In the case of transforming legal services, the conventional wisdom on how to deliver services operates as an obstacle that must be overcome. By now it has reached the point of absurd denial of the new world. We all know full well that it is convenient to stick to a service model that has not been proven to be outdated – despite being out-priced or costly. Maybe it is because it seems to be the everlasting winning model. This is also the general counsel's mistake. To speak for myself, I cannot hang on to only a gatekeeping role. One cannot face the 'more for less' burden and complain about how not to achieve business requirements. Meanwhile, a number of general counsel are reluctant (it is a buyer's market, remember) to take on board entrepreneurial legal service providers or to implement new service models for delivering in-house legal services. So law firms repeat the 'happily by the hour' wisdom, while most general counsel still pay by the hour.[7] What did I do to overturn this conventional wisdom? I bridged the implementation gap, played double and transformed legal departments.

3. The transformational legal department

The concept of the transformational legal department – as I named this kind of change – is based on my previous experiences as a legal professional, an executive director and a general counsel. On the side I read books and picked up some ideas and figured out how to apply them. Not at random, but with a clear focus: one needs quality to establish an outperforming legal department.

---

7 *Unbundling a market: the appetite for new legal services models*, Allen & Overy, 2014.

3.1 Quality

Like any other professional, legal counsel understand the importance of quality. When delivering legal services, they strive to reach the highest level of legal quality. However, this single level of quality is not nearly enough. A legal counsel needs to deliver more than just brilliant legal advice on a state-of-the-art level. The legal department can no longer present itself as the company's legal gatekeeping cost centre. Today every professional is constantly challenged to contribute to the company's profitability. Therefore, when solely driven by professional excellence the conventional legal professional neglects this business requirement. Tomorrow's legal counsel not only feels noticeably responsible for the company's success, but delivers the outperforming legal services and therefore adds value. So what comes next? My tutor, Louis Bunt, explained that modern legal counsel must take into account five key indicators to address professional quality.[8] He uses the model shown in Figure 1.

Figure 1: Five key indicators of quality in the legal profession

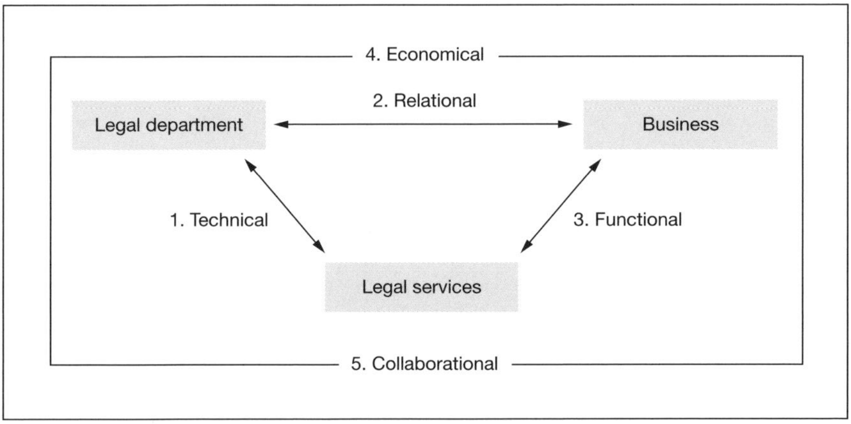

The model helps to show that besides the legal (ie, technical) quality, a legal counsel must synchronously meet the expected standard on how to relate with internal and external clients. They expect client-centred and connecting behaviour, including communication in a clear, non-veiled manner so that non-legal persons can understand the solutions provided. Besides these technical and relational qualities, the legal department must take into account the usability of the legal services (the functional quality). Does the result and outcome of the state-of-the-art legal work meet the (underlying) expectations of the client? The thing is that superb technical quality does not automatically imply high functional quality, although legal professionals often expect this to be the case. We must deliver state-of-the-art legal services that meet the required technical, relational and functional qualities. But not at any price. From the business's perspective, the legal counsel must deliver value for money and from a general counsel's point of view, the legal department's services must meet the

8 Louis Bunt, *Seven Qualities for Professional Services*, Breda, 2014.

economical standards. Last but not least there must be a level of collaboration (a trustworthy partnership) that adds on from the company's cultural perspective. I am convinced that by using this model any legal department can make the leap and reach a level of outperforming services. This is how my legal departments succeeded.

3.2 Perceptions of quality

I aimed to prioritise the value of the legal department services. I knew that the quick wins and first benefits were to be found in-house. Strategic (not just legal) advice is considered the highest-value output of the legal department. It reflects the core services that the legal department provides for any company. It is this kind of advice that directly adds value to the company's projects and overall strategic goals. For this kind of highly valued work, understanding the business is a critical success factor. Therefore, the legal department – as any support service – had to respond effectively to wishes and needs, while in the meantime reflecting organisational and business goals, and guarding the legal boundaries.

With Stephan van Gelder, chief executive at Integron, I co-created specifically for the legal department an internal customer satisfaction research survey.[9] At present, Integron is one of the leading research and consulting firms on customer satisfaction surveys. This internal customer satisfaction research enabled me to make my legal department more aware and more effective. It equipped my team with the knowledge it needed to work on the further development of our services. My legal department became more aware of their responsibilities towards their internal customers. We furthermore strengthened our relationship with them and increased our added value. What exactly did Stephan and I do?

First of all we needed to know what questions to ask the legal department's internal customers. The questionnaire could not cover only the technical (legal) quality. Most (internal) clients are non-legal and therefore unable to assess the technical/legal quality; they simply rely on that quality as a given. As a legal counsel, one is considered to be able to deliver good legal services. It is not surprising that clients give high rates for technical quality. As a matter of fact, if we look closer at their rating, they intuitively assess not just this technical quality but – based on perceptions – also relational, functional and commercial quality. Therefore, the survey also had to take into account the functional, relational, economical and collaborative qualities. Could we do that? Yes: in early 2011 we developed and conducted an internal customer satisfaction research survey that took into account the legal quality and the process, but also the issue of human contact. In addition to the overall level, the survey drew a distinction between specific customer groups in order to ensure focus on specific improvements. The survey was conducted with the legal department's objectives and image in mind.

The legal counsel themselves answered the online questionnaire. They were asked to rate themselves – but through their customers' eyes. They had to write down how their customers would rate them on the five quality indicators (see Figure 2). They were modest and thought that an overall score for customer satisfaction would be 68 (on a scale of 0 to 100).

---

9 This survey can be made available on request.

Figure 2: Perceptions of quality

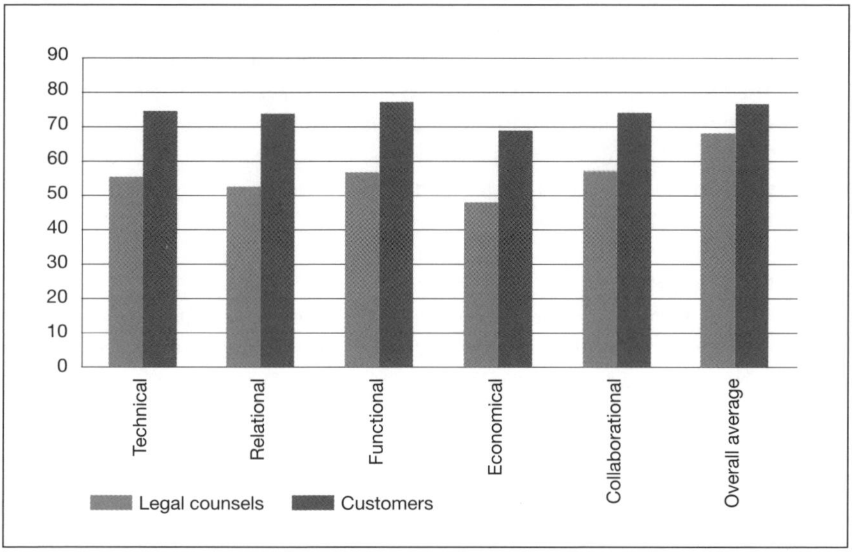

At the same time the research revealed internal customers' expectations and how satisfied and loyal they were to the legal department. We were pleasantly surprised: our internal customers rated us higher than we expected on every quality. Their overall average rating was a well-received 77%. We learned a few things: first, there was no reason to feel sorry for being a legal professional; secondly, we had happy customers; and thirdly, we could still improve customer satisfaction by 23%. Furthermore, we realised that legal professionals tend to prefer to be better safe than sorry: a client who rates at '70' is not disappointed but satisfied. Finally the results made us aware of how to manage expectations and increase customer satisfaction on certain qualities. We therefore needed to change. We had to believe in our added value, our personalities and our values. We also had to go further beyond traditional legal counselling. For me, to change a legal department and increase added value one has to make the individual legal counsel aware of his possibilities – to change the play in the middle of the game.

I did not further analyse the internal customer satisfaction research survey, make benchmarks or write a masterplan for the future of the legal department. Instead I held in-depth conversations taking into account the survey results with every legal counsel, the internal customers, the stakeholders and some of the company law firms. I tried to understand their mindsets, beliefs, principles and values. I wanted to identify their fears, threads, dreams and goals. And while having those conversations I enlarged the purpose of the company's vision for the (near) future from a mutual point of view. I jotted down the key elements for delivering services, scribbled some notes on behaviour and drew a picture on the organisation of work. By then, everyone involved knew that a change was going to take place. More importantly, every member of the legal team knew that they were the ones changing.

But the challenge is not simply to identify change, or even fundamental change. One needs to identify the point at which the change becomes so profound that it rewrites the rules. That is where transformation takes place – if you want it to. This has nothing to do with saying yes to change, but all about individuals doing things. Therefore, I sat down with my legal counsel and agreed with every one of them what their contribution should be to that change; how they would change. We linked personal planning, performance and personal rewards to the achievement of our company's strategy. They all had a personal plan in place. That is how the transformation started.

4. My blueprint

So here is my blueprint. I used it to make a difference; you can use it to make the leap. I must admit that to have a blueprint is not enough; the applied transformation is by interpretation and will have its own applied experience – or not – depending on how brave you are on your journey. Bearing in mind that the past does not remain a reliable guide to the future, my legal department had to reach out and relate. This is a matter of personality and how added value can be created.

I invited the legal counsel to share their thoughts on tomorrow's legal practice and how they would contribute and – as a team – outperform their peers. How they would surprise their (internal) customers by over-delivering without under-promising. Within two years they became a high-performing team, by getting out of the box of self-deception.

To reach a higher level of integrated quality I asked the senior legal counsel in person what they needed to be able to reach a new level of practising the business of law. In early 2011 they told me that they were wasting time on repetitive tasks that should be done by less-experienced legal professionals. They needed to take care of the more complex legal issues. I invited them on an adventure. I started a specific traineeship for young legal professionals. This PGGM traineeship has been specially developed for top talent with an academic background. The selected trainees set out on their own journey and I simply watched them leave. We created a safe environment for learning and making mistakes to make them feel comfortable. Bar one, they all succeeded. The youngsters were guided by the experienced legal counsel. At first the legal counsel thought it would merely be time consuming, but it turned out not to be the case. The youngsters were clever, eager, devoted, motivated and persistent. They simply went every extra mile. They picked up on the tasks that were not to be done by the senior legal counsel, thereby creating what the senior legal counsel needed: time. This enabled the senior legal counsel to take up the complex and strategic legal issues.

The next step was to change the common perception of legal counsel as cost centres. I started to brand the legal department, the legal counsel and myself. We shifted the internal customers' focus from law firms to the legal department – by building relations based on quality. The legal department no longer needed to assign law firms on every major deal. The senior legal counsel were in a new position; they could – and they dared to – do it themselves. And that is where another personal change took place. They left their comfort zones, picked up other skills and joined the business deal teams. By acting proactively and swiftly and offering business solutions, they became collaborators in running the business. There was not much left for the law firms to do other than offer some expert legal opinions. We successfully changed the nature of the game. And we saved some considerable money too – since 2011 external legal spend has dropped by over 40%.

I furthermore differentiated between legal activities. I used Michael Porter's value chain model for inspiration.[10] I took a closer look at PGGM's primary activities and how the legal support could best add value. The legal department did not wait for things to go wrong; we prevented things from going wrong. Standardised legal content became available for business purposes. Legal counsel were embedded in the business units to deliver direct legal assistance and guidance at the right time. The legal counsel – especially the senior counsel – also helped to avoid legal risks and trouble by creating more awareness among their internal customers. Thus, more legal activities were carried out at a lower cost. I made the legal department and law firms deliver legal services with a business perspective in mind. After a two-year period of investing in human capital (the traineeship), the headcount could be reduced.

At the start of the traineeship I introduced a mentoring scheme aimed at guiding the younger legal counsel in their work. I asked the experienced legal counsel to give guidance to help the young legal counsel reach a higher level of performance – to show them the dos and don'ts in the practice of legal business. I added something important: I introduced reverse mentoring. The young legal counsel were invited to share their insights and experiences (after all, they are the millennial generation) regarding the legal services provided by the senior legal counsel. Thereby another double interplay was introduced.

The legal counsel changed – simply by genuinely wanting to do more than just deliver outstanding legal quality. They help our company and their colleagues to achieve results and be successful. They focus on the business requirements with a strong legal touch. Today they deliver practical solutions instead of legal memos. They work with the internal customers in close collaboration on strategic issues. They are to be found where business takes place. They are business partners at an early stage in the decision-making process. They also maintain the highest standard in legal quality, because it is an essential condition for a trustworthy relationship with internal customers. Those internal customers – as their colleagues – also strive for the best services to be delivered, by involving the legal professional as soon as is necessary.

At the end of 2012, PGGM's legal department's average score for internal customer satisfaction increased on three key performance indicators: on relational quality – how we provided services (7.9 to 8.2); on the usability of our advice and products (7.7 to 8.1); and on our interaction with clients and our business orientation – collaborational quality (7.5 to 7.7).

5. It is about delivering service!

When thinking about the future of legal services, there is a temptation simply to think about introducing unique structures or outsourcing or innovative ways of

10 Michael Porter, *Competitive Advantage: Creating and Sustaining Superior Performance*, New York, 1985.

billing. However, for me it is more or less a matter of how law firms and legal departments deliver their services.

Since the first predictions on the future (or end) of lawyers and whether they would be replaced by robots, many have recognised the importance of taking a much broader view and considering why it is that general counsel have moved their work from traditional firms to other law firms and legal service providers in the first place. From a business point of view, legal services need to be adaptive, highly responsive and business savvy. The legal department must be able to meet the expectations on all the five required qualities. It therefore has to keep up with new concepts for delivering legal services. Besides the personal touch of the legal counsel and their change in attitude, the transformation of a legal department is about how to deliver legal services. In order continuously to outperform, a legal department must be able to adapt to new (maybe even innovative) technological concepts for delivering services.

Frey and Osborne wrote an interesting paper on the future of employment.[11] It shows that the pace of technological innovation is still increasing. I believe that it is this pace that is disrupting legal services. Frey and Osborne argue that legal writing, among other tasks, will soon be automated, echoing what Susskind wrote in 2008. Today, Chrissie Lightfoot promises lawyers a future if they are willing to embrace techniques without neglecting the importance of being genuine.[12] This makes sense because Frey and Osborne also predict that 'the art of persuading' will not be replaced by robots. Bespoke advice and highly complicated deal-making is still an art worth paying for. The flipside of this coin is that legal activities can be (and, more importantly, should be) automated. When general counsel look closely at their legal activities, they can recognise the possibilities for increasing their added value and reducing costs through technological innovation.

Companies and their legal departments are looking for more accessible, efficient and client-friendly legal services. If that means replacing (parts of) the bespoke traditional services with e-legal solutions, then that is fine by me. At PGGM, contracts and supportive legal services are embedded in the automated procurement chain. Occasionally, bespoke legal advice is given on demand. Now we are exploring possibilities in more complex supply chains. The aim is to standardise services that do not need to be done by a legal counsel in person.

Many traditional law firms believe that what they decide to offer is what matters, but it is not enough to offer state-of-the-art legal advice in order to establish a long-term relationship. What worries me is that these law firms hardly ever ask how their client wants them to deliver their legal services. For a number of years I discussed an idea for document assembly with added legal advice to be delivered by a law firm. This idea meant that the law firm had to provide services in a different way. The idea did not come to fruition. However, a group of general counsel picked up on the idea and within a few months they had executed it. This example shows that the

11 Carl Benedikt Frey and Michael A Osborne, 'The future of employment: How susceptible are jobs to computerisation?', Oxford, September 17 2013.

12 Chrissie Lightfoot, 'Tomorrow's naked lawyer: NewTech, NewHuman, NewLaw – How to be successful, 2015 to 2045', *Entrepeneurlawyer*, London, 2015.

challenge for law firms revolves around their ability and willingness to change to their customers' needs. We all know that robots cannot take over the legal profession, but the evolution of lawyers and the growth of e-legal solutions prove that legal departments have to adapt and adopt new ways of providing legal services for their companies.

6. The evolution of legal counsel

Legal experts have existed since the days of ancient Greece and Rome, and today we find them everywhere – conventional legal counsel (not many), today's legal counsel and even tomorrow's legal counsel. There are already game changers in (in-house) legal services. They are driven by the proliferation of technology in our everyday lives. I believe that what started as a slow process is turning into an ever-faster-moving transformation.

Companies such as Axiom are streamlining basic legal processes for corporate clients. Others, such as LawyerLinQ in the Netherlands, are creating new legal marketplaces for businesses, threatening the traditional corporate law firm and legal department structure. In 2005, with USG Legal Professionals, I introduced an outsourced legal department for corporate clients, leaving the conventional law firms puzzled. It was not legal knowledge, but how to use and apply that knowledge using technology that made a difference. These early adopters of legal services based on the use of technology are moving on, keeping themselves ahead of the pack. This is where some legal departments – such as mine – can be found. I am willing to explore and to try (and often fail) new methods.

Cloud-based solutions in legal systems are on the rise. These kinds of solution are more efficient and less expensive than hosting in-house. General counsel from Dutch multinationals and an IT service provider are exploring the possibilities for a contract management solution in the Cloud. It is also important to share this knowledge with other general counsel.

Slowly but surely court appearances will be conducted virtually. In the Netherlands, it is already possible to access legal advice with the tap of a button. More and more legal services will be packaged up and delivered instantly to consumers and businesses with minimal bespoke legal work.

Our society is always online and more connected by technology than ever. This hyper-connected world affects the conventional structures for delivering legal services. More and more legal services will be delivered online, facilitated by the use of technology and mobile devices. This is exactly what I will try to introduce further in the near future.

The rate of innovation is increasing, with hundreds of new legal startup companies emerging every year. This will continue to affect the way legal departments operate in the future. That is why I take the future seriously. I want to be adaptive and able to anticipate things to come. The question is no longer 'more for less', but rather how fast can you alter and deliver efficient, affordable legal services to meet business requirements.

The years to come will present an interesting landscape for today's general counsel. Will you step up to the challenge and evolve to the needs of your company?

7. My approach to change

I adopted a mixture of two strategies to make my legal department meet business requirements. I introduced methods for conducting legal work in a more efficient and effective way. Furthermore, I collaborated with other general counsel and law firms on the development of instruments, such as document management and compliance.

I introduced strict document management policies, looked at workflow processes and took a more proactive approach to legal spend management. Our legal department moved to an almost paperless environment. Legal counsel now use iPads, intranets and SharePoint technologies. We have better document management and contract life-cycle management, and product-based solutions in place. I pick up on alternative sourcing methods to become more efficient. Through the use of IT tools combined with professional discipline, the legal workflow was altered to meet the required integral quality standards.

I am on the brink of introducing more self-service for non-legal users to create legal documents using standard-clause libraries at my company. Why is this important? It saves the business and the legal department time. It makes our company more responsive. The time saved can be used to deliver more value-added services in the field of ever-increasing regulatory matters. It also means that a law firm is often not necessary to provide me with these services. Basically, technology (or robots) is in place at the bottom of the pyramid and this reduces the overall legal spend.

Furthermore, I am exploring opportunities to integrate legal activities within operational systems for the core business of our company. This supply chain management approach is enabling the legal department to become more efficient and effective. If you know where the weakest link is to be found, you can handle legal risk before it occurs.

8. Outlook

The roles that (in-house) lawyers play today have changed, and in the near future the changes in the field of legal services will accelerate. Robots will not take over the law firm or legal department, as legal professionals will be keen enough constantly: to adapt and reinvent themselves; to embrace opportunities presented by technology and the new legal landscape; and to leave the vertical tradition of the artisan law firm behind and expand horizontally by unbundling legal activities. Soon lawyers and legal counsel will no longer perform all the legal work because much of it will be conducted by sophisticated computer software. General counsel must be ready, willing and able to adapt to ever-changing business requirements. I embarked on a process of change, which might not be the same as you have chosen but which ended up focusing on the main tasks of in-house counsel – that is, to contribute to the success of the company. No matter what the future holds, ultimately the human element is irreplaceable.

General counsel: leaders in the legal arena

Christian Rau
DaVita HealthCare Partners, Inc

1. Introduction

What distinguishes a truly outstanding legal department from an average one are the hearts and minds of its lawyers and supporters. Picking the right people and then developing them and keeping them motivated is key. While the market is flush with talent (both junior and more experienced), not every new lawyer will add real, long-term value to your team. Building upon analytical minds with brains and plenty of technical expertise – and sometimes an ego to go with it – today's general counsel must develop their team members' business acumen, project management capabilities and soft skills so that the legal department can shine both in the 'engine room' and the boardroom of the corporation. Balancing a flat hierarchy feel and collegial environment with the functional and geographical matrix necessary for efficient information flow and rapid decision making is crucial to keeping corporate lawyers motivated – not to mention attractive compensation models and advancement opportunities. If running a legal department is akin to herding cats, engaging the hearts and minds of your team for the long term may well be the ultimate leadership challenge for general counsel in the 21st century.

In the corporate world we often hear the phrase "our people are our most important asset", but this is particularly true with regard to the in-house legal function. A competent, engaged and loyal member of the legal department can make a world of difference when it comes to enabling compliant growth, managing legal risk and protecting the reputation of the enterprise – three of the key functions of an in-house legal department. And many such members working together will create a group dynamic that will be productive, uplifting and motivating for clients and lawyers alike.

2. Recruit

Bringing lawyers[1] in-house is one answer to the ever-tricky question of whether to 'make or buy' legal advice. Developing and leveraging legal expertise within a corporation, creating proximity, trust and synergies with internal clients and being able to rely on a more attractive and predictable cost structure count among the factors which are often quoted in favour of in-sourcing legal work.

1 It is solely in tribute to limitations of size that this chapter focuses almost entirely on attorneys. This shall in no way imply that paralegals, contract managers, assistants and other members of the legal staff – all of whom together make up a great legal team – are of lesser importance.

Yet, before you post an advertisement on a legal search website or call your headhunter, you should ask yourself and whoever in your legal organisation has your ear a number of crucial questions, such as:

- Why exactly are we creating this position?
- Have possible alternatives to creating a permanent position been properly explored?
- What is the precise profile of the new position?
- To whose budget is this position being allocated?
- Is this position reasonably crisis-proof or do we risk losing it in the next economic downturn?

2.1 Whom should you hire?

This will firstly depend on the size, structure and tasks of your legal department or legal departments (in case you oversee a legal function composed of several sets of lawyers which may be more or less independent from each other). Then you should consider and pressure-test two important selection parameters: skills (generalists versus specialised lawyers) on the one hand and seniority (lawyers without much practical experiences versus experienced lawyers) on the other. Some questions to consider:

- Are you looking for a newcomer who can be taken under the wing of an experienced colleague or do you want to – or have to – take on somebody who must quickly tackle complex legal assignments and even manage other lawyers right from the start?
- Is the position located at the company's headquarters or in a satellite office, perhaps in another jurisdiction and time zone?
- What will the reporting line be and how many layers will separate the new hire from you as the general counsel?
- Is there time for the new colleague to be properly onboarded or is it an emergency hire?
- Does your company have a policy of hiring only lawyers who already have a number of years of experience, perhaps with a respectable law firm, or are you generally comfortable hiring a lawyer fresh out of university?
- What about a preference of promoting from within when more senior positions are being filled?
- Are outsiders just as welcome as members of your legal function who have been rising through the ranks?

2.2 Looking for the right fit

The good news is that universities and law schools keep producing graduates in large numbers every year. Most law firms do not grow at the same pace. Attractive public sector jobs for lawyers are limited; as a consequence there are numerous candidates out there. The not-so-good news is that there continues to be if not a war for talent, at least a serious contest for the most suitable in-house lawyers. Finding the right fit between your needs and the candidate's abilities and expectations is key. Some more questions to consider:

- Why are lawyers pursuing an in-house career such as they might leave their law firms and come knocking at your door?
- What do they know and what do they think about your company and the industry in which it operates?
- How do they view the legal job that is on offer; what do they expect of it?
- What makes them tick; what makes them happy, preferably in the long run?

These are some key questions that you and your recruitment team should think and talk about before the hiring process gets under way. Most legal departments will need a fair amount of 'lawyers' lawyers' – meaning colleagues who are really good at and strongly and consistently interested in dealing with substantive legal issues (ie, analysing legal problems, drafting agreements and briefs, giving specific legal advice etc). They should probably make up the lion's share of your legal team at any given time. Depending on the tasks of your legal department, its size and also the business model of your company, additional skills and interests may be required or useful. If a candidate already has relevant project management experience (one of the typical skills that an in-house counsel must develop – see section 3.1 below), easily relates to balance sheets and financial modelling or is an above-average communicator, all these features will be valuable add-on qualifications – provided, however, that the new recruit does not leave the impression that lawyering is really no longer at the centre of his interests. It is not surprising that some lawyers tend to lose their lust for the law over time; that they would rather organise projects, manage processes and/or people. That is fine – provided that you and your department know about it and are able to make good use of these preferences. But do make sure that a deeper inquiry into the core areas, past and present, of each candidate's professional passion and strong suits is part of the hiring, and that you clearly convey your expectations of the likely content of the job on offer.

Of similar importance is finding the right balance between your company's corporate culture and a candidate's possible appetite for titles, hierarchy and fringe benefits, or keener interest in work–life balance, flexible working hours or the opportunity to do *pro bono* work. Individual preferences vary quite widely, both individually and across age groups. They are worth exploring. The key is to find the right fit, manage expectations and avoid surprises – on both sides.

2.3 The hiring process

Like any recruiting, legal recruiting is not an exact science. It can be learned and perfected. The degree to which other functions – namely human resources (HR) – are involved will differ from company to company, but it is advisable for the general counsel to tap into whatever meaningful knowledge and resources HR can offer, all the while retaining the final word as to which candidate gets offered the position. After all, HR is itself a service provider and in the given circumstances the legal department is its client. Moreover, if the candidate does not work out as hoped, such misstep will ultimately be the general counsel's responsibility and become part of his report card.

Lawyers are – if not by nature at least by training and conditioning – not the easiest recruits to deal with, and perhaps they should not be. Be prepared to see both lawyerly qualities and idiosyncrasies, such as analytical skills, scepticism and surprisingly frequent streaks of irreverence towards internal rules and well-established corporate traditions, surface in the hiring process.

The hiring process should be clear, swift and fair. Everyone will benefit from that. First, the job profile should be clear – to you, the candidates and relevant third parties (such as headhunters). It should allow for both an absolute evaluation of candidates (if I had only this candidate, would he make the cut?) and also a solid comparison between several contestants (candidate X is stronger as to our criteria 1 and 3, while candidate Y ideally fulfils criterion 2). Then, the process should be well organised and tightly run, taking into account busier and slower phases of the business year, as well as foreseeable periods of absence of key decision makers. Have a reliable core team, know how many rounds of interviews – including group sessions and one-on-ones – you are planning for and give the advancing candidates an indication of what to expect and how long you estimate the process to be. More is not necessarily better and simply throwing more people at a (hiring) problem will not guarantee a better result nor be the best use of everyone's time. It is most unlikely that if five people have been unable to give a clear up-or-down recommendation after a total of three rounds of interviews, two further rounds with five more people will do the trick.

While approaches to interviews differ, there is nothing wrong in asking candidates legal, subject-matter-expertise-related questions or putting them in front of brief case studies or risk scenarios. Interaction, presentation and other communication skills should also be tested, preferably in real-life corporate-world situations, which are often characterised by limited access to facts, time pressure and the necessity to rely on teamwork. Reviewing a sample work product may also be a useful source of information, at least for more experienced candidates. Obtaining at least three references should help to round the picture and mitigate the risk of hiring the wrong person.

In the end the decision will hinge on the best available prognosis of the candidate's skills and personality, his passion for this specific job at this specific company and the best fit between him, his key clients and the corporate culture of his future employer. As previously mentioned, the final decision is and should be yours. If you have doubts, do not hire that person. It may be frustrating at times, but finding the best available person for the job is worth your time and energy.

For every successful candidate there will be several who are turned down. People talk, lawyers are not shy and today's electronic media make it easy to spread negative news about employers. Openness and transparency towards the other shortlisted candidates and, when appropriate, a brief and polite explanation as to why they did not receive a job offer will be understood, appreciated and remembered. Do not let yourself or your company become associated with a pattern of confused, overly bureaucratic or otherwise unpleasant hiring practices.

2.4 Hiring is general counsel work

No matter how big and far-flung your legal function, recruiting is something that the general counsel can never totally outsource or lose sight of. You should involve yourself, at a minimum, in shaping, understanding and approving the job description and in understanding the strength of the candidates whom you have attracted. And, if at all possible, you should be involved in the final decision as to which candidate is actually offered a job. If your department is small or you have to fill a key position (eg, a head of litigation), this is a no-brainer. But even if you are running a complex, international and multi-tiered legal organisation, you should view recruiting as one of your core responsibilities since the heads, hearts and hands of your people matter. Being able to add a competent, dedicated and loyal lawyer to your team can make the difference in the next project or the next crisis, not to mention the fact that whatever the new recruit does – or fails to do – will be and become part of your responsibility.

At recurring intervals, a little soul-searching and a critical look in the mirror may also be in order. Are you and all those who have a say in the hiring process comfortable hiring truly excellent candidates – that is, people who are as good if not better at certain things than those who hire them? If you have doubts, remember the truism that only A people are comfortable hiring A people, while B people tend to hire C people, not to speak of those whom C people will want to hire. Protect yourself against this risk of a slippery slope towards technical mediocrity and – only seemingly – comfortable 'yea-sayers'. Hire the best you can get and when in doubt, over-hire. The challenges that this creates are manageable (see section 4 below) and preferable to those brought about by hiring people who can barely fulfil their tasks, who have little development potential or who might become overwhelmed with their job and its ever-growing requirements.

One final thought on recruiting: nobody is perfect and maybe it was not a match made in heaven after all. Make sure you and the people you rely upon get to know the new colleague and his behaviour on the job quickly and thoroughly so as to decide – preferably within the applicable and customary trial period – whether he is a keeper or whether you should part ways, swiftly and professionally, in case things do not work out as planned.

3. Retain and motivate

Hiring costs time, money and management attention. However, losing a member of your team is often disruptive, distracting and can negatively impact team morale – not to mention the need to find a replacement and start yet another hiring process. It is therefore in your interest to retain the members of your department – particularly those who have the potential to be high performers and good team players. Retention is good, but retention without motivation is not good enough. Legal work remains, to a large extent, brainwork, which is and can only be done by humans. Many lawyers are intelligent and analytical people, but winning (or, as cynics would say, 'renting') their brains can only do so much. What will set your legal department apart is the level of inner engagement that you can generate and maintain within your team. Creating and maintaining an atmosphere of sustained high motivation to do one's job, to do it well and to derive pleasure and meaning from it makes the difference and opens the door to the league of high-performing legal departments.

3.1 Onboarding

So the new legal recruit has joined the legal organisation. If that organisation has a certain level of maturity and the recruitment occurred in the ordinary course of events, there is probably a process in place which will familiarise him in a somewhat systematic and orderly way with his new employer, its business model, its mission and core values, as well as with the key players with whom he will be interacting. But even if you are a start-up with limited processes and procedures, it is good to invest the time to onboard the new colleague to the best of your abilities. It is an investment well worth the effort and time. Yes, legal work is brainwork, but it is also true that in order to add value and gain professional satisfaction from the job, the new colleague must internalise a couple of things which may have become so second nature to you and the other old-timers that you might not consider them worth mentioning or explaining – for example:

- What does the company do exactly and in what markets is it active?
- What are its main areas of growth and risk, what are its future opportunities and threats?
- What does the legal function do, what are the key internal clients expecting of it and what is it measured against?
- What were its past moments of legal glory – or gloom – and what lessons have been learned – particularly from the latter?
- Who are the neighbouring functions and who are key stakeholders with whom the legal department frequently interacts, and at times clashes?

Part of the first 6–12 months on the job should also be an assessment and a first round of development of the newcomer's basic service skills which go beyond technical legal expertise. Many lawyers who move in-house will have to learn how to translate their legal knowledge into actionable advice within a corporate environment which typically has a short attention span and vastly prefers PowerPoint slides or crisp emails over lengthy paper memos. Other professional skills such as the ability to work as a team, prioritise, manage projects and work across functions, time zones and cultures need to be analysed and brought to a level which helps the new hire become more effective early on, while giving him a first taste of the specific professional satisfaction that an in-house legal job at your company can bring. As new members gain more experience and seniority, advanced and more tailor-made development programmes (see section 4 below) will enhance these skills and advance personal growth.

Legal hirings are sometimes prompted by emergencies or they may come in the wake of a crisis where the existing lawyers are overstretched and busy putting out fires or responding to government action. The temptation may be high to let the new colleague, who has so successfully convinced everyone of being a self-starter during the job interviews, dive in head first and then sink or swim without much introduction or mentoring. But everyone – truly everyone – benefits from a thorough onboarding and orientation. Whenever possible, assign a sufficiently senior colleague to the new hire, if only as an informal coach or mentor. Last but not least, new attorneys should be paired with experienced assistants, just like new assistants often benefit the most from working with more seasoned attorneys.

3.2 Motivation

How does one motivate lawyers? Is there a recipe or even a magic formula? How do you get into your colleagues' heads and should you? If leading a legal department is akin to herding cats, the task of keeping things running smoothly with people motivated and satisfied might seem like a daunting one. However, three pieces of advice should help you with that challenge. They relate to the organisation of your legal department, the tools with which you equip your lawyers and, last but certainly not least, the atmosphere that you create and help to maintain, and which hopefully permeates your legal department through and through.

(a) Organisation, reporting lines and hierarchies

Legal departments come in all shapes and sizes. Very few of them have been developed in a well-thought-out, systematic and efficient way. In an ideal world and by consciously reflecting the structures of the overall organisation which the legal department serves, lawyers should be allocated geographically, quantitatively and -- subject matter-wise – where they are needed and where they can add the best value. Alas, the reality is often starkly different and more in line with company structures that have grown in leaps and bounds and are full of regional peculiarities, 'legacy' issues and non- or semi-integrated structures. Support functions such as legal departments will often not have been allowed to grow (or be reallocated) in sync with business needs or changing risk profiles.

With that in mind, consider the following: assuming that your company is active in more than one market and has more than just a head office, chances are that sooner or later there will have to be lawyers in more than one place and one country. You will typically need a core team at headquarters, which will address high-priority issues and matters surrounding corporate governance, corporate finance and the like. At the same time the senior line managers in the field – those powerful and self-confident regional chieftains – will almost invariably prefer to have a lawyer down the hall whom they can talk to, spontaneously and face-to-face. Some of them may have even hired one in the past – often without consulting you or your predecessor.

Striking the right balance between lawyers at headquarters and lawyers in the field defies an easy solution, but as a general rule lawyers work much better in groups of two, three or five colleagues rather than as lone rangers. Nobody can know everything, and sound in-house legal advice tailored to a client's needs is often the product of close teamwork. So cluster if you can. Maybe you can use a regional hub and create or develop a small legal team there.

Strong business managers tend to be demanding clients who like to push the envelope, take risks and often consider cutting corners. As welcome as this entrepreneurial drive may be in principle, in order to balance it against acceptable financial and reputational risk, every company needs strong and business-savvy lawyers who, while perfectly aware of their role as service providers, feel comfortable speaking 'truth to power' and drawing a line in the sand that the company must not cross. It is hard to imagine a set-up in which lawyers can do that without knowing that in those hopefully infrequent but unavoidable cases of friction or conflict they can rely on a general counsel who will back them up – if necessary all the way to the chief executive and the board. This in turn requires a level of professional independence that can be safeguarded only by having all lawyers report (disciplinarily) into lawyers and not into business leaders – and with the general counsel reporting into the chief executive and also being empowered to make himself heard in front of the board. Only then will a company receive the best advice in difficult situations; only then will you be able to develop the type of team spirit that will keep your lawyers motivated; and only then will you have a handle on the hiring process and the allocation of new colleagues within a far-flung organisation.

The relative flatness of your legal department – both in real terms but in particular how it is perceived day to day – will also be a motivational factor for your team. Whether you are hiring a more seasoned candidate – maybe even a partner from a law firm – or a youngster who is expecting plenty of group interaction, open floor plans and the unabashed sharing of crowd intelligence, lawyers do not take easily to layered organisations with numerous bosses and sub-bosses – and the protocol, the attitudes and the distractions that come with them. Many prefer a distinctly egalitarian approach, much like in a (fictitious) law firm with only partners of different seniority and no associates. Neither are lawyers easy graders of the performance of their peers, including their former peers and newly minted superiors. For every person who receives one of the coveted hierarchical promotions in a stratified legal organisation, there will be several who will wonder and grumble why it was not them who got the job and whose motivation and performance may suffer.

Moreover, with every hierarchy layer you create, you also build in – whether you like it or not – a filter for the speed, accuracy and purity of information that trickles up to you.

It is therefore advisable to think most carefully about a legal organisation where information, advice and opinions (and a good sense of humour) can flow freely, while maintaining functionality through a clear and effective allocation of tasks, responsibilities and working groups – particularly if your team is large and regionally diverse.

(b) Skills and tools

The in-house legal function is a classic service function, and without a successful and thriving business there is really no reason for in-house lawyers to be there. Lawyers do not come cheap, so it is in everyone's best interest to create an environment in which they perform optimally. This is all the more true in an era where lawyerly skills, such as the ability to process large amounts of information swiftly, provide realistic risk assessments and give pragmatic advice, are becoming ever more valuable – not least so as to help brave the tidal waves of data, information and pseudo-information which wash over today's corporate decision makers day in, day out.

A lawyer's main tool is his brain. That remains a true statement but it is incomplete. In order to be effective, efficient and motivated, in-house counsel need additional tools. These include a workplace which allows for concentration and interaction, as well as adequate administrative support. Reliable information exchange and interaction facilitated through computers and mobile devices is as much part of a 21st-century lawyer's toolbox as are electronically available samples, forms and precedents which are tested, up-to-date and user-friendly and available in the office, on the road and at home. Strong legal skills and reliable tools tend to feed off each other.

Technology is not every lawyer's strong suit and quite a few of us have often been followers rather than leaders in this field. Regrettably, it is also true that for most businesses the lawyers' specific information and data-processing needs are not a first-tier priority. So it is no wonder that when it comes to document management or communicating with outside law firms and their platforms and tools, in-house legal departments have frequently been given short shrift by IT departments or been left to their own, sometimes primitive or improvised, standalone solutions. But do not underestimate the effect that intelligent, intuitive and up-to-date tools have both on lawyers' output and on their job satisfaction.

(c) Atmosphere

Maybe the most important – albeit truly intangible – motivating factor within an in-house legal function is the atmosphere in which these countless hours of concentration, brainwork, drafting and wordsmithing, risk assessment and advice unfold.

It is not easy to feel the pulse of your team when you are constantly tied up in meetings with key clients, the board, outside law firms, auditors or other stakeholders – or when major parts of your legal team work on the other side of the globe. Neither is it easy to generate good vibrations within legal services in a long-lasting, sustainable way. But it is worth trying. Not only is a professional, positive and spin-free atmosphere uplifting to virtually all of us, but it is also the single most powerful motivating and stabilising factor for your team. Consider the following questions:

- Do you have a universally understandable vision or an aspirational goal as to what you think life within your legal department should be like?
- Can you formulate that goal in two or three sentences?
- Is that goal known to and shared by the vast majority of your team members?

Maybe you want to take a moment and think about the overall mood, the energy level and indeed the atmosphere in your legal department and its different offices:

- How do people treat each other?
- Do they act differently towards the bosses than when interacting with their clients, their peers or their assistants?
- What is the workload like and is it evenly distributed?
- Do people greet each other when they come and go, do they have lunch or a coffee together, and is there room for a private chat, a joke, an easy laugh?
- When was the last time you sat down to listen and talk to each of your colleagues?
- What do you know about them and does it matter to you?
- What are your instruments, if any, for gauging the morale and spirit within the legal team?

Companies and company cultures differ, so do personal styles. Therefore there probably is no 'one wavelength fits all vibes' kind of solution to the legal department atmosphere challenge. But set out next are some building blocks which seem to resonate well with most in-house counsel.

Integrity: We serve our company, its leadership and its employees – but always within the confines of the law. We advise on the law and do not shy away from shedding light on the grey areas – but we refuse to ignore or bend the law, come what may. What is more, we are open, measured and forthright in our communications, both external and within the legal function. We hold ourselves to high professional standards in what we say and what we do. We recognise that as lawyers we are unlikely to win many popularity awards and that respect – sometimes through gritted teeth – may often be the highest praise that we can ever expect from our clients.

Fair play, teamwork and meritocracy: We work together and alongside each other as legal service providers and, whenever possible, as partners and trusted advisers of our clients. At the same time we will never forget that we are part of the legal team. We respect each team member with his strengths and weaknesses, and help each other out whenever we can. We know that every team member counts. We do not badmouth each other, either in public or internally. We do not go behind each other's backs; we do not jockey for recognition or advancement at the detriment of a colleague. Dirty tricks, political behaviour and spin have no place in our midst. When there is a problem or disagreement we find ways of addressing and dealing with it, openly and constructively. We can look up to our legal department leadership because it has earned our trust. Promotions, advancements and opportunities are based on merit and the senior members of the department use every opportunity to verify that talent, teamwork and strong performance are recognised.

Feedback: We value and solicit feedback – first and foremost from our clients but also from our legal colleagues and other stakeholders (eg, within a 360-degree exercise). We live with the fact that client feedback may at times be clouded by overly quantitative considerations (how much, how fast, how cheap?) or by wishful thinking (no bonus unless you win this litigation), and we trust that the often invisible part of our work and performance – notably managing and helping to avoid the materialisation of risk – will eventually be recognised and rewarded.

Leadership by example: Every single member of legal services does – at least to some degree – actual legal work, including some of the more tedious and less attractive kind. There is no cast of managers who just allocate legal work to others or outsource it. Senior members of the legal function take on difficult and complex assignments themselves, see them through to completion and hold themselves accountable for the end result. They use every opportunity to share their knowledge and experience with other members of the team and work just as hard – if not harder – as the more junior team members. Positive results and praise will be shared with the team, while accountability for possible mistakes and shortcomings will be absorbed by the team leader. There is a systematic allocation of tasks and responsibilities and continuous communication within the team. Upon completion of a project there are robust debriefs and 'lessons learned' sessions. Success is recognised and celebrated – together.

Sharing and living the above values and adding your own interpretation and style to them will go a long way towards keeping your team together, even in the inevitable rough and dry patches through which companies and their legal departments have to go from time to time.

4. Develop and reward

Traditionally, there seemed to be limited room for job development in the in-house legal function. People would join, do their job, perhaps specialise in an area or two and often settle into something of a routine. Once in a blue moon, advancement to a more senior legal position – complete with a noticeably higher salary, bigger office and more face time with the upper echelons of the company – would be on the cards. If the company was promoting from within, the nod would often go to the lawyer with the longest tenure in the organisation. Career development became largely a game of demographics and endurance.

Well, it does not have to be that way and thankfully it mostly no longer is. A global economy with high risks and attractive growth opportunities, increasing legal regulation and enforcement and, last but not least, corporate scandals and the ascent of compliance have catapulted a number of in-house lawyers from the relatively steady backwaters of old into the inner circles of corporate seniority and decision-making. Legal departments have grown in size, sophistication and strategic importance.

This new normal creates both opportunities and necessities. One should not assume that lawyers (eg, from law firms) can go in-house mainly to 'shift down' and have a quieter life. Neither is it realistic to believe that in-house lawyers will forever just grind away and perform at their best if they do not see a job perspective and also a bit of variety and excitement in their day-to-day work. This is even more true as Generation Y works its way through the ranks.

Career development and growth mean different things to different people. If you get your hiring and onboarding process right (see sections 2 and 3 above), you will know about the preferences of your legal team members and you have hopefully managed their expectations wisely so far. But while each member of your team must ultimately be the one who drives his own professional career, you are the one who should think about, prepare and offer development and growth opportunities for as many members of your team as possible. Their ambitions and their willingness to challenge themselves will vary quite considerably, but most members of your team will be looking for one or more of the following areas of development, growth and reward – if you let them.

4.1 Remuneration

Money is hardly the primary motivation behind an in-house legal career – and it should not be. There are certainly many more opportunities to make large amounts of money (eg, as a lawyer-turned-entrepreneur, as a partner in a profitable law firm or, possibly, in the financial industry). By the same token, in-house counsel should be given an overall attractive financial package which is commensurate with their skills and performance, no matter how difficult it may be to assess and measure them. Fairness, both in comparison with their peers (not least those who were hired after them) and with other comparable functions in the company, will go a long way towards having your colleagues focus on things other than their next payslip or their yearly bonus. Otherwise there are two options: an in-house counsel who constantly thinks and complains about being underpaid should check whether there are other opportunities within the corporation or pursue his career elsewhere.

4.2 Managing staff

Earlier in this chapter a cautious approach to creating multiple levels of hierarchy in the legal function was advocated. However, in order for this concept not to backfire, businesses must avoid one serious mistake which has hurt a number of in-house legal departments to date: by following a rigid and misplaced 'to advance in your career you must be managing other people' type of logic, some companies literally force lawyers, including those who neither want to become a boss nor are particularly good at it, to jockey for a team leader, group leader or another one of those positions, rare as they may be, which command the magic reporting lines and personnel responsibility. Once there, these poor colleagues are often quite unhappy with the implications and the human side of their added management tasks, while creating frustration and low morale among their – equally unhappy – reports. Therefore, there should be two types of career track for in-house counsel: an attractive subject-matter-expert track for most and a leadership-and-management track for the relatively few who, aside from being and remaining strong lawyers, are really good at and actually want to take on additional responsibilities as people managers and supervisors. Up to a certain level both tracks should allow for similar advancement, rank and pecuniary rewards.

4.3 Job content

As previously mentioned, most members of a legal department should be 'lawyers' lawyers' – that is, people who, by way of example, relish the idea of drafting their next complex legal document, of flying out for the next round of negotiations with a difficult joint venture partner or of poring over hundreds of pages of fine print to make that crucial litigation case bulletproof. Job development, growth and reward for them will typically mean giving them tools and opportunities to do their legal job better and granting them ever-increasing levels of subject-matter authority. They will hence benefit from continually more challenging assignments in which they can learn from and interact with experts and sharpen their skills.

Most of these colleagues will value autonomy and, over time, may work best with relatively little supervision and certainly no micro-management, but always the ability to use you or another member of the senior legal team as a sounding board. Enable and, if necessary, train them to present professionally to senior leadership as the project lawyer in charge and resist any temptation to steal their thunder by presenting their work products in your own name. If you abide by the above, you should count these valuable brains and hearts among your high-performing, stable and satisfied team members.

While some team members will like the path towards specialisation and autonomy, others will get a kick out of a broader portfolio with varying assignments and possibly a rotation to another office of your company, perhaps by linking up with a project or business development team. Or what about a job swap with or secondment to a law firm or financial institution? Not all companies will be able to provide for such opportunities, but they are not as fanciful or as hard to organise as they may sound. It is worth thinking about these career opportunities – particularly with a view to your younger and mid-career team members.

4.4 Professional development

If somebody who has proven his mettle and is a keeper wants to pursue a specialised training programme or even an advanced degree such as an Executive MBA or LLM abroad, do not just turn that request down. Yes, this will create yet another organisational challenge (who will replace him? will he come back? will we have a position for him then?), but if the thus-added competencies and skills are aligned with your and the company's overall goals, one should welcome such initiative and find ways to communicate it as a sign that the legal function with all of its bespoke tailoring of legal solutions for clients will also be creative and flexible when it comes to bringing the best out in its own members – even if it requires at times some tailormade solutions on the home front. Not only the younger members, but all members of your team will be likely to appreciate such thoughtfulness, imagination and engagement on your side.

Many corporations have internal development programmes for their high potentials. Make sure that the high potentials from the legal department have a chance to participate in those too.

And what about the less adventurous and perhaps more mature members of the legal function? Can they serve as mentors and coaches to new recruits? Can they add value by revising crucial templates, give training and legal updates to key clients, or represent the company in an industry association? A bit of creativity can help to devise avenues for everyone's development and the professional satisfaction that comes with it.

4.5 Recognition

Last but not least, let us mention some other rewards which help in our day-to-day activities. Again, a little thinking outside the corporate box may help, as even seemingly small signs of acknowledgement and thoughtfulness count. How often do members of the legal team get an honourable mention in an internal company publication or receive a public thank you from you or their key internal clients, perhaps accompanied by a small gift? What about other ways of recognising team members who go beyond the call of duty? Why not have them shadow you for a day, have lunch with you or accompany you to a legal conference (and blog about it to the rest of the team)? Why not let them chair the next monthly internal legal team meeting? How about eking out some face time for that outperformer or young high potential with your chief executive or chief financial officer? The opportunities are there – if you help to create them.

5. Summary

Our fast-paced and sometimes confusing corporate environment, which is constantly emitting an overload of information and communication while being in dire need of guidance and advice, needs the legal function more than ever. Lawyers will not be out of a job any time soon and machines will not replace them in the near future. Heads and hearts will continue to matter and they are the differentiating factor between a decent and a great legal department. Even more so than in the past, finding the right fit when recruiting, keeping your team members engaged and motivated, and helping them to grow throughout their career is your challenge as a general counsel in the 21st century.

Finally here are 10 key messages and takeaways:

1. It is all about the right people and the right mindset.
2. Remain close to each hiring.
3. When in doubt, over-hire.
4. Cluster if you can.
5. Maintain flat hierarchies – and a flat-hierarchy feel – as much as possible.
6. Onboarding and learning in-house skills early on is vital.
7. Strong skills and good tools feed off each other.
8. A healthy, fair and meritocratic atmosphere is the strongest motivating factor for your team.
9. Help every member of your team to develop.
10. Be demanding – and generous.

Managing workloads into the future: corporate legal operations efficiency

Paul Smith
Eversheds LLP

1. Introduction

In large corporations the 'more for less' mantra is being chanted ever louder, bringing pressure to bear on internal legal departments in many ways. The purpose of this chapter is to examine these pressures and provide solutions for greater operational efficiency. The topics covered include:

- the preparation of an operational strategy;
- the optimisation of internal resource;
- the management of external resource, as indicated by an analysis of the cases of DuPont, Tyco, FMC Technologies and the International Air Transport Association (IATA); and
- the demonstration of success through metrics and measures.

2. Strategy

The starting point is to define what the internal department is there to do – what services it provides to the corporation and how it interacts with its shareholders. It is remarkable how few legal departments have a defined strategy which everyone in the department understands and can articulate.

A general counsel was recently put on the spot by the chief executive officer (CEO) of the corporation, who said: "I've been thinking. We have a compliance department which keeps us straight on the law; a contracts department which prepares our legal contracts; and when we have a major transaction or a major piece of litigation, we bring in an external law firm. So what does the internal legal department actually do?" A defined strategy can help to answer this question for both the department and the wider business.

A good starting point is for all members of the department to meet and discuss what they all do. The next step is to discuss whether what the department actually does is aligned with the strategy of the business. In many legal departments – particularly long-established ones – it often becomes apparent that tasks are being performed for historical reasons, rather than necessarily being a priority of the business going forward. A strategy document is a good way of aligning the purpose of the legal department with the strategy of the business. Having the CEO or chief operating officer (COO) brief the legal team on the evolving strategy of the business is also helpful.

Client surveys are integral to the process of preparing a strategy; however, many legal departments are reluctant to ask their clients for feedback for fear of a negative reaction. The surveys need not be complicated and the aim is to ask users of the legal department a number of simple questions, such as the following:

- How would you rate your experience on a scale of 1 to 5?
- What additional services do you think should be provided?
- Over the next year, do you expect a greater or lesser need for the services of the legal department?

Many legal departments are pleasantly surprised by the results of these surveys, which often demonstrate delight with the work of the department and an expectation of needing more services – particularly given concerns about greater regulatory pressures, personal liability, anti-bribery legislation and competition laws.

Strategy documents and client feedback are useful tools when seeking a greater budget for the department. Another useful tool for obtaining budget is to look at any previous financial settlements and regulatory fines which the corporation has had to pay as a result of compliance breaches. The sales revenues which would have to be generated to meet that cost can then be calculated. Greater investment in preventive actions by the legal department would reduce that sum.

As well as specifying what services the legal department provides, it is helpful to state the services it does not provide. Given the department's limited resources and the practical impossibility of covering everything, this is vital. However, in practice, many of the tasks carried out are really the function of other departments. A tool which is commonly used by consultants is process mapping. The aim is to look at how the department is organised and, in particular, to identify the various tasks which are undertaken and map the steps which are taken to achieve the end result.

An analysis of the maps can reveal inefficiencies; unnecessary steps can then be eliminated to reduce wasteful effort, duplicative actions and other unproductive tasks. Process maps can also show the workflows to and from other departments. What often emerges from such analysis is that other departments send incomplete work to the legal department, taking the view that the legal department will complete the necessary work. By identifying these issues, the legal department can put gatekeeping measures in place to ensure that it performs only the tasks which it is expected to do. Once all of the workflows have been analysed, it is then possible to move from mapping the department as it is to how it ought to be.

3. Optimising internal resource

The cost and efficiency of internal legal departments are under scrutiny like never before. In general terms, it is more cost effective to employ internal lawyers than to utilise external lawyers. Nevertheless, it is impossible for most legal departments to cover every legal issue in every location in which the corporation has needs, and so a balance must be found between what is insourced and what is outsourced. A good deal of benchmarking data is available in the market and there are consultants who specialise in benchmarking legal departments. Comparisons are usually made between departments in the same industry and between the number of internal lawyers and the corporation's revenues.

Most legal consultants will use the analogy of a triangle. At the apex of the triangle is the critical legal work which could fundamentally affect the business, such as a hostile takeover, 'bet the ranch' litigation or major regulatory investigations into, for example, bribery or price fixing. This work is high risk and not cost sensitive, and usually accounts for approximately 5% of the department's legal work. At the base of the triangle is the routine commodity work, such as real estate leases, debt collection and routine litigation, which usually accounts for approximately 25% of the legal work. In general, this work is not overly risky or cost sensitive. The 70% of legal work in the middle is the general work of the legal department which must be carried out day to day and covers a broad range of issues where cost and risk are more finely balanced.

Looking at this triangle, the general counsel – or in larger departments the legal COO – will need to decide which work should be carried out internally and which work should be outsourced, balancing risk and cost factors. This equation varies dramatically between different legal departments: some take the view that the internal function should undertake the high-risk strategic work and outsource the more routine, while others believe the opposite, with varying degrees in between.

To get the balance right, the starting point is to look at the tasks that the legal department currently performs and where it carries out those functions. There is an increasing trend for employees of major companies, including in-house lawyers, to move to more cost-effective locations rather than central city locations. Cost savings can also be made by optimising the space that the legal department occupies. With regard to the tasks performed, analysis often reveals – particularly in more mature legal departments – that highly paid internal lawyers are often carrying out routine work at a higher cost than that would be charged by an external lawyer. Moving this work would free up the expensive internal lawyers to undertake more strategic work or to be restructured.

Coverage of both legal support and geography is another important part of the equation. As corporations continue to expand geographically, legal departments are asked to provide greater support across increasingly challenging and complicated jurisdictions. Again, a balance must be achieved between what can be provided internally and what needs to be outsourced. There are also different operating models: some corporations have strong central legal departments, while others are highly decentralised, with lawyers embedded in business units in diverse locations. Analysis is required to determine the right balance and the most efficient way of working.

Central to all of this is the legal budget. The truth is that most legal departments do not know how much they spend. Internal costs can be identified, but external legal spend is much more difficult to ascertain. Preparing a legal budget is an art form; comparisons can be made with previous years' spending, but it is much harder to forecast what might be coming down the pipeline in the future (eg, potential corporate mergers or regulatory investigations). General counsel often budget for what is known at the time of preparing the budget rather than trying to anticipate what might happen. Legal costs associated with a merger, for example, will usually form part of the transaction costs rather than coming out of the general legal budget.

Many general counsel are under constant pressure to justify their costs to the management of the corporation. Budgets are often reduced year on year and money for the recruitment of additional staff is hard to obtain. One solution to the issue of headcount is to avoid permanent hires, and there is a growing use of temporary staffing suppliers to in-house legal departments such as Axiom and Eversheds Agile, which provide qualified lawyers and paralegals on short-term contracts. Many legal departments also insist that their external law firms provide low-cost or free secondees.

4. Managing external legal spend

Much of the debate surrounding the optimisation of legal departments has concerned the control of external legal spend. There was an active discussion within the profession before the financial crisis in 2008, but real change accelerated after that time. Power in the legal market shifted from the law firms to the legal departments. In contrast to other service industries, it was the suppliers rather than the buyers who had the upper hand. Many legal departments wanting to respond to the pressures they were under were reluctant to challenge the law firms they instructed for fear they would upset them. When faced with greater pressures, they responded by seeking discounts from the hourly rates that law firms charged rather than embarking on more strategic and structural reforms of their relationships with their external firms.

Now, more far-reaching changes are taking place, and four examples are set out next.

4.1 DuPont

The pioneer in this area was DuPont, the oldest company in the United States and a global leader in agriculture, energy, food and life sciences. DuPont responded to pressures on the legal department as long ago as the early 1990s with the creation of the groundbreaking DuPont Legal Model. In the teeth of an earlier economic recession, all business functions within the DuPont Corporation were challenged with taking out millions of dollars in cost. The legal department addressed the challenge by looking at what colleagues in the manufacturing function were doing to take out costs.

What it learnt was that colleagues viewed their suppliers as long-term partners rather than a series of one-off transactions. Their suppliers were vital in keeping the production process moving and both sides appreciated their mutual interest in each other's continuing success. Dealings with suppliers were viewed as long-term relationships based on trust, transparency and openness. Critically, those relationships were with a few suppliers through which DuPont could maximise its buying power by obtaining large discounts in return for substantial volumes of business.

The members of the DuPont legal department – like those of many other legal departments – were allowed to instruct whichever lawyer they wished, including friends and former classmates. Again, as in many other departments past and present, invoices were paid without discussion. But the DuPont legal department then followed the lead of their manufacturing colleagues and decided to reduce the number of law firm suppliers by following a process of convergence. Amid considerable resistance from their law firms, they embarked on a tender process setting out the basis upon which they would deal with law firm suppliers. Some firms howled in protest, with one saying that it had acted for the corporation since the Civil War era. Some firms refused to take part in the process at all. At the conclusion of a lengthy selection procedure, the number of law firms both existing and entirely new which would be used by DuPont was reduced from 460 to 30. A formal panel of firms was established, with the presumption that most external legal work would be sent to those firms. Subsequently, DuPont concentrated its buying power in a number of international jurisdictions by sending all of its work to one preferred firm in each country. Many other companies have subsequently gone down the route of reducing the number of external firms that they use by creating smaller legal panels and driving up the discounts they can achieve.

The rise in the number of legal departments moving away from unrestricted use of external lawyers to a more formalised panel arrangement has been accelerated by the growing importance of internal procurement departments. The job of procurement is to get the best value for money from the corporation's suppliers. Commodities such as stationery, office equipment and travel services are obvious targets, where external contracts are regularly put out to tender with the principal aim of driving down the price.

Many in-house lawyers do not consider the procurement function to have any role in the selection and engagement of external law firms; selecting which lawyers to instruct on a particular matter requires a detailed knowledge of their credentials and track record. However, as we saw from the triangle earlier, such considerations do not apply to all types of legal work, much of which is repetitive and routine, and which could be capably dispatched by many competitors.

Procurement departments view the engagement of law firms as expensive supply contracts like any other supply contracts, which should be subject to the same rigorous competitive process. At one extreme, some corporations have permitted the procurement department to select which law firms can be used with little or no input from the legal department. In other corporations, the legal department has successfully resisted the involvement of procurement in the appointment of law firms.

In many corporations the relationship works best when both departments are involved in the selection process. Procurement can bring a rigour and discipline to the pitch process in formulating requests for proposals and establishing the metrics by which success can be measured. Establishing scoring criteria and negotiating rates, and cherry-picking from the various proposals to come up with the best possible deal, all add value to the process for the corporation. The legal department must be satisfied that the chosen firm is capable of performing the work to the right level of quality. Where it goes wrong is when procurement selects a firm solely on the basis of the cheapest price.

4.2 Tyco

After the DuPont model came the Tyco Legal Model. In 2006, US corporation Tyco was emerging from a turbulent period in which a number of its directors had been found guilty of fraud. The corporation's reputation was severely tarnished; it was under intense regulatory scrutiny and subject to multiple lawsuits. Tyco operated in a number of diverse industry sectors, including fire and security services, health and electronics. Hundreds of companies had been acquired across the world and Tyco was a large, sprawling empire employing hundreds of external law firms with little or no control on costs.

A new legal team was appointed with the goal of restoring the corporation's reputation. The new general counsel was determined to establish the most efficient way of managing the legal function and optimising its performance. His key priorities were increased legal compliance across the world, operational efficiency and managing cost. In the United States, because of the size and complexity of the jurisdiction, Tyco decided to appoint sole firms for particular subject areas such as labour law, intellectual property and product liability. To achieve this, it pursued a rigorous tender process.

When looking at Europe, the Middle East and Africa, Tyco – like DuPont – decided to go down the sole supplier route by geography; but rather than appointing by individual country, it ambitiously appointed by entire region, replacing 280 law firms with just one across 40 countries.

To optimise efficiency, Tyco carried out a gap analysis to identify its own internal resources and the needs which would have to be outsourced to the external firm. This was carried out on the basis of legal and geographic coverage, and the exercise revealed that there were major gaps which the external firm would have to fill.

The process of deciding which firm would be appointed was carried out as a joint exercise by the legal and procurement departments. The legal department decided which firms would be invited to tender and the request for proposals was prepared jointly. Initially 12 firms were involved in the process; following various written submissions, this was reduced to six and then two. The two firms made a formal pitch in person to representatives of both departments. Throughout the process the two departments identified various elements of the proposals which they liked and disliked. The final agreement with the appointed firm was an amalgamation of the various competing bids.

The procurement department managed the pitch process and determined the metrics by which success would be measured. Throughout the entire process and after the firm was appointed, the procurement department continued to negotiate on all elements of pricing. In order to formulate its bids, Tyco provided the competing law firms with details of the fees paid to the existing law firms by legal subject matter and by jurisdiction in the previous two years, with the caveat that this information was likely to be inaccurate. The legal department's criteria were based on the quality of the law firms and their ability to service Tyco in the various legal subject matter areas and by geography. The firms' track record in managing cross-border work was also critical. Given its recent history, Tyco also wanted the firm to be able to provide an overreaching compliance role across the region.

What emerged was the Tyco Legal Model, which was groundbreaking in terms of its scope and ambition. As at DuPont, this was to be a long-term relationship based on trust between the legal department and the external law firm.

To address coverage, the law firm provided a large number of lawyers on secondment to Tyco in various jurisdictions, until such time that Tyco could recruit additional internal resources. Where the law firm had gaps in its coverage and capability, other law firms were appointed; some of these were new and others had previously worked for Tyco, but all were managed by the external firm.

Critical to the success of the Tyco Legal Model was the agreement of a protocol whereby the external law firm and its subcontractors could not carry out any work unless this had been approved by the legal department. If the firm did carry out any work without approval, it would not be paid for that work. The in-house lawyers would decide whether work would be performed internally or outsourced, and the protocol provided for every piece of work to have a brief scope of the work required and a budget for costs. To date, more than 500 external lawyers have handled over 6,000 matters for Tyco, including 2,000 litigation cases.

As to costs, the Tyco Legal Model provided that the routine work (defined as 'in scope' and largely contained in the bottom 70% of the triangle referred to above) should be carried out for a fixed fee. Law firms pitching for this work prepared their bids on the basis of the previous spend on the existing firms, as stated above. Where the firm had the capability to carry out higher-end transactional and major litigation work towards the top of the triangle (defined as 'out of scope'), there was a presumption that the law firm would be appointed, although Tyco reserved the right to appoint other law firms for this work. This work was carried out at discounted hourly rates.

Through efficient management of the work of both the legal department and the external firm, there was a dramatic reduction in the legal spend on 'in scope' work, dropping by 40% between January 2007 and September 2011 (see Figure 1). As the law firm gained the trust of Tyco, it carried out more and more 'out of scope' work, such that 75% of the firm's fees are now derived from the higher-end work. The contract between Tyco and the firm has been renewed four times, as evidence of the continuing success of the partnership.

The creation and use of data has been of great importance to managing the relationship and reducing legal costs. With only one provider, it is possible to have an overview of the legal work; this is more difficult with multiple suppliers. As all matters are initiated through the protocol and tracked as they progress, it is possible at any one time to see how many matters are open, the fees billed and the costs spent versus budget. The data can be analysed by subject matter, by business unit and by country. It is also possible to track such data as the top 10 litigation matters by level of financial exposure, and this can all be presented on one dashboard. This is an excellent tool for the legal department to demonstrate to management their progress on managing legal spend and dealing with compliance breaches. As well as dealing with the latter, the law firm provides an ongoing preventive training programme covering such matters as anti-bribery and price fixing.

Initially the law firm developed an IT platform to handle the tracking of cases, budget, billing and reporting, which it named the Global Account Management System. Tyco subsequently utilised an external program from an external vendor and the firm now inputs data into that system.

A number of different approaches have been used to reduce legal spend – in particular, the use of heat mapping, whereby legal costs in various jurisdictions can be analysed by subject matter and by reference to the level of risk and size of resources in each country (see Figure 2). As a result, comparisons can be made to see whether the spend in particular areas is disproportionate and targeted cuts can thus be implemented.

Figure 1: Basic scope fees ($000) charged under the Tyco Legal Model

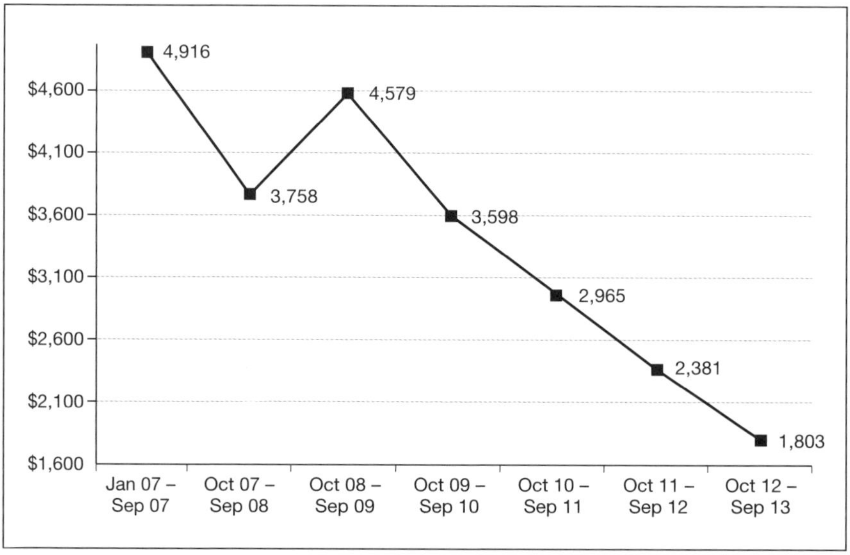

4.3 FMC Technologies

Another interesting model relating to managing external law firms is that developed by US-based oil and gas support services company FMC Technologies. FMC has a small legal team with legal needs across the world. Its model is known as the Alliance Counsel Engagement System, which provides for the delivery of cost-effective legal services by rewarding law firms through reference to their performance, based on feedback from the legal department.

As a result of its law firms having 'skin in the game', FMC believes that it receives a superior legal service. A fundamental element of the FMC model is the legal department's insistence on keeping total costs down by buying as little legal service as possible from its law firms.

The law firms are paid 80% of their bills, with the remaining 20% at risk. Bonuses are paid up to 120% if there has been outstanding and exceptional performance. FMC's main international law firm averages 108% of invoice value. An important criterion for determining reward is the efficiency with which the firm performed the matter. Factors to assess efficiency include responsiveness, goals achieved, effectiveness and predictive accuracy.

Figure 2: Main areas of Tyco legal spend by country

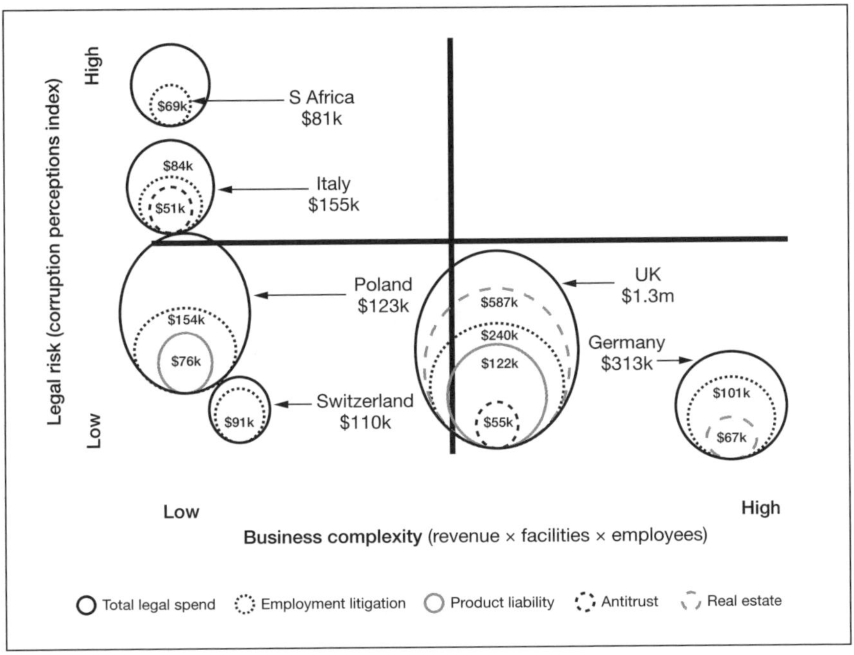

4.4 IATA

The latest development in the growth of these global efficiency and optimisation models has been the establishment by the International Air Transport Association (IATA) of a single-firm model for the Middle East and Africa, covering more than 70 countries across all legal subject matters. This model is a hybrid of the earlier models discussed, with one point of contact at the law firm who manages all the work carried out by the firm and its subcontractors. Again, no work can commence without an agreed record of instruction from the legal department and the provision of a comprehensive budget which cannot be exceeded without further client approval. Following a review of past and projected workflows, the law firm provides across all jurisdictions a single flat hourly rate for any work which is carried out in the country. Like the FMC model, there is a withholding mechanism such that 15% of the value of the bill is retained on all bills to be repaid at six-monthly intervals, provided that the law firm performs to expectations against six criteria, including commerciality, accuracy of budget and matter outcome. If the law firm performs above expectations, it is possible to earn up to 30% of invoice value (ie, a 15% bonus). A detailed service level agreement is also in place which specifies key performance indicators for the law firm, which are regularly reviewed.

IATA has found that this collaboration model is providing consistent, quality legal service with predictable costs in two challenging jurisdictions.

5. Demonstrating success through metrics and measures

Having used some of the optimisation tools referred to above, it is vital that the legal department communicates its success to the business. This in turn leads to a wider debate about how the legal department can demonstrate that it adds value to the corporation, rather than being simply a cost centre. The old adage is true that what gets measured gets results. Most legal department metrics relate to tracking spend against budget, but there are many more measures which can be used, such as:

- recording reductions in cycle times (ie, how long it takes to complete a matter, such as standard contracts or routine litigation, from start to finish);
- recording the number of training events completed; and
- detailing the number of early case assessments carried out in litigation cases to determine at the outset of a case the strategy going forward and the likely cost.

DuPont carries out an annual survey of its external law firms and other legal suppliers in order to demonstrate to the corporation the value derived from its external suppliers. The DuPont Annual Benchmark Survey tracks a range of measures, such as:

- whether a supplier has bought products and services from DuPont;
- savings made through discounts on hourly rates and the use of fixed fees;
- staff secondments to the legal department; and
- the levels of work conducted by the law firm partners and associates to demonstrate that work is being delegated down to the most cost-effective level of attorney.

DuPont has also established a pioneering legal recoveries programme whereby the legal department and the external law firms identify opportunities for the corporation to generate revenues by pursuing claims. Such claims have included:

- claims against utility companies for losses caused by power outages;
- a more aggressive approach to enforcing trademarks and patents;
- maximising insurance claims; and
- better enforcement of warranty and indemnity clauses in corporate acquisition agreements.

French tyre company Michelin has pursued a similar programme to bring in revenues to counter the 'cost centre-only' argument.

One newly appointed general counsel asked to be located in the finance department rather than the legal department, in order to demonstrate to management the value he could bring. At an early meeting discussing challenges to the cash flow he volunteered that he could help the position by advancing the settlement of a case and bring in the revenues sooner. From then on he was part of the team. As one business person famously said: "The legal department communicates in Word and the rest of the organisation uses Excel." In addressing the pressures of achieving more from less, the need for more effective communication from the legal department has never been more important.

Finally, here are several examples of where a legal department might be able to recover costs or increase income, to the benefit of the business:

- Customer fails to take product at rate quoted;
- Power outages at sites;
- Supplier supplied raw material not in specification;
- Disagreement over services in M&A transaction;
- Audits of contractors or licensees revealed improper charges or underpayments;
- Contract manufacturer made out-of-spec product;
- Customer fails to fulfill contractual commitments;
- Tax assessments challenged;
- Anti-dumping and duty suspensions;
- Breach of contract to purchase product if buyer invested in a plant expansion;
- Disputes resolved by future business;
- Patent infringement;
- Customer's failure to honour take-or-pay provision of contract;
- Misrepresentation in advertisement made by competitors;
- Breach of commitment to purchase products in return for special incentives;
- Goods damaged in transit;
- Extension of patent rights;
- Distributor's refusal to pay for product deliveries;
- Breach of M&A warranties;
- Non-payment by customers;
- Insurance recoveries in litigation;
- Trademark infringement/counterfeiting;
- International trade;
- IP dispute leading to renecotiation of patent licence agreements; and
- Class action claims.

Legal standard setters

Jochen Deister
DMZ Legal
Carsten Reimann
Xenion Legal

1. Introduction

This chapter highlights the challenges faced by general counsel when trying to deliver high-quality service and work products against increasing time and budgetary constraints. In order to succeed, it is key to categorise work strategically according to priority and importance, and then apply consistent standards for the actual product.

A real-life case from Germany is employed to describe how using an approach in line with an International Organization for Standardization (ISO)-based process can help general counsel to fulfil their tasks more effectively and efficiently.

2. Challenges and pain points

The need for increased effectiveness and efficiency is a challenge that general counsel progressively face. Keeping on top of (more or less) routine work and still retaining time for truly crucial tasks seems to be an increasingly insurmountable endeavour.

This was the situation at one of Germany's DAX 30 corporations.[1] The legal department at headquarters level has been around for many years; the lawyers are experienced and know their company and their law. Yet sometimes they find it hard to answer seemingly simple questions such as: Who exactly is doing what in the team and why exactly do we need this many people? Another ever-increasing challenge is the struggle to justify internal spend. For this company this was triggered by an internal audit request to reveal everything about external legal spend – for example:

- Why do you have such high costs in certain countries?
- Would it be better to do more work in-house?
- Would it be better to give some tasks away?

The general counsel was searching for solutions. She tried to monitor closely the hours billed by external law firms with a strong view to reducing them. She even hired an external service provider to support this hour/cost-cutting exercise. However, the law firms were not amused and she received numerous calls from senior partners wanting to discuss business rather than provide business advice. The provider also did not really ease tensions as originally promised. Vibes went from bad to worse – and the whole operation quickly turned political and proved once again that not all legal areas are created equal.

She considered which other options were available. Metrics and benchmarking

1 The following is based on a real-life case.

came to mind; however, on closer inspection, the general counsel discovered that rankings and recommendation handbooks are usually compiled by journalists and young researchers. These resources could not help her to match price with performance in daily business matters. They are mostly about top lawyers acting in crisis situations. Finally, she started reading surveys reporting what the 'average company' does: how many lawyers compared to what turnover; and what ratio of in-house and external counsel work etc. Some studies are more detailed and give results broken down by region and industry sector. At the end of her reading, she found little consolation in telling her internal audit team that some competitor firms also pay high legal bills in some countries. Obviously 'the average' is not much better off either. Still, she did not want to be average; 'average' is just another term for 'gone tomorrow'. She wanted a solid base for her own legal function; a starting point from which she can improve through what her team experiences and learns every day.

Finally, she found her own approach going forward: legal quality management.

3. Key driver for sustainable growth

A modern in-house team wears two main hats. On the one hand, it is a service provider to the management as well as to the sales, purchasing and other departments. From this angle, its role is to support the growth of the company. On the other hand, the legal team is the 'clear conscience' of a company, ensuring that the legal framework of business actions is known and adhered to.[2] This perspective adds sustainability to the balanced mix: if the company grows but breaks all laws in the process, it will not be around for long. However, if the company focuses only on protection, there will hardly be any progress because every opportunity comes with a risk. In essence, the general counsel of the 21st century is a key driver for sustainable growth. General counsel who lean too much on either side of opportunity or risk will not achieve their full success potential.

4. Quality – but fast and efficient

Clients demand quality work from the legal department. Even though the legal field is extremely nuanced, clients want their lawyers to give them clear advice that is spot on and correct. Thus, 'quality' is defined by the clients of the law department as being right and as leveraging the legal framework to support growth in a sustainable manner. Negotiating a favourable deal or developing a contract template that reduces risk while still being acceptable to a customer or supplier to allow for a quick turnaround can achieve this. Lengthy meetings and discussions about legal topics are things of the past. However, this tactical focus on 'getting ink on the paper' is accompanied by the more discreet task of ensuring that there will still be a company tomorrow. The management or the board of directors can best assess this piece of work and this level of quality. However, all clients want their lawyers to respond quickly – and not to spend the war chest on outside counsel advice.

---

2 It is up to each individual company to decide how far it will take this requirement. While the authors have a clear opinion, for instance, on how a compliance department should be organised, this chapter focuses on the broader picture and so generally assumes the legality function to be a subset of the overall legal function in a company.

5. Critical thinkers – and more?

Lawyers are trained to think – and to think critically. While this criterion is a key component of any definition of an external attorney, in particular it is the successful in-house counsel who prides himself on having this attribute. As the old German saying goes, "*lever dot as slav*" ("rather dead than be a slave"), and lawyers alike should noisily withdraw rather than toe an undue corporate line – despite being an integral part of the corporate value creation chain. However, the downside of this heroic self-perception is that earthen principles such as the cost-benefit concept are hard to convey to lawyers – whether internal or external. In light of ever-increasing cost pressures in normal operation mode, in-house counsel display a respectful willingness to adopt change. This is highlighted first and foremost by the advent of discussions on what the value proposition of the lawyer actually is. Quality management is the answer.

6. Legal quality management

In addition to seeing themselves as members of a free profession, lawyers are analysts. They are trained and able to deal with form and content. The study of law provides for heightened awareness and thinking in formal and material categories. This in turn forms a perfect base for handling procedures and processes, their documentation and improvement. Suddenly we are at the primary core of quality management. However, lawyers have not really understood this proximity and often utter a flawed and ill-informed reluctance ("I'm only about quality – don't bother me with quantity measures").

However, this is only half of the way. A well-functioning legal department must not only define processes and implement them. In addition, an essential ingredient of success (and part of a quality system) is to measure effectiveness (does the process achieve its goal?) and efficiency (can we achieve the desired result easier, faster or cheaper in another way?). The resulting data must then be analysed and used in the continual improvement of the quality management system.

Thus, the main objective of a quality system for a legal department is to produce the right products, which ultimately translates into customer satisfaction.

7. The three 'states' of work of a legal department

When sifting through the many operational processes and exceptions, there are three main scenarios at work in any legal department: normal operation (known as 'steady state'), larger transactions and crises.

7.1 Steady state

First, examples of the steady state are legal support of the procurement or sales team (eg, by drafting and negotiating contracts). In addition, a critical shareholders' meeting or a product recall would fall into this category. In essence, the steady state is characterised by repeatable (smaller) projects.

7.2 Large transactions

Secondly, a major transaction would extend the scope of the project and require additional resources, as well as a closer legal risk analysis. Primary examples are acquisitions and divestitures. A major litigation (eg, for a key patent) would meet these criteria. These large transactions have in common with the steady state the fact that repeatable processes are applied, but the scope is much larger and thus more often justifies a deviation from an otherwise standard process to suit the particular deal at hand.

7.3 Crisis

Thirdly, a crisis is a 'live or die' situation for the company. While a product recall should usually be part of the steady state, if it concerns the core or only product of the enterprise, it falls into the crisis category. Thus, the differentiator is the impact: if failure would be lethal, then the company is in crisis mode. Another example would be a substantial antitrust claim because of the potentially high fines (up to 10% of the global group revenue under EU laws). In the future, privacy law infringements might also fall into this subgroup. Not only is the negative PR an increasing factor, but a draft EU regulation exists that will adopt a regime of fines derived from the antitrust practice.

8. Developing processes for each state

Developing a clearer understanding of the tasks of a legal department is, however, only the first step. After establishing the task categories, it is necessary to allow for processes and work packages below this level. A quality management standard would primarily look at the normal operation and larger transactions.

8.1 The suitability of crises for legal quality management

Dealing with a crisis requires the highest degree of tailor-made response. There are processes for crises – for example, whom to inform and who takes the lead (eg, the chief financial officer for the threat of bankruptcy or the general counsel for a major patent litigation). However, due to the varying external factors (eg, government investigations, judicial attacks from competitors and hostile takeovers), such emergencies are exceptions.

8.2 Processes for the steady state

It is much more productive to look at the first two states and develop processes for those. If looking at the steady state, the normal operation (ie, the principle of 'good is good enough') would be the guiding principle. A quality management system can be efficiently and successfully established on this basis. In particular, building a continual improvement loop will ensure that lessons are not only learned but also reflected in an improved process. Understood in this way, legal quality management is closely related to the build-measure-learn loop of the Lean Startup movement initiated by Eric Ries and Steve Blank.[3] Popular in modern and fast-paced industries such as high-tech, this loop is a variation of the plan-do-check-act cycle developed by W Edwards Deming with respect to automotive manufacturing in the United States and Japan.[4]

---

3 While we consider this concept also to be excellently suited for the legal profession, the time for a minimum viable product in terms of a legal document has probably not yet come.

8.3 Processes for large transactions

Despite their often very individual scope, even larger transactions can also be structured into process steps. This area possesses the greatest potential for including external suppliers (ie, law firms) into the processes to ensure the right balance across quality, time and cost.

9. Principles of legal quality management

Each organisation pursues an adequate purpose, taking into consideration the requirements and expectations of customers and other interested parties (eg, employees, suppliers, owners and shareholders). Based on these strategic requirements, each organisation strives to gain a competitive advantage in the most effective and efficient manner to achieve, maintain and improve the overall organisational performance and capability.

Quality management standards such as ISO 9000:2005 and 9004:2009 join quality management principles to the achievement of those objectives – and the same is true for legal quality management. The application of these principles not only provides direct benefits to increase the quality capability, but also makes an important contribution to cost and risk management. Benefit, cost and risk trade-offs are decisive for the organisation's success.

Thus, the principles set out next should govern every legal department and its individual approach towards legal quality management.

9.1 Customer orientation

Organisations depend on their customers and therefore should understand the current and future interests of customers in order to meet their needs and strive to exceed their expectations. The legal department is primarily focused on the internal customer (eg, the management, procurement or sales department). This often leads to a cluster of diverse customers with competing interests. Impartiality, backbone and communication skills are required to create a balance.

Legal quality management can serve to identify and prioritise the divergent needs according to objective criteria. The key criterion is whether an activity adds to driving sustainable growth. Many internal activities are just that – activities that keep people busy but have little to no impact on the outside.

Thus, the legal department's view should expand beyond the internal customer. External customers are of key relevance – not just for the company, but also for the primary mission of the legal team to support sustainable growth. The role of a modern in-house lawyer is not simply to find the right legal solution (ie, a 'given' or 'hygiene factor' in the proper economic terms); in addition to purely legal considerations, the corporate lawyer must take into consideration aspects such as

---

4 This cycle is based on the notion of continual improvement. We believe that legal functions – at least in steady-state mode – should be seen as part of the legal services supply chain which can be improved from the customer's perspective. Consequently, this asks for quality management to encompass techniques of supply chain management and modular sourcing. While these principles seem to be further implemented in the Anglo-American legal world, in continental Europe traditional lawyers are often still used to 100% production depth in legal services. We think that this is now changing with the next generation of MBA-trained general counsel moving in.

customer satisfaction and the general reputation of the company.

Try this simple exercise the next time the legal team gathers: leave two seats free at the table, one for an internal customer of your choice (eg, finance, management or sales) and one for an external customer of the company. Then ask yourself before and after each agenda topic whether it was relevant and beneficial for them. If the answer is that the customer has fallen asleep or died of boredom, then you might reconsider the prioritisation of that topic. Also, avoid the common mistake of perceiving that everything needs to be done for the customer. That is the mantra of inexperienced sales people and is far too short-sighted. If you do something to satisfy customer A, then you have no resources left for customer B. Or, if you give your product away for free (the ultimate customer benefit), you will have no money left to produce or improve it, to support the customer etc. Justice in an individual case is often injustice for the other cases.

9.2 Leadership

Leaders establish unity of purpose and the organisation's direction. A leader should create and maintain an internal environment in which people can become fully involved to achieve the organisation's goals.

Leadership of the legal function often means backbone. It is important to stand up against a wrong decision, even if it means being the sole voice. The mission of the legal team also to take care of the sustainable side of growth ultimately mandates this behaviour. After voicing concern, the legal team needs to find the right balance between when to commit to the majority business decision and when to further escalate. This part of leadership is again supported by the right priorities that are defined in legal quality management.

9.3 Involvement of team members

Employees at all levels form the organisation. Their full integration into its mission and goals allows their skills to be used for the organisation's benefit.

Legal quality management also provides for processes that not only enable involvement of the right people in the right projects at the right time, but also grant employees processes to develop professionally and personally. Once again, a learning organisation in the spirit of the build-measure-learn loop is quintessential.

9.4 Process-driven approach

Any desired result is achieved more efficiently when activities and corresponding resources are managed as a process flow.

This is usually a hard principle to embrace for legal teams, as lawyers seem to have an inherent tendency to see their work as art rather than mundane deliverables. While a good legal work product essentially requires creativity and grand vision, this does not mean that only chaotic work practices lead to superb results. Quite the contrary: a process-driven approach ensures that ample time for creativity is available because all other non-essential pieces are developed faster and with less effort. If, on the other hand, every work package was treated as equal, time would quickly run out and ultimately nothing would be achieved.

The beauty of legal quality management is to identify those categories of use cases where a process-driven approach is most likely to lead to results – and where another approach is more suitable. The three states of a legal department illustrate this point excellently: routine work (steady state) is much more receptive to processes than the non-repetitive individual crisis scenario (which is not to say that a crisis occurs only once in a company's lifetime; however, it will dramatically change its appearance and individual challenges).

9.5 Systems approach to management

Interrelated processes must be identified, understood, directed and controlled from a systems perspective to contribute to the effectiveness and efficiency of the organisation.

The essence of this complex model is that processes have an impact on other processes and systems (ie, the world inside an organisation is complex). When managing the legal function, these interrelated consequences have to be borne in mind.

9.6 Continual improvement

The continual improvement of the organisation's overall performance constitutes a permanent objective of the organisation.

Life without learning is death. Any organisation – large or small – must commit to constant improvement and constant learning in order to adapt to current and future challenges. A process in legal quality management in particular is not static. It will initially be developed, but then must be continually open to changes. Those changes can be in the environment (eg, the company shifts from business to consumer to business to business, or a new regulation is promulgated); external (eg, the customer requires a different output, such as short email instead of long memo); or internal (eg, a key expert takes up a new role).

Continual improvement and thus adaptability is the key benefit of legal quality management. Quality management is often misunderstood as a one-off effort. On the contrary, the initial setup only provides the groundwork for further enhancement and change.

9.7 Principle-based approach to decision taking

Effective decisions are based on the analysis of data and information.

A current disadvantage for the argumentative position of a legal team is the lack of factual evidence and research. By pursuing a view of 'quality matters most', legal teams have driven themselves into a corner where they cannot add significant data to a decision. Simple questions – such as what the cost or even price of a particular legal service is – are often met with blank stares. When asked to assess the 'legal risk' of a contract, many lawyers do not have an adequate answer.[5]

At least, legal quality management puts in-house counsel in a position to gather fundamental data (eg, process times). This does not mean that these aspects are key performance indicators and that once legal quality management is in place the

5 As a side note, we do not believe there is such a thing as 'legal risk'. Rather, we think that all risks are ultimately business risks and that some require a closer legal evaluation than others.

general counsel can slap a price on every task or detail his team's added value. Nevertheless, it is the first step towards fostering a more data-driven culture that will ultimately benefit the legal team, not only to the outside but also to the inside in terms of a better prioritisation guideline or identification of improvement opportunities.

9.8 Supplier relationships for mutual benefit

An organisation and its suppliers are dependent on each other. Relationships for mutual benefit increase the ability of both sides to add value.

External law firms are clearly key suppliers for in-house teams. However, advanced legal teams pursue a more diversified approach to a make-or-buy decision. They leverage the whole spectrum of external supplier relationships (eg, by working with interim legal solution providers[6] or seconded associates from firms). Professor Richard Susskind has proposed a much more diversified model of legal work.[7] A legal team will have to consider which services it considers core and which are commodities. These are the exact questions that would require answering in the assessment of the work packages that make up a category such as steady state or large transaction.

10. A legal quality management roadmap

What is required for legal quality management? First, documenting the processes and the thinking behind them is relevant. Secondly, the definition of processes and work packages is at the core of a legal quality management programme.

10.1 Documentation is everything – almost

Not only does documentation ensure that the great work in assessing and defining processes and procedures is captured, it also serves as a basis for sustainability: new colleagues have an easy reference for how tasks are to be performed – and why. Also, and importantly, future improvements have a baseline to start from. The version history will allow for quick guidance if ideas have already been tried in the past. This ensures that continual improvement is really only improvement – and not the repeating of the same mistake twice. Thus, the importance of documentation cannot be underestimated.

The scope of the documentation should be appropriate for the size and risk profile of the organisation, its complexity of products and processes, and the competence of its employees. As a minimum, the following set of documents must be created:

- a description of the quality policy and quality objectives (including scope of the quality management system and justification for any exclusions of requirements); and
- a quality management manual containing:

---

6 Greenstone Miller, Jody and Miller, Matt, 'The Rise of the Supertemp', *Harvard Business Review 2012*, available at https://hbr.org/2012/05/the-rise-of-the-supertemp. In the interests of transparency, Carsten Reimann owns and operates such a flexible legal solutions company so we are fully convinced that this model reflects (part of) the future of legal services.

7 Susskind, Richard, *Tomorrow's Lawyers*, Oxford University Press, 2013.

- a description of processes, including:
  - control of documents;
  - control of quality records;
  - control of non-conforming products;
  - corrective action; and
  - prevention; and
- meta-processes, including:
  - internal audits; and
  - a description of the documentation process, in particular the versioning and approval procedure.

This might initially seem like a significant amount of documentation work – and it will be. However, when it is considered that it is going to be the basis for future endeavours, it quickly becomes a worthwhile investment. It is required for the efficient operation of the quality management system and processes. The documentation takes into consideration:

- effectiveness;
- ease of use;
- required resources;
- information management; and
- interfaces with customers, suppliers and other interested parties.

Processes are captured in the quality management handbook, also known as the QM manual. Creating a QM manual shows the organisation and its process landscape with the aim of controlling the nature and activities of the organisation and representing internal and external interests.

10.2 Documentation of processes in a QM manual

The documentation of processes is at the very heart of the legal quality management system. This is where the core ideas, procedures, documents and interfaces are defined. The following serves as a rough overview of what can and should be captured.

First, a meta-description gives insight into how a customer-oriented organisation is going to be built, how documents are created, approved and maintained, and what the key interfaces are.

Secondly, the responsibility of the leadership is key for a working legal quality management system. Leadership refers both to the overall company management and the general counsel or head of legal and his senior team. The task of this group of senior people is to provide for the efficient use of the available resources and for decision-making based on facts, and to ensure that special attention is paid to both customer satisfaction and the needs and expectations of other relevant interested parties. A quality policy, quality management system and quality goals also have to be initiated by the leadership and agreed by the team and key interested parties. The leadership should also establish the role of a legal quality manager who has overall responsibility for the project.

The description of customer orientation comes next. It is essential to evaluate the needs and expectations of customers and interested parties with respect to product characteristics, environmental impact, service, price, life cycle costs and product liability. This evaluation aims to ensure that:

- requirements and expectations are understood;
- key features of the legal products are identified;
- opportunities and competitive advantages are used; and
- weaknesses are reduced.

Interested parties may be customers and end users, people in the organisation, owners and investors, as well as suppliers and partners of the part of the company's operations affected by the legal products.

Responsibility, competencies and communication are an integral part of a legal quality management system. Employees need to be assigned clear responsibilities with the aim of motivating them to participate in the achievement of quality objectives. Communication guidelines also need to be defined.

The quality management system needs to be regularly audited for its effectiveness and efficiency. This section establishes which processes are used (eg, a snapshot of key processes and spot checks of others) and who is responsible for the audit.

A big part of the QM manual is the resources section. Resources not only encompass personnel but also infrastructure, environment, information and external partners. With respect to personnel, first competency levels need to be determined for respective tasks. In this respect, a major portion of the QM manual focuses on continual education, both as an offering and as a process for ensuring effectiveness and efficiency.

However, the key passages of the QM manual concern the legal product development. This section covers the actual work products of a legal team. They can take many shapes and forms, including:

- a contract;
- participation in a negotiation;
- litigation management;
- project management of an acquisition;
- support of a shareholders' meeting; and
- oral or written advice.

This section divides each process into planning; customer orientation (what is the benefit for the customer? why should we do this in the first place?); procurement (external partners, inbound know-how transfer); and product realisation with the sub-phases of direction and controlling, as well as validation.

The QM manual also contains a section on measuring, analysing and improving the processes. In this part, the foundation for further data analysis is being laid. Customer satisfaction is a key indicator in this respect, but it needs to be procured in an objective and repeatable manner. Internal audits and corrective measures form the close of the QM manual.

11. Summary

Establishing a legal quality management system is by no means an easy process. It requires hard work in all phases – from planning, assessing the status quo, categorising the work packages and tasks, developing the standard, and consolidating and approving the document. Furthermore, the QM manual is a live document that has to be reviewed regularly and improved. However, new tasks can be added much more easily if the foundation is laid properly. The overall benefit of a more transparent and data-driven legal management system is tremendous. A solid legal management system is the basis for any benefit assessment. Without a legal quality management system, there is hardly any chance of developing the legal function into what it should be: a value driver for the organisation.

Once you have established a solid legal in-house function that is well organised and can be managed like other well-run business units (rather than by *ad hoc* communication without mid-term planning and transparent performance data), the way is free for adding further improvements beyond your own core people and making your team's life easier. Some ideas: add readily available information technology to support the way you work (rather than buying software which tells you how to work). You have done your homework. You set the standard driving your organisation's effectiveness and efficiency. Expect the same standard of others. In many industries, supplier audits have proved a good exercise for enhancing cooperation and ensuring quality.

BYOS – Bring Your Own Standard!

The legal disruption dilemma: a case study on new service

Filip Corveleyn
Felix Rackwitz
Tools4Legal GmbH

1. Introduction

'Innovation' is the buzzword of the day. With the rise of legal process outsourcing providers in the early 2000s, the legal market saw a first wave of innovation. The United Kingdom's Legal Services Act 2007 heralded a second wave. Incumbent law firms and new entrants are trying to come up with an answer to the ever more important challenge of 'more for less'. This more-for-less deal is being enforced by an increasingly powerful in-house function. Much of the innovation today is happening in the so-called 'common law market'. The first signs of a trickle-down effect can now be noticed in continental Europe, although it is still very much early days.

In this chapter there is consideration as to why it is so hard for law firms to come up with real product and service innovation. We contend that the underlying issue is the difficulty in business model innovation for law firms. We share our experience of providing a new legal service delivery model, based on business model innovation, including the steps we have taken to move away from the known paths and venture onto new ground. This illustrates a new approach: instead of focusing on the legal issues at hand, there is a focus on the business problem the client is facing.

2. The current state of the legal market

Over the last decade or so, the legal market has experienced a number of important changes. Each of these on its own does not represent a paradigm shift; however, combined, they make for quite a dramatic shift in the status of today's legal market. In our view, the combination of these changes will start to have an increasingly important impact on the legal market as we know it.

First, increasingly more lawyers have moved from a law firm setting to in-house legal departments. With them, they take know-how and practical hands-on experience of how law firms work, and hence they are much better equipped to manage their outside counsel. Secondly, the position of the corporate or legal counsel has significantly grown in importance. Thirdly, there has been a strong drive towards outsourcing law firms' back-office work. This last movement started with the early dawn of legal process outsourcing providers between 2000 and 2005. Working as an outsourcing partner for law firms or directly with clients, typical legal process outsourcing providers such as Integreon, Pangea3, Quislex etc quickly captured market share[1] (estimated at $1 billion in 2010) and in doing so created a new legal service delivery model. Law firms today increasingly operate their own captive form of outsourcing standardised work.

In parallel, we saw the birth of alternative law firm models – most successful in the example of Axiom Legal (2000). For more background on this, see our white paper on the Legal Innovation Matrix.[2]

And finally, a younger generation of senior associates and partners are starting their own venture, further fragmenting the market on the supply side. This highly fragmented and dispersed supply offering on the one hand and a more concentrated and focused demand side on the other has further increased the current challenges that law firms face.

The professional services firm business model runs into a huge problem when faced with this shift in power from the supply side (law firms) to the demand side (corporate counsel). Clients are increasingly trying to enforce a new deal. Most often, this is labelled today as 'pressure on price' or 'more for less', as phrased by Richard Susskind and Mari Sako.

However, pressure on price is only one step towards a more diversified market offering. Price wars have never helped any industry, and downward spiralling prices never end up serving supply and demand sides in the long term. Pressure on price seems to indicate that there is a growing lack of other differentiating factors between law firms. This has two major implications: new entrants can capture market share more easily if they enter the market with a clear value proposition, based on a different business model. This in turn implies that the competition will further increase, putting even more pressure on the incumbent law firms.

Clients will come to expect legal service providers to provide new and innovative ways of product and service delivery. And this is where the law firm business model clogs up. It cannot deliver, as we will discuss hereafter.

3. Innovation in the legal market

The legal market today is evolving rapidly – particularly the UK legal market.[3] Some might even be as bold as to say that it is being disrupted or on the brink of disruption.[4] This trend is made possible because of increased modularity of legal services and know-how: legal work can be increasingly deconstructed into its constituent components (popularly labelled 'unbundling'). The technical term for this market shift is 'vertical market disintegration'. This market disintegration creates opportunities for new entrants into what used to be the exclusive playing field of law firms.

Now, 'innovation' seems to be the buzzword of the day. But should law firms be innovative? Or, better stated, how innovative can they be? It has become clear that there is a huge obstacle preventing law firms from being truly innovative. Richard Susskind has labelled it as follows: "It is not easy to convince a group of millionaires

---

1 Friedman R, 'The impact of LPO you might not have noticed' in *Law Practice Today*, American Bar Association (2012).

2 Corveleyn, F and Rackwitz, F, *The Legal Innovation Matrix*, Bucerius Law School, Hamburg/Germany (2014). See also https://ua.linkedin.com/company/tools4legal-gmbh

3 'Innovation nation report' by Legal Futures and Thomson Reuters, 2015; and 'Innovation in the City report' by Legal Futures and Thomson Reuters, 2015. See www.legalfutures.co.uk/reports

4 Christensen C, Wang D and van Bever D, 'Consulting on the cusp of disruption', *Harvard Business Review* (2013).

... that their business model is wrong." This quote captures the essence of the problem: the underlying business model.

But why should a law firm want to be innovative? Well, today, most companies and most companies' legal departments are still run by non-digital natives (ie, people born before the age of the internet took over). This is about to change. In the very near future, digital natives on both sides of the table (ie, in-house counsel and law firms) will take over and they expect services to be delivered in quite a different way.

Moreover, whereas lawyers used to 'make law' and companies and in-house counsel used to 'buy law', nowadays companies increasingly make law themselves and buy more smartly or use law firms for a second opinion or as an insurance against potential future issues arising.[5]

Frustration is already growing in the legal industry among buyers of legal services regarding the rather old-fashioned and traditional way of service delivery by law firms. Based on our own research, we see three main reasons why law firms are struggling to adapt:

- The law firm business model is inherently flawed.
- The law firm management model makes change management particularly challenging.
- There is a lack of focus.

Let us briefly explore these three reasons next.

3.1 The law firm business model is inherently flawed when dealing with changing demand

The (leveraged) business model is inherently contradictory to the increasing market demand of more for less.

The law firm's business model is rather simple and builds on the combined idea of selling expertise in time units and leveraging a pyramid of contributors – from support and junior level up to highly experienced people – and much sought-after expertise (with, of course, the odd exception of highly specialised niche firms, for example).

The opaqueness and obfuscation of legal know-how and the experience built up by lawyers internally has made it possible, for quite some time now, for law firms to operate this (sometimes highly leveraged) model profitably.

They still continue to do so today. Rather successfully. This is because, so far, no one has come up with a good alternative to charging for knowledge in time units. With the growing pressure on price, a multitude of consultants and software providers have thrown themselves into the field of what is called alternative fee arrangement consultancy or spend management software, trying to solve the issue of pressure on price or the more-for-less dilemma that law firms increasingly face. Other solutions consist of using formal procurement processes to buy legal services.

Although paramount and instrumental, the application of and search for alternative fee arrangements only lays bare the visible part of the wound, not the

5 Sako, M, 'Make-or-buy decisions in legal services: a strategic perspective' (2010); and Sako, M, 'General Counsel with Power' (2011), Said Business School, University of Oxford, 42.

illness itself. It is often said that many lawyers still think that once the dust of the financial crisis of 2008 has settled, things will return to normal before long. This might be a fatal mistake. Things have actually changed rather fundamentally in our view. The first signs of real change are still weak, but they are here to stay. Moreover, it is our opinion that they will most likely gain momentum rather quickly.

Why does this mean that the law firm business model is inherently flawed? Look at it this way: the buyer of legal services is increasingly requesting law firms to provide more for less (ie, try to be more efficient). Now, when you introduce efficiency into a law firm's leveraged business model, you not only reduce revenue but also directly impact the bottom line.

Understanding this dilemma is important. In our view, the future buyer of 'legal' will want to buy legal services and know-how in a much different way (see above on digital natives). This means that in order to connect with these clients, a law firm should change its service delivery model and maybe even explore product innovation. However, this means introducing efficiency – not only in the back office of the law firm, but also in the front office (ie, where the service is delivered and the benefit is passed on to the client).

If you wish to change the service delivery model to clients or come up with a sustainable product innovation, you first need to address the underlying business model because otherwise, as we explained, the risk is that you will cannibalise your existing business.[6]

Alternatively, if this cannot be done from within the existing structure, maybe then you need to look at setting up hedging structures.

3.2 The law firm management model does not facilitate change management

Although many large law firms now have a professional management structure, even for them change management requires a lot of time, money, effort and energy. Change management is always difficult. Introducing change into a management model built up (essentially) out of a collection of various profit centres, with internal rivalry (see section 3.3 below) and to a varying degree relatively high levels of management freedom and decentralised decision structures, is even more difficult – particularly when you are or have been earning above-average returns for decades.

3.3 Lack of focus

Another problem arises within the boundaries of a law firm. Expertise and experience[7] are often not shared but kept inside the intra-firm module because of what Pitelis refers to as intra-firm rivalry.[8] This kind of organisational modularity or near decomposability creates knowledge silos that inhibit architectural innovation.[9] Much like Kevin Spacey shows us in *House of Cards*, law firms today and the way they are organised also know a high level of antagonistic intra-firm conflict: internal politics and fights.

---

6 Johnson W, Christensen C and Kagermann H, 'Reinventing your business model', *Harvard Business Review* 86, pp50–59.

7 Maister D, *The Advice Business* (2005), chapter 2.

8 Pitelis N, 'A Behavioural Resource-Based View of the Firm', *Organizational Science* 18:478–490 (2007).

This means that time, energy, money and resources are diverted away from what is happening in the market and lost in both intra-firm and (increasingly) inter-firm competitive fights. One result: failure to spot opportunities creates opportunities for new entrants to capture market share and transform the way in which legal services are delivered.

4. Innovation: the road to new business

4.1 Can law firms innovate and what is required for them to innovate successfully?

When asked, lawyers will mostly state that business development means being close to your clients, knowing them, being responsive and creative, etc. It requires good sector knowledge, being proactive, understanding the market and being visible. All of this is true; however none of these skills provides a unique selling point.

We contend that the road to new business development will require rather different capabilities, currently most often non-existent within law firms.

We are talking about skills such as project management, process insight and lean process management, workflow knowledge and understanding the difference between digital innovation,[10] virtualisation[11] and automation. More importantly, the unique selling point which a law firm could derive from these skills is finding a specific way of combining people, know-how and technology.

As stated above, to apply these skills successfully, a fundamentally different business model is required.

4.2 The paradigm of the business model and how to solve it: how can law firms truly innovate?

If the core of the paradigm lies in the business model, then the key to a solution can be found there as well. It is often stated that some parts of corporate legal work are not highly technical, but rather standard and commodifiable. Many lawyers still contest the commodity factor of their daily work. They often argue that each contract will have its own typical aspects, that each negotiation is different, each transaction specific.

However, the underlying process is not. Even more so, the experience of one or two lawyers may be very case specific. But when you look across the playing field to all law firms and all lawyers dealing with similar contracts, negotiations or transactions, one might find that such experience may well be wrong (see discussion above about new skills relating to process and project management).

The first step towards a complete overhaul of the legal service delivery model is not to ask what the legal pitfalls are or where the legal risks may be hiding, but what

---

9 Henderson *et al* 1990 and Zedtwidt 2003, as cited by Sako, 2010.

10 Digital innovation has three key characteristics: (i) reprogrammability, allowing a wide array of functions; (ii) homogenisation of data, separating the content from the medium; and (iii) its self-referential nature, creating positive network externalities, reinforcing the digital innovation (Yoo, Y, Henfridsson O and Lyytinen K, 'The New Organising Logic of Digital Innovation', *Information Systems Research* 21(4), December 2010).

11 Virtualisation is in essence the digital online (full or partial) translation of what are currently mostly physical processes.

the actual client's business need is. "What actually is the job to be done?" is the question that Harvard professor Clayton Christensen frequently puts forward in his publications, which perfectly frames the core challenge.[12]

5. Example: how Tools4Legal developed its innovative new legal service delivery model

"What is the job to be done?" was the starting point for what would later become our first jointly developed cloud-based solution.

This first request was rather serendipitous. The idea for this first solution was not developed on the basis of sophisticated market research or in-depth legal know-how. Instead, our research and development focused on getting to grips with techniques of design thinking, process unbundling and workflow analysis. We developed a three-layer model that allows us to break down a business process into its constituent parts and rebuild it in a way that maximises efficiency while safeguarding legal quality standards. The ultimate goal is always to hand back control to the legal counsel while freeing up valuable in-house counsel time.

Once the methodology was in place, we simply asked a number of general counsel of large corporations about their daily frustrations and received quite a response. Asking a general counsel about his daily worries and carefully listening to the response was the first step towards building a new type of solution. Instead of going through customer relationship management-driven questionnaires aimed at selling more hours or bringing partners from other practice groups into the game, we wanted to know what could be done better in terms of processes and project management. We drilled down into the data of how things were done, by whom, when, etc. We also observed in detail how the buyer of legal services was actually dealing with the problem in practice. Analysis of process mapping carries the risk of mapping the process as it should be, not as it is. We wanted to know the process as it was. This is called 'follow me home' (for successful examples of this approach, see the story about Intiut and their accounting product Quicken).[13]

This commitment to understanding the real client issue and the real client need was what the client needed. Subsequently, this led to the co-creation of the first Tools4Legal product.

5.1 Step 1: Data mining and analysis

We first looked into the historical data available on how the client and their legal counsel have been operating in certain areas of their practice – in particular in the high-volume/low-value field. Using the Pareto principle, we drilled down into the granular level of countries, actions, workflows, volume, variety and variability of work.

12 See for example Christensen C, *The innovator's dilemma*, 271 (2000); and Christensen C, Wang D and van Bever D, 'Consulting on the cusp of disruption', *Harvard Business Review* (2013).

13 Radjou, N and Prabhu, J, *Frugal Innovation*, Chapter 1 (2015).

5.2 Step 2: Rearrangements of work streams

Once the data set was clear and conclusions could be drawn, we started to recompose the work streams. This recomposing exercise was based on design-thinking exercises, with fast prototyping and physical workflow experience, as well as the application of industrial lean Six Sigma techniques,[14] eliminating the not-value-adding and unnecessary 'waste' within the existing and established processes.

5.3 Step 3: Development of a web-based service

On the basis of the basic blueprints for a redesigned workflow, we co-created and developed the reworked work streams into a web-based service – a legal application where the business process is encapsulated in the software.

The actual development time was a mere eight weeks, from starting with the challenge to finishing with a first prototype. Our legal service design approach used techniques of design thinking and the six step: *Understand – Observe – Point of View – Ideate – Prototype – Test-process* followed by scrum programming.[15] This service design process is not yet known in the world of law firms.

Without the active support of an innovative and trusted client, this development in such a short time frame would not have been possible. We are most grateful and indeed lucky for all the client support we received from our first global US-based multinational.

5.4 Step 4: Go live

The first real test came in October 2014, when version 1.0 of our web service went live in a pilot project in two test jurisdictions: Belgium and Germany. This first test in the real world would show whether the process we had co-designed with our client would be generic and sufficiently robust to handle incoming client requests using a standardised business process, irrespective of local legal rules. We are happy to report that it was.

As previously mentioned, the key to redesigning workflows is not to think of them as 'legal' workflows (which would be back to case-centric thinking again), but to start from the client business workflow. Once that becomes clear, the legal work flow is moulded and placed where it really adds value, cutting away waste.

It requires full comprehension of the complete value chain of work (both in-house and out-of-house), as well as all stakeholders involved, all practical steps to be taken, all communication to be exchanged, all information needs and requirements and, in particular, a good understanding of how timing plays into all of these elements.

It is also important to understand that our three-layered unbundling/rebundling model and the four-step process we use to build new service solutions is generic and hence can be used for a variety of legal issues and requirements, irrespective of language and jurisdiction (truly cross-border).

---

14 Brown, T, 'Design thinking', *Harvard Business Review*, June 2008, pp 84–96.
15 For more information see: www.hpi-academy.de

5.5 Findings from our analysis

From our initial analysis, the following pain points were identified:

- *Lack of oversight:* the management of the different country workflows was managed by one experienced in-house lawyer. Much of his time was spent on purely managing workflows.
- *Lack of repeatable process:* the processes used in all countries were not standardised as most often the processes were lawyer-centric and not client-centric.
- *Lack of control:* the client had no full control over the process in the sense that there was no proper backup plan or process in place. If the key in-house person were to fall ill or leave the company, the company would have no solid process to fall back on.
- *Lack of external project management:* requests kept coming in for topical information. As there was no single point of information (no one-stop shop for information), this often resulted in time-consuming fact-chasing missions.

A simple example may clarify things further. The client complained: "So, we did 65 transactions in country X last year and still do not have templates readily available." How would it be possible to cover all countries in the whole of continental Europe but for the help and sustained efforts of one (very knowledgeable) in-house lawyer? That was at the same time a major company risk. One in-house lawyer spent nearly one third of his time (400 hours per annum) on dealing with the management of repetitive matters and still received high annual bills from external law firms.

5.6 Information technology for the sake of information technology – automation for the sake of automation

The starting point for Tools4Legal and the client was never to build an IT solution. Nor was it to automate legal work. Let us be honest, IT solutions are already out there. However, when looking for the right technology to build our solution quickly, we took ample time to survey the market. The IT development market is currently also undergoing its own disruption. Where IT development used to be the playground of IT wizards or large platform players such as SAP, nowadays programming and development have become more accessible and commonplace. In addition, much like legal work, the actual development of software is becoming more and more prone to commoditisation.

We required and found an IT solution that would allow us to develop robust and reliable solutions in record time (to achieve client buy-in), without sacrificing the usability and user-friendliness of the user interface. The key performance indicators of 'easy to understand' and 'easy to use', relating to client experience, were paramount.

The feedback we received on most of the IT solutions currently used by legal departments is that they are often built by IT for IT. This has some important implications. Many IT solutions currently on the market required an important investment in development and testing. Once on the market, these have a lengthy lifespan to ensure a healthy return on investment. Tailoring these solutions to specific needs as a legal counsel then becomes rather burdensome and expensive. Moreover, as these solutions have often been developed with more than one user in mind, more than one legal counsel reported that most IT solutions are overdeveloped and over-engineered. Sometimes even worse, originally designed with other purposes in mind they were re-engineered to suit other (read legal) purposes at the end of the initial product life cycle. This has made many legal counsel wary of buying into an IT solution. Fast prototyping was therefore even more important for us.

Automation, virtualisation or digitisation of processes and documents should never be pursued without a clear goal. The goal Tools4legal pursues is putting control back into the hands of the client, through making the processes more effective and the user interface a friendly place to be.

Whenever a design decision is taken, we ask the question of whether it really improves the service delivery and client experience. This is tested, and real-time client feedback helps continually to improve the user experience.

5.7 The preliminary results of our first solution

During the pilot phase of the application of the ICT Tools4Legal tool, users' time internally in the legal departments has been freed up significantly (down 64% in the pilot phase) and they have simultaneously remarkably managed to drive down costs for the actual legal spend (down 33% in the pilot phase) without pulling all options in terms of optimisation of the processes. At the same time, quality measurably increased as a result of processes that are much more streamlined and robust. The predefined key performance indicator of usability of the tool was at 74% (with a target of 60%) as the interface of the custom-built software solution is self-explanatory and requires minimum training.

6. Some guidelines on innovation: thoughts and suggestions

As previously stated, innovation for law firms requires first and foremost a rethink of the business model. Service and product innovation require fundamentally different business models.

Why should a law firm embark on building an application that, for example, covers all countries in continental Europe for one client, even those where this or that client has just one or even potentially no business incidents in any given year? Economically that does not make sense. However, many corporate clients share the same issues. Developing a generic solution that works for one client yields one that works for many clients. Repetitive work across the board pops up not only in one company, but in many companies.

Enabling such a service innovation requires a thorough rethink of the underlying business model. However, as we said before, as a law firm you may find it difficult, nay, sheer impossible, to trade in leveraged time billing for volume-driven (lower-margin) services, as this might undercut your existing business.

This would indeed be the short-term view. A suggested approach here could be to look into setting up hedging structures, to experiment with and try out new business models, potentially giving birth to new service delivery ideas or product innovations. For all the reasons mentioned above, business agility and innovation will become increasingly important in an ever-changing fast-paced business world.

Moreover, Clayton Christensen argued in his book on disruptive innovation that incumbents often fail to respond in a timely fashion to new market threats because they underestimate them. However, they will initially be proven right as the incumbent law firm will take what Christensen calls the right business decision for the business at that time. This somewhat weird paradox holds a very powerful truth. A successful business and successful law firm will listen to its clients and try to meet their needs as best it can, while maximising profit in doing so. This in turn takes away much, if not all, incentive for change.

As Christensen made clear, disruptive change usually comes about when market incumbents are overshooting the market (too complex a product offering), while new entrants provide inferior solutions, often at very low prices (and hence uninteresting margins) and often in emerging markets first on the principle of 'good enough'.

As described in detail in another publication,[16] providers that merge IT and legal process knowledge to a tailored managed service might become an interesting alternative for general counsel to highly qualified law firms when it comes to dealing with legal commodity. The underlying business model is the answer to the growing demand for transparency and control as it fundamentally differs from the 'billable hour' in the legal world.

There will no doubt always be a demand for sophisticated legal advice. But at the same time we are going to see a change on the demand side and general counsel are going to enforce a new deal based on the drivers identified by Susskind: market liberalisation in the legal field; the constantly growing application of information and communication technology in law; and the more-for-less challenge. This change is not going to happen overnight.

7. Conclusion

We are of the opinion that, in the future, general counsel and legal departments will steer their legal operations in a fundamentally different way to the way it is experienced and practised today, with less email traffic and fewer phone calls – particularly with their external service providers which they have to pay and coordinate at the same time. Access to information and being in control are key, and service providers to general counsel and legal departments – no matter whether these are traditional law firms or new alternative providers of legal services – will be forced to provide their clients with new solutions covering the changing demand. However, the solution will most likely not be countless new extranets provided by every single law firm as we saw a decade ago with data room solutions as an additional service (another case-centric solution at that time). The new solutions by service providers such as Tools4Legal might point towards this new direction with the service

16 Corveleyn, F and Rackwitz, F, *The Legal Innovation Matrix* (2014).

innovation merging business ease of use in legal and single-point outsourcing, with more applications and services to be launched in the future.

For law firms, this means three things, as set out next.

7.1 Question your business model and think openly about whether and how to change it

As discussed, the main issue lies in the contradiction between the future market demand and the current business model. Law firms will have to reinvent their business model. This means that, as a law firm, you may want to ask yourself the following three questions:

- What should or will be our customer value proposition?
- What is the right profit formula for that value proposition?
- From the two questions above, what business needs in terms of key resources and key processes are required?[17]

When considering a new business model, you may want to review one or more of the following options.

You could opt to maintain the existing business model and structure, focusing on tailored and specialised work. This will leave a rather large proportion of your current work out of scope. This work can be picked up through a newco structure with a different business model. This newco can then be used to handle the high-volume, low-variable type of work (a so-called hedging structure or 'ambidextrous' approach).

However, in some jurisdictions, this approach might run into certain legal or governance issues because of regulatory restrictions. Here you might consider collaborating with outsourcing solution providers. They can provide back-office innovation that can be (partially) passed on to clients.

A third option might be to create a new collaboration model between service providers of legal commodity work. Each can then focus on what they do best, benefiting from each other's strengths and compensating for each other's weaknesses.

7.2 Invest in new skills

Most lawyers will have spent considerable time studying before obtaining their law degree, after which may have followed years and years of hard work, more study and so on. Keeping up with client work, legal developments and management tasks already requires considerable time. How can you convince the lawyers to make time in their already-overloaded schedules to adopt these new skills? It might be a good idea to bring in some new blood – people with an open mind about the business of law; people who are happy to challenge existing ways of thinking and who bring in their own business expertise. This in turn requires effective leadership (see below).

---

17 Johnson W, Christensen C, and Kagermann H, 'Reinventing your business model', *Harvard Business Review* 86, 2008, pp 50–59.

7.3 Lead and anchor success early on

Change is one of the most difficult things to bring about. Successful change management initially requires the following elements (see also Kotter's eight steps):

- *A shared sense of urgency:* your organisation needs to understand why it needs to change or why certain changes are important for the survival or success of the company or firm.
- *A guiding coalition:* you will need a small group of people leading the way.
- *A clear strategic vision:* if you cannot share and explain your vision in a convincing manner, all change efforts will remain without success. This vision and how it should be lived through the organisation needs to start at the top and work its way down.
- *A list of volunteers to support the first steps:* change does not happen overnight, nor does it come automatically. You need to work on it, day after day. That is why you need a set of volunteers at each level of the organisation, supporting the change and making it happen, day after day after day.
- *An enabling environment:* change can only thrive if the organisation allows it to. You need to provide a framework within entrepreneurship where change is actively supported, not just condoned.
- *Anchoring and celebrating short-term wins:* if you want change to be successfully recognised internally, you need to celebrate the first wins. When drawing up your change process plan, provide for specific results to be shown and celebrated early on. These will help to convince your organisation that the path of change you have chosen is indeed the right one.

After these first six steps, you can hopefully start to accelerate the change process and prepare to institutionalise it.

The role of information technology in shaping and supporting global legal operations

Scott D Rosenberg
Project Leadership Associates

1. Introduction

For today's global general counsel, the proper administration and development of information technology should be considered a primary area of management oversight which needs both focus and understanding. Few people within corporate IT departments are highly familiar with or appreciate the unique business requirements and supporting technologies needed by general counsel and their legal teams in creating and running a high-performing legal department. As is often the case, technology serves as the mechanism through which both practice and operational best practices are achieved. Therefore, it is incumbent on the global general counsel to have more than just an appreciation of technology; he must consider knowledge in this area to be a major competency and computer literacy to be a defining skill.

Establishing one's credibility as a digital native and not a digital naïve has often proved challenging for the 21st-century general counsel. Fortunately, many forums now exist to improve one's knowledge of the various software and systems that can improve legal practice and promote operational efficiency. Even so, the real obstacle for most legal departments is not the skill level of the general counsel and his legal management team, but the fact that many of these corporate executives will not personally exploit the software and systems they purchase to their fullest capabilities. This should not prevent things moving forward. The greatest impediment to technology use and success is not aptitude, but attitude. Where one sees oneself on the Rogers' technology adoption curve (see Figure 1) is often a determinant of the desired benefit that the general counsel expects to achieve – and is willing to risk – in pushing forward with technology investment.

Historically, general counsel too often position themselves as late majority adopters – even laggards – at the tailing end of the bell curve (although many think of themselves as being nearer to the front end). Certainly, the need for mitigation of risk and its resulting exclusion to information access promotes conservative legal and business practices. Yet, it is the general counsel who is willing to integrate technology tightly into legal and operational best practice processes – and not simply 'repave the cow path' – who typically sees the greatest return on investment.

Figure 1: Rogers' Technology Adoption Curve

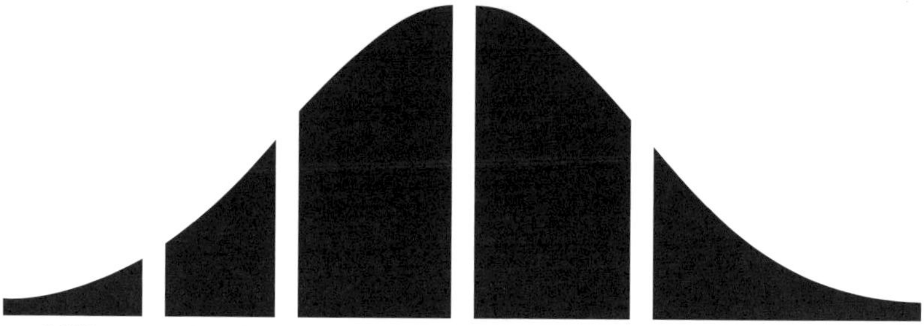

When strategising on the role and positioning of information technology within his legal department, the general counsel should be familiar with, even appreciate, answers to many of the questions outlined below. Having thought through and developed a well-crafted strategy or position in each of these areas will prove important in creating a roadmap for any future successful deployment.

2. Payback for IT investment

Regardless of aptitude or attitude, technology continues to become more and more important to legal departments as a primary instrument for ensuring collaboration, sharing knowledge, achieving efficiency, controlling cost, mitigating risk, measuring performance and promoting value. How the use and function of technology has evolved and will continue to contribute to the future globalisation of the legal function will be discussed in the context of each of these objectives. Technologies in support of each objective are highlighted in bold.

2.1 Knowledge sharing: Creating a culture of contribution, collaboration and 'oneness' within the legal department

One of the goals of the general counsel is to create an environment in which people come together to share lessons learned and work product in an atmosphere of trust, and where everyone feels they are contributing to the bottom line. All general counsel desire to establish a cultural awareness that reflects and is in alignment with their vision for a high-performing legal function. But global general counsel have an even bigger challenge – how to do so in light of disparate geographic, demographic and cultural differences. Fortunately, a category of applications is being used by many legal departments today to centralise information and serve as an authoritative source repository through which staff – both within and external to the law department – can store, search, leverage and collaborate on work product. Information sharing can occur even in consideration of security access needs of individual practice groups or matter types. This software is referred to as document or content management systems.

Another means of connecting those within the legal function is through the development and use of a legal intranet – typically a site within the overall enterprise intranet. These typically take two forms – client-facing and lawyer-facing. Client-facing websites are generally integrated into the solution used by all lines of business to communicate who they are and what they do. It can be an effective means for providing access to a company's legal policies and protocols, as well as a directory of those within the legal department to whom requests for legal service can be made. Lawyer-facing websites are often referred to as collaborative portals or knowledge management systems, through which expertise can be shared and transferred between in-house counsel. This is a mechanism for use by general counsel to communicate happenings, expectations and results.

No matter the chosen product, developing a workable matter-centric computing platform should be the ultimate goal. The idea is to create an environment in which all information is centered on its related matter or project, and where lawyers can get what they need, where they need it, without much clicking from place to place. Creating such a platform has until recently proven problematic – particularly due to difficulties in linking structured and unstructured information. Most have found the organisation and management of unstructured (or text-heavy) data (ie, documents and emails) to be much different from the management of a structured (or fielded) database.

Moving software to the web and data into the Cloud (ie, cloud computing) has made – and will continue to make – it easier to promote knowledge sharing. Free from limitations of hardware, location and time zone, corporate counsel now have the ability to work from anywhere, at any time. General counsel can think of allocating work based on the best skill sets rather than the best access to technology. Data stores can represent the work product of everyone considered part of the legal function – all in a centralised repository. Corporate IT departments can reduce support costs while clients and vendors can become part of the information workflow process. In effect, know-how can be pooled and distributed.

2.2 Process efficiency: Streamlining and standardising legal and business best-practice processes

Provided it does not increase legal risk, the global general counsel is always looking to improve process efficiency. As a typical example, insurance companies often need to share information across multiple constituencies – the claims department, the legal department and staff counsel offices. Often, legal information related to a claim is stored in separate databases, each with its own inclusionary security protocols. These siloed repositories can prove problematic, causing lawyers to have to exert significant effort in providing information access upon request or when deemed necessary. These issues might be more about culture and protocol than they are about technology limitation; yet, this tolerance towards 'need to know' information sharing often flies against the general counsel's desire to create a culture of openness within the legal team. At its extreme, such an environment can even lead to information hoarding. Should this be the case, the general counsel will be well served to remind others that everyone works for the same company (and law department), and that software configuration – in consideration of privilege and security needs, of course – should promote process efficiency through standardisation and transparency.

One application that can help to bring efficiency to legal processes is a relational database management system. Commonly referred to as matter management systems, these tools can be used to enter data pertinent to a particular unit of work or project – called a 'matter' in legal parlance. Once entered, pieces of data pertaining to summary information, people, events, notes and strategies can be assembled, sliced and diced in a myriad of ways both to search and report on work performed. Relevant data can be accessed and manipulated in ways that greatly reduce lawyers' time – for example, eliminating redundancy in work product creation and minimising time spent in searching for relevant information. Workflow functionality within these tools helps to move information from Point A to Point B more efficiently and effectively than existing manual processes. Audit trails pointing to what changes were made by whom and when they occurred reduce the risk associated with having several people collaborating on a matter.

A matter management system is one of the core foundational technologies within a legal department and a tool the global general counsel often uses to oversee his internal and external teams, including outside counsel. It can be used to assess practice performance, identify direction and trends, and facilitate day-to-day operations management. With the additions of electronic billing and document management functions, these tools are commonly thought of as 'legal enterprise resource planning' solutions, similar in nature to that of SAP or PeopleSoft to the general operations of the enterprise. In fact, Gartner recently coined the term 'enterprise legal management' when referring to this type of software.

A similar yet separate tool is the enterprise contract life-cycle management system. Although a matter management system can track contracts as a unique matter, agreements in this context are often those managed solely by the legal department and limited in volume. But what of the contracting process throughout the enterprise? At a minimum, it can be argued that the general counsel should provide guidance. More and more, general counsel are held to be directly responsible for all contracts from whatever source – at least at an architectural level. No matter the level of accountability, the general counsel should be concerned about efficiencies and risks associated with the global contracting process. When thinking more holistically – for example, 'buy-side' agreements managed by the procurement department or 'sell-side' agreements management by the sales department – an enterprise contract life-cycle management system is designed to meet the needs of the entire enterprise, including the legal department. As solutions geared specifically to the contracting process, enterprise contract life-cycle management software contains features and functions in support of creation, storage, workflow, notification, search and reporting of contracts across their entire life-cycle (see Figure 2).

Figure 2: The contract life cycle[1]

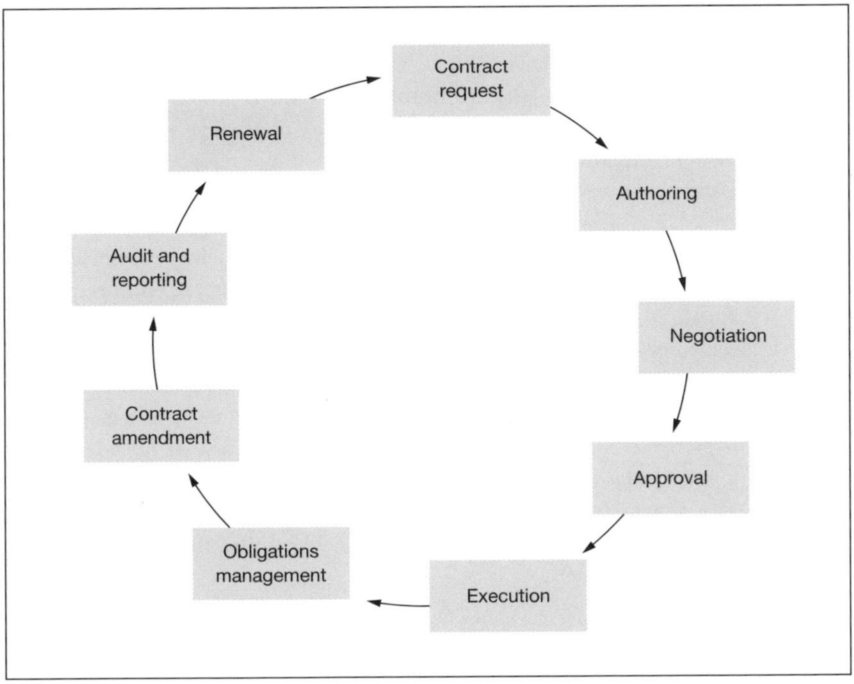

2.3 Cost control: Improving management of legal spend

Matter management and electronic billing systems are being successfully used to monitor legal spend, manage budgets and analyse performance. These tools help third parties (ie, external law firms and other vendors) to deliver legal bills securely for review and payment. The result can bring significant cost savings and compliance with outside counsel guidelines.

The prevailing solution to managing this objective is the electronic billing – or e-billing – function within the matter management system. This tool has two primary functions: the automation of invoice processing; and the analysis and effective use of legal spend.

The push to automated invoice processing has become fairly straightforward; outside counsel are likely to have already been required to participate. In exchange for invoice information received electronically and in an industry standard format (legal electronic data exchange standard or LEDES), invoices are processed faster and with greater precision. In return, firms are paid faster, improving their cash flow. The general counsel obtains a wealth of financial information that can be used to manage matter, firm and departmental budgets, assess firm performance and make educated decisions regarding appropriate resource allocations.

1 'What is Contract Management Software?', *Selectica*, available at www.selectica.com/resources/guide/contract-management-guide#.VS15zPnF_IY

Historically, the general counsel's use of this information has been more limited to monitoring and baselining legal spend. However, the promise of e-billing remains great and, in fact, these tools are constantly evolving to incorporate features and functions that truly can be used to minimise spend and change behaviour. Analytic engines are now more graphic (think dashboards), powerful (ie, adoption of true business intelligence methods and architecture to analyse 'big data') and useful (eg, pooling all expenditure under management of a vendor to compare and contrast rates and performance). Many vendors cite a fairly quick return on investment (ROI) in purchasing these solutions. A recent article states as follows:

> *The hard savings from adopting technology are fairly easy to project. For instance, departments that implement e-billing systems often experience savings through standardization of invoices, which allows validation against guidelines and comparisons of rates and fees. The data from recent studies show a yield of two to four percent within the first two years from correcting basic validation errors. But the data these systems generate can also spur initiatives that result in reduced costs through improved efficiency. Better access to useful data leads to improved reporting and analysis, which the department can use to find opportunities to reduce spend.*[2]

The general counsel would thus be wise to consider both quantitative and qualitative assessments of success when determining the value brought through technology investment.

2.4 Risk mitigation: Reducing risk associated with decision making and regulatory compliance

Many perceive the general counsel to have greatest impact in his role of legal risk manager. In particular, executive leaders turn to general counsel to protect them and the company from litigation resulting from bad business practices. When identifying and mitigating legal risks, the global general counsel has a key role to play. In particular, he offers:

- a direct and deep understanding of the organisation and its objectives and business practices as a whole, since his work spans all functional areas;
- an ability to challenge operational practices on the basis of well-defined legal principles and precedent, and:
- the independence and detachment which come from membership in an independent profession and a fiduciary duty to act in an ethical capacity.

One important way in which general counsel can both monitor and assess risk is through the implementation and use of technology. A legal department uses many tools to manage risk, but one of the most notable, and arguably where the greatest investment occurs – at least in the United States – is in the field of electronic discovery – or e-discovery – and litigation readiness. Litigation readiness is not just about having tools and processes to deal with major litigation. Quite the opposite: litigation readiness is about being prepared to deal with litigation-related issues (eg, claims, incidents, investigations, as well as lawsuits) that you know are going to

---

2 Robin Snasdell, 'Projecting the ROI of Technology', *Law Technology News*, December 17 2014.

come through the door as part of the normal course of conducting business.

How and where a legal department chooses to invest within the electronic discovery reference model (see Figure 3) needs to be given serious consideration by today's global general counsel. E-discovery processes and policies must be validated and/or engineered to ensure a legally defensible, forensically sound position that will hold itself up to scrutiny by the courts.

Figure 3: Electronic discovery reference model

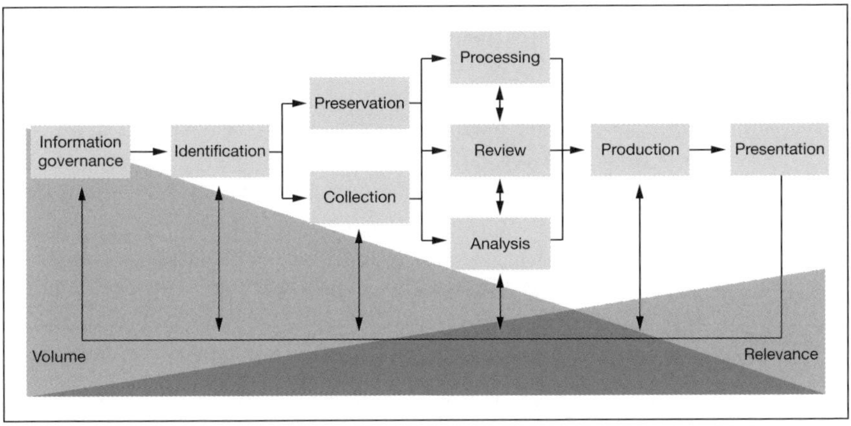

While most companies either have or are working on well-thought-out processes and policies in oversight of the left-hand side of the electronic discovery reference model (information governance, identification, preservation and collection), the right half of the equation is typically left to outside or panel counsel to support and manage. The factors that determine the extent to which the entirety of the e-discovery process is managed inside or outside include:

- type of industry;
- size of operations;
- potential exposure resulting from claims; and
- risk profile.

As a general rule, highly regulated, large, exposed and risk-averse organisations have more investment in e-discovery methods and technologies. This can lead to the hiring of e-discovery support staff or the outsourcing of e-discovery functions – legal process outsourcing is now big business – and investment in data processing and production tools.

Whether or not reliant on outside vendors or law firms, two key areas of process focus should be in support of proper information governance, including records management systems and litigation holds. With emphasis on proper records policy, many legal departments use their document management systems to 'manage in place' the retention and destruction of corporate records in accordance with corporate records retention schedules. In this capacity, the general counsel can act as a good corporate citizen, blazing the trail for others to follow; this is important as the legal department often has a hand in drafting and developing records policy. As important, general counsel can leverage tools already used within the legal department to manage work-in-process documents as corporate records. It should always be remembered that a well-thought-out information governance strategy means that most documents never end up as evidentiary materials.

How best to manage so-called 'litigation holds' is usually a question of volume. A 'litigation hold' (sometimes referred to as a 'legal hold') is a process used to preserve all forms of relevant information when litigation is reasonably anticipated. For those companies of a highly litigious nature, legal holds are frequent and the adoption of stand-alone software specifically designed to oversee the life cycle of a hold is prevalent. For those companies where holds are more sporadic and infrequent, many matter management systems allow a distinct matter type to be established or have a separate 'module' through which litigation holds can be recorded, custodians notified and activity monitored.

Another area of risk for many companies has to do with the proper use and leverage of intellectual property. Intellectual asset management systems are tools designed to manage patent, trademark and domain name portfolios. Although individual trademarks and/or patents can be managed through a matter management system, most portfolios of any size or complexity will require a separate solution. As intellectual asset management systems provide true portfolio management – including jurisdiction-specific rule sets – and workflow capabilities needed to support a high-volume IP practice, general counsel find these stand-alone products to be a worthwhile investment.

2.5 Performance measurement: Using analytics to assess practice and vendor performance

In the world of legal technology, analytics is hot. Similar to a corporation's manipulation and use of big data, the general counsel and his leadership team are shifting their focus from capturing data (ie, invoice information) to aggregating financial, operational and performance information to spot trends, optimise resources and make business decisions.

Over the last several years, software vendors and legal consultants have geared up to help general counsel figure out how poorly they have been spending on legal services. There are now products and services galore designed to gather information already being tracked by the legal department and – using advanced analytic techniques – to paint a picture regarding how much is being or should be spent relative to what other firms are charging for matters of a similar nature. But the real question for every global general counsel should be: why are you not working with vendors already doing this on their own? If more emphasis was placed on evaluating and selecting vendors that can prove they have systematic processes and tools in place that give you greater insight into how they price services and manage your projects, you would be given the visibility – and certainty – needed to make better resource allocation decisions.

In effect, the burden shifts from the legal department being reactive in assessing spend to the law firm being pre-emptive in proposing pricing. Just maybe we can reduce the need for in-house counsel to also serve as financial analysts.

2.6 Value promotion: Selling the value of the legal department to clients and executive management

One of the greatest operational challenges faced by the global general counsel is proving the value of his legal department to executive management. In today's world of 'do more with less', many general counsel are faced with having to justify headcount and legal spend. Everyone intuitively understands the need for lawyers, but how can this effectively be articulated? This is especially difficult when, as is often the case, one needs to prove a negative (ie, that something very bad never happened because of lawyer intervention). How does one put a dollar value on risk avoidance?

Although one can quantitatively measure performance (see section 2.5 above), often it is the qualitative expression of work effort that has the most resonance. By way of example, Kim Rucker, executive vice president, corporate and legal affairs, general counsel and corporate secretary at Kraft Foods Group Inc, has her lawyers periodically contribute to a report called the Value Tracker – a simple and easily constructed Microsoft WORD table in which each new row describes a value-based activity, monetary impact (cost savings or revenue generation), dates of occurrence and who should be given credit. She does not limit recognition solely to the legal department; anyone participating in these value-based activities is included. She does not make use of this report frivolously; it is something she can pull from her 'back pocket' whenever anyone questions the efficacy of her legal team. As part of their performance goals, her staff understand the importance of maintaining this report – adding new line items and removing those that are dated – not as a means of measuring them but of demonstrating the value of the legal function as a whole.

3. The modern-day IT platform

With the prevalence of technology solutions in the marketplace, several questions must be answered in formation of an IT architecture that meets both business and technical requirements. Often, the global general counsel will enlist the assistance of his corporate IT department or that of independent technology consultants in defining an appropriate information architecture. Regardless of the architect, the general counsel must have an appreciation (at minimum) or understanding (at best) of an infrastructure's impact on information access, management and data security. In fact, creation of a well-thought-out and strategic technology plan will include answers to the questions considered next.

3.1 Should legal applications be located on premises or in the Cloud?

Software on premises is the traditional approach to information access. Hardware is built-out and on location in corporate data centres; software is installed and run on computers connected to those data centres. The customer is responsible for the security, availability and overall management of on-premises software, although vendors generally provide after-sales implementation and support services.

Maintaining on-premises software is often more expensive than on-demand, internet-accessible software – software in the Cloud – because it requires in-house server hardware, capital investment in software licences, in-house IT support staff and longer implementation time. However, on-premises software is considered more secure, as the entire volume of software and data remains on the organisation's premises.

3.2 If in the Cloud, should this be a private or public cloud?

Done effectively, a cloud-based, 'virtualised' infrastructure can offer advantages over traditional data centre build-outs in areas of performance, scalability and even security. As organisations develop their strategies for implementing cloud computing, many corporate IT departments are facing a choice: to deploy a private cloud or leverage a public cloud. So what are the differences between the two and which is right for you?

Simply stated, a private cloud is infrastructure through which hardware and software is hosted and managed by the company; essentially, it is an extension of an enterprise's traditional data centre and a non-shared resource. A public cloud is infrastructure through which hardware and software is hosted and managed by vendors, sometimes referred to as 'software as a service'; it is available for use by other organisations, although in a highly secure manner (see Table 1).

Table 1: Public vs private cloud

Public cloud	Private cloud
• Hosted at a service provider site	• Hosted at either an enterprise or service provider site
• Supports multiple customers	• Supports one customer
• Often utilises shared infrastructure	• Does not utilise shared infrastructure
• Supports connectivity over the intranet	• Connectivity over a private network or the internet
• Suited for information that is not private	• Suited for information that needs a high level of security
• Can be cheaper than private cloud	–

Both public and private clouds have management implications. By choosing a public cloud solution, an organisation can offload much of the management responsibility to its cloud vendor. In a private cloud scenario, there is significant demand on resources to specify, purchase, house, update, maintain and safeguard the physical infrastructure. Financially, deploying a private cloud can also create a large initial capital expense, with subsequent investment required as new equipment and capacity is added.

In a public cloud scenario, capital expense is virtually eliminated; the financial burden is shifted to a fee-for-service, often based on utilisation and data volume. Maintaining and securing public cloud infrastructure is the responsibility of the vendor, enabling the customer to streamline IT operations and minimise time and money spent on system upkeep.

3.3 Should legal applications be purchased or licensed?

As a rule of thumb, a licensed or annual subscription pricing model is less costly in the short term and can be designated an operating expense, often avoiding a higher level of financial scrutiny by the finance or corporate IT teams. This model can also facilitate a shorter-term investment with fewer consequences should the legal department decide to move in a different technological direction. In addition, licensing generally means receiving the benefit of software updates as they come online.

However, the overall cost of licensing can be much higher in the longer term. Most vendors charge via an annual subscription pricing model that year on year will result in greater overall expenditure. Of course, this increased cost should be offset by the cost of not having to rely as much on in-house IT support for assistance (the licence includes support as opposed to a separate charge).

Figure 4: Typical law department systems

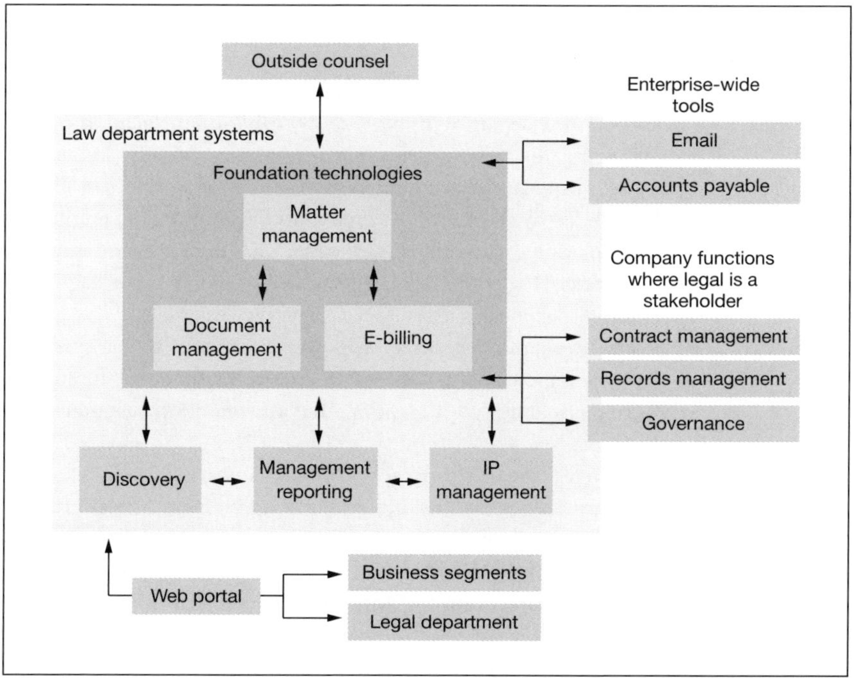

3.4 Can a single product do it all?

As a starting point, legal departments typically rely on three primary tools to serve as the architectural foundation for their information management needs. Together, the use of matter management, e-billing and document management solutions are often referred to as 'enterprise legal management' (see Figure 4).

The extent to which these three functions can adequately be found within a single product is dependent on the needs of each organisation.

3.5 How can work product best be managed?

Although it is generally accepted today that both matter management and e-billing functionality are consolidated within one application (in fact, it would be difficult nowadays to buy one without the other), the management of legal content (eg, email, documents, etc) – can be achieved in several ways, including through the use of the following systems:

- Legal matter management systems:
  - Pros: all data within one database; no additional cost;
  - Cons: usually a two-step process of saving a document and then importing it into the system; limited functionality in comparison to a dedicated legal document management system;
- Legal document management systems:
  - Pros: documents are centralised and directly associated with their related matters ('matter-centricity'); robust functionality (including strong email management) and workflow geared to specific needs of lawyers (eg, security, versioning and collaboration); familiarity by in-house counsel (used by most law firms);
  - Cons: may be different from the corporate standard; another system needing to be learned by in-house counsel and maintained by the corporate IT department; more costly (investment in additional hardware and software);
- Enterprise content management systems:
  - Pros: in use by the rest of the organisation (resulting in potential for greater collaboration with others and easier maintenance and support by the corporate IT department); less costly (taking advantage of existing enterprise licence);
  - Cons: no matter-centricity; workflow less geared to the specific needs of lawyers (eg, security, versioning and collaboration); limited ability to force compliance with corporate records retention schedules and policy.

3.6 What about the need for integration with other systems?

There are two primary forms of integration: application integration and data integration. Application integration is a direct connection between separate software programs; often, this integration is provided through a vendor-developed and published application programming interface. While seemingly a simple form of connection, issues can arise when integrated products need to be updated or swapped out. A more holistic solution is data integration, where data can be exchanged between – even among – applications irrespective of the software. Creating a data layer through construction of data warehouses, data marts or some form of integration appliance or middleware can provide a more solid foundation for information exchange and analytics.

4. Deploying information technology to promote business transformation

Although the global general counsel may not need to be a technology expert, his ability to leverage investment in technology – often a significant spend – is dependent on his ability to effectively manage change. While many put tremendous effort and energy into defining system requirements and the selection and implementation of software, these activities have little meaning if, at the end of the day, people are not using the tools provided. Policy around change management will play a critical role in determining user adoption and leverage of technology. In his capacity as project sponsor and champion, the general counsel can have the greatest impact on ensuring technology adoption and use.

By sheer force of authority, staff will make use of software if it is mandated by the general counsel (of course, the flipside is true: without said mandate, there is often little hope of adoption). Many, in fact, take this approach. However, should the general counsel prefer a lighter touch, there are – at a minimum – two critical strategies that will help with user adoption and promotion of best practice processes – what consultants refer to as 'change management'. Falling under this designation are principles of anytime, anywhere access to legal information via use of cloud computing, and a focus on personal, real-time training and ongoing support.

5. Best structure for IT support

No general counsel and – by extension – legal department can effectively select, implement and support technology without input and buy-in from the chief information officer and – by extension – the corporate IT department. The degree to which they need to or should be involved is a question every general counsel must address. The answer may determine the likelihood of successful deployment.

5.1 Role of corporate IT department in the budget process

Let us begin with the start of any technology initiative: the budget. In an optimum setting, budget for technology capital and expenditure is under the control and supervision of the legal department. In such a case, the legal department brings in the corporate IT department to assist in assessing needs, defining requirements, selecting software, deploying systems and providing ongoing support after implementation. The relationship between the legal and corporate IT departments is of a partnering nature; the legal department defines its needs and wants and is willing and able to pay for them. The corporate IT department assists, making certain that technology expenditure is in alignment with corporate standards, but willing to deviate should the legal department show a reasonable business case for deviation.

Unfortunately, this dream state is just that – a dream. The more typical scenario is one where technology budget is under the control and supervision of the corporate IT department (not the legal department). In such a case, the following paths are likely to result from a request for expenditure:

- The corporate IT department communicates that there is no legal department budget. There are several variations here, from allocating nothing to the yearly budget cycle to pulling back at any point during the year. As the legal department is a corporate cost centre, it ranks relatively low on the budget 'totem pole' in relation to a business unit's technology requests for expenditure.
- The corporate IT department provides a preliminary budget. It allows the legal department to identify its needs, define its requirements and select software. Upon selection, final vetting and approval must be provided by the technology audit/authorisation committee. The committee comprises a group of people who have yet to be involved in the evaluation and decision-making process, and thus have no contextual understanding for how conclusions were reached and decisions attained. The committee claims that similar software is being used in other areas of the company and thus does not approve the legal department's request for expenditure.
- The corporate IT department prefers more analysis to be performed and pushes the request further down the road. Wait until next year.

One would hazard to guess that more legal technology projects have failed to get off the ground as a result of corporate IT department budget control than any other rationale. Keep in mind that, at any point, the global general counsel, given his rank and role within the senior management structure, can overrule the corporate IT department – and often the chief information officer. If – and this is a big if – he so demands it, it will happen. Yet, for many reasons, general counsel are often unwilling to invest the political capital needed to get their projects approved. Regardless of political affinity, there are some suggested rules of the road for getting final approval (see Figure 5).

These suggestions may seem like common sense, but unfortunately, very few general counsel establish these ground rules.

5.2 Role of corporate IT department in the implementation process

The intent here is not to bash the corporate IT department. Quite the opposite: successful technology projects begin and end by involving the corporate IT department in their implementation. In this capacity, the corporate IT department can play many roles – project manager, business and technical analyst, trainer, even help desk support. To achieve the most benefit, it is important that these roles are clearly explained and understood by all. The relationship must be an open and honest partnership. The legal department must feel it is getting timely attention and the corporate IT department must feel its advice is being considered and its contributions recognised.

A suggestion for getting the most from the partnership is to dedicate corporate IT department resources to the legal department, if only for project duration. Asking for assistance in defining goals, requirements and logistics – right from project inception – is likely to increase the probability of gaining corporate IT department buy-in and advocacy as the project is pushed forward. Providing the corporate IT

Figure 5: Ground rules for successful technology project initiation

1. Insist that the legal department be allocated and allowed to manage its own yearly technology budget – like every other corporate line of business.
2. Insist that the legal department leads efforts in identifying its own needs and development of a business case for technology expenditure. The general counsel should make known his personal desire to push the project forward and provide a projected ROI and realistic roadmap for completion.
3. Insist that the corporate IT department assigns a liaison to the legal department to serve as business and technical adviser to the project team. The chief information officer or decision maker within the corporate IT department should periodically be apprised of progress throughout the project.
4. Insist that any request for expenditure follows the corporate IT department standards and protocols (if any). These must be identified and well understood prior to beginning any project.
5. Once a request is made, insist that any decision regarding project viability be made within a reasonable time frame. The corporate IT department should provide rationale should the project be rejected and not the other way around – that is, the legal department should not have to provide rationale for its acceptance (other than projected ROI, of course).

department a seat on the project steering committee is yet another way to validate their contribution.

5.3 Role of vendors and consultants

Often, bringing consultants onto the project team can provide many benefits and improve success rates. Independent consultants provide systems expertise and experience in understanding legal processes and system configurations that span many legal departments. Given that they do this type of work all the time, they bring a level of expertise that cannot be provided by corporate IT staff. Many times, the sheer fact that they are outside the company provides them a level of credence that no internal staff can provide.

The very best consultants not only have a deep technical understanding of specific tools, but can also create and communicate a vision for how their use will forge a desired future state. To do so requires thinking holistically, across practice groups and geographic locations. It requires identifying the 'big picture' as well as developing a plan for getting others to buy in to its legitimacy. Thus, in selecting the right consultant, the general counsel would be wise to choose from among those who can be both strategic and tactical in approach.

5.4 Best methods for ongoing IT support

Once the project is completed, it may seem a bit daunting to have to deal with the myriad questions and issues that are likely to arise as a result of process and policy change. Fortunately, the global general counsel need not go it alone. Many general counsel form technology steering committees that meet periodically to review project(s) status, resolve support questions and confirm budget needs. Members include representatives from the corporate IT department who play a vital role in translating technical specifications into laymen's terms. The technology committee often insists on service level agreements with the corporate IT department; these serve as an informal contract defining expectations relating to ongoing types of service, performance measurement, problem management and issue escalation procedures. It is also a good idea periodically to establish goals and review the performance of the corporate IT team as one would any internal member of the legal department.

6. The need for continual improvement and innovation

In his book *Tomorrow's Lawyers*, Richard Susskind refers to a key challenge for legal professionals to identify and grasp the opportunities afforded by emerging technologies. He cautions against "irrational rejectionism" – the dogmatic and visceral dismissal of a technology with which the sceptic has no direct personal experience. Instead, he calls upon lawyers to go beyond automating current working practices that are not efficient: "the challenge is to innovate, to practise law in ways that we could not have done in the past."[3]

One method for assessing how effective technology has been in achieving continual improvement and innovation is making a comparison of capabilities relative to a proposed 'maturity model' of process proficiency (see Table 2).

7. Conclusion

Today's general counsel should take command of defining a technology roadmap that is both strategic in purpose and opportunistic in reach. Most importantly, he must not let perfection be the enemy of good. There may be existing technologies that can be optimised or better leveraged. There may be process efficiencies that can quickly be brought to bear simply through project sponsorship and vocalisation of expected benefits. There could be significant and immediate cost savings to be made just by letting others know they are being watched. Whatever the near-term benefits, today's general counsel should strive for long-term continual improvement and innovation that is disruptive to both practice and business operations. For, as Mark Chandler, former senior vice president and general counsel of Cisco, so eloquently stated: "The opportunity is there to recognize the business realities that will be driven by new technology. We can seize the chance to offer more value to clients. We can seize the opportunity for our own employees to be more engaged and productive. Our mutual success depends on it."[5]

---

3 Richard Susskind , *Tomorrow's Lawyers*, Oxford University Press, 2013.

4 'Legal Department Optimization: Leveraging a Maturity Model to Achieve Operational Excellence', *LexisNexis White Paper*, 2015.

5 Mark Chandler, Northwestern School of Law's 34th Annual Securities Regulation Institute, January, 2007.

Table 2: Example of technology maturity model[4]

	Manual processes	Deployed technology	Integrated information	Data-driven decisions	Predictive results
Area of Proficiency					
Knowledge management	Spreadsheets	Standard reports	Dashboards	Analytics	Scenario modelling
Communication	Email	Matter journals and documents	Matter calendars	Shared KPI accountabilities	Real-time alerts
Matter governance	Manual, one-off	Billing guidelines	Comprehensive matter visibility	Matter project plans	Collaborative decisions
Budget oversight	'Blank cheque'	Matter-level budgets	Aggregated budgets	Variance analysis	Data-driven forecasts
Vendor management	Anecdotal	Requests for proposals	Preferred firm panel	Law firm scorecard	Law firm optimisation
Matter Pricing	Hourly	Rate discounts	Alternative fee structures	Strategically negotiated fees	Win-win pricing

Compliant customer data handling: a challenge for IT service providers

Dennis Grabherr
Hewlett-Packard Company

1. General introduction

For most companies that exploit innovations of the digital revolution, the efficient handling of customer data is fundamental to their commercial success, but also represents their Achilles' heel if measured against increasingly complex contractual and international statutory restrictions. The compliant handling of customer data represents a major issue for legal as well as IT departments, and a thorough understanding of the related problems is a must for the in-house counsel involved.

In the chapter these issues are explored from the point of view of an IT service provider operating in the business-to-business space, as it is fair to assume that with an increasingly complex delivery infrastructure, many IT service providers are not yet in a position to ensure that their 24/7, follow-the-sun global service delivery models handle entrusted corporate customer data in compliance with all applicable contractual, legal, regulatory or governance obligations.

In order to avoid contractual liability for breach of contract and fines for – for example – information security breaches and related reputational damage, all IT service providers must ensure that their customer data is handled with integrity and in a compliant and safe manner.

Based on practical in-house experience, this chapter not only outlines the typical causes of non-compliant customer data handling, but also lays out a set of possible organisational and cultural risk-mitigation measures for introduction across an organisation.

In order to frame future business models which are capable of compliant customer data handling, it is not only imperative for the legal and IT teams to be joined up and brutally transparent in their processes, but also that buy-in and full backing from top management are unconditionally required.

2. Introduction to data handling

It has never been more important for IT service providers – and general counsel – to know what data an organisation has, where it is stored, who has access to it and how it should be classified. Yet, as data creation and collection increase every day, this has never been more difficult to assess.

Customers entrust their IT service provider to handle their data with integrity and in a compliant and safe manner. Irrespective of the data type (eg, business critical, personal or governmental), the customer will define how it should be processed. In addition, local laws are likely to dictate how data is to be managed.

Based on practical in-house legal and compliance experience, this chapter takes a closer look at the challenges surrounding compliant customer data handling from the perspective of a typical global IT service provider offering complex bespoke services to its business customers. It not only discusses the typical causes of non-compliant customer data handling, but also outlines a set of specific organisational and cultural risk-mitigation good-practice measures for introduction and interdisciplinary enforcement across an organisation.

Given that legal/compliance risk is the driver behind the challenge of achieving compliant customer data handling and therefore overall ownership must remain with the legal/compliance function, it must be clearly understood that this challenge can be mastered only on the basis of joint leadership of – and fully transparent collaboration between – the lawyers and their technical counterparts responsible for service delivery. In other words, this is also a plea to bridge, urgently and effectively, the understanding gap between the often fundamentally incompatible legal and IT worlds that still exist.

Given the condensed scope of this chapter, it does not cover domestic statutory law requirements or all possible IT compliance aspects. It should also not be understood as a static recipe for compliant customer data handling, as the best processes are dynamic and require constant evaluation and tweaking.

The insights presented may also help in making risk-based decisions about how much an IT service provider – and not just the legal/compliance function – should spend on compliant customer data handling as a strategic investment in client relations and client trust.

The following definitions will be useful in the further course of this chapter:

- 'Customer data' means all types of data of customers as contractually defined. It can include confidential customer information (eg, emails, strategic plans, customer network information etc) and personal data about the IT service provider's employees, its customers or, if a government customer, its citizens.
- 'Customer data handling' means what the IT service provider does in managing and processing (including obtaining, accessing, storing, transferring and destroying) customer data.
- 'Customer data handling requirements' means the obligations for the handling of customer data placed on the IT service provider (a) contractually by a private or public sector customer and/or (b) according to law or regulation.

IT service providers are in the customer data handling business. Customer data is typically hosted in, accessed from or transferred to many countries around the globe. Given the 24/7, follow-the-sun global service delivery infrastructure with help desks and data centres scattered all over, the complexity of compliant customer data handling is increasing at a breathtaking rate.

Over the past few years customers have become much more demanding with regard to customer data handling restrictions and, in parallel, global privacy and data security regulation are rapidly growing tougher, more detailed and more fragmented.

The internal governance of an IT service provider typically requires that all business must be in compliance with contractual as well as statutory obligations. Getting customer data handling right is key, not only for delivering business sustainability and financial and compliance goals, but also in order for the IT service provider to help avoid potentially severe civil, criminal and financial consequences, reputational damage and – worst of all – loss of customer trust.

It is essential to ensure that, as a trusted business partner, the IT service provider complies with the customer data handling requirements agreed upon with its customers. This is integral to the service that the IT service provider provides.

The legal and operations teams of IT service providers need to understand better all contractual and legal restrictions regarding the geographic transfer of – and access to – entrusted customer data. Technological change is happening at such a pace that traditional silo-based functional sign-off processes – still widely in use, with only cosmetic changes – have reached their end-of-life stage and have not yet been replaced by truly cross-functional collaborative approaches, which are unconditionally necessary to identify and address customer data-handling-related risk. Furthermore, in service and supply arrangements the IT service provider needs to maintain alignment between what has been promised and what is delivered operationally, on an end-to-end basis.

The litmus test for customer data handling compliance in an IT service provider should be as follows: is it possible in your organisation that service design and delivery functions provide final sign-off without a detailed match of service design and intended actual service delivery against any/all contractual and statutory customer data handling requirements? In reality, the detailed service design is often only completed after contract signature without considering customer data handling requirements. Given traditional silo structures, few feel responsible or accountable for bridging this obvious gap and many traditionalists – often even incentivised by diametrically opposed bonus schemes – perceive the customer data handling compliance goal as a redundant hurdle instead of a strategic facilitator in the process of creating a sustainable business model and unique selling point for the customer.

In summary, the objective of customer data handling compliance is to help ensure that: (a) the IT service provider agrees contractually only to such contractual customer data handling requirements which the IT service provider is actually capable of delivering compliantly; and (b) the IT service provider can effectively comply with statutory obligations.

3. Assessment of customer data handling compliance

Assessing whether the service delivery arrangements of an IT service provider are compliant with customer data handling requirements can be performed only through a holistic, interdisciplinary (ie, legal and technical) analysis of a representative sample of live major IT service provider customer contracts and their corresponding service delivery.

For the purposes of the customer data-handling compliance assessment, a relational database containing all the product, system, user and location data should be used. That data can then be overlaid with the specific contractual customer data-handling requirement data in the form of abstract 'logical rules', which allow a set of reports to be produced from the database that show the following:

- which systems hold what restricted customer data;
- where these systems are being accessed;
- who is accessing these systems (both IT service provider and third parties); and
- which specific customer data handling requirements are being breached.

On the one hand, such an interdisciplinary assessment is a non-trivial, resource-hungry and time-consuming process, but on the other hand its output – if done thoroughly – provides unique and necessary insights that help to transform the IT service provider into a more data-handling-compliant organisation.

The input to the relational database should be provided by the following three work streams:

- Legal review of the selected IT service provider customer contracts, including the multitude of related IT service provider supply agreements, to identify customer data handling requirements and determine the degree to which these have been flowed down;
- Determination of how the relevant customer data is being processed in hundreds of delivery systems within the IT service provider's system stack, specifically:
  - What products or services are being supplied to the relevant customer?
  - What systems are in use to deliver those products (eg, capturing orders, fulfilling the service, managing the service, billing for the service, etc)?
  - Where are the systems in use physically located and hosted?
  - Which users have access to the relevant customer data in the systems?
  - Where in the world are those users accessing the systems?
  - Which company is the relevant user employed by (IT service provider full-time equivalents or IT service provider supplier staff)?
- Analysis of how the relevant customer data is being processed in the systems of potentially hundreds of suppliers to deliver the service, and who has access to the relevant data.

A high-level summary of the interdisciplinary customer data-handling compliance assessment process should include performance of a legal customer data handling review of the selected IT service provider customer and supplier contracts to identify – specifically for each contract – the following elements:

- customer data handling requirements in customer contracts;
- contractually defined customer data types as referred to in the identified customer data handling requirements;
- a list of contractually pre-approved suppliers as well as a list of suppliers actually in use for service delivery;
- the contractual consequences of breach of identified customer data handling requirements; and
- determination whether customer data handling requirements have been effectively flowed down to IT service provider suppliers.

Furthermore, on the systems side, the following analysis must be undertaken:

- Analysis of the IT service provider's internal system stack, to identify those systems managing or processing one or more of the customer data types for the purpose of delivering each customer's specific service scope;
- For each IT service provider and IT service provider supplier system, identification of geographically distributed user access profiles for each IT service provider user and supplier user; and
- Identification of the international host location for each IT service provider internal system stack in use for service delivery purposes.

By gradually feeding all such data into the relational database, it is possible to create an accurate and detailed view of the total number of contractual breaches of customer data handling requirements caused by the IT service provider's current service delivery.

It cannot be emphasised enough that the success of such assessment depends on the following factors:

- cross-functional top-down support and buy-in (eg, legal, technical, operations, procurement etc);
- executive sponsorship combined with the firm intention of making use of the insights gained to drive organisational transformation and behavioural change towards higher levels of customer data handling compliance; and
- continued (throughout the entire project) intense coordination and collaboration between the joint legal and technical project leads.

Clearly this analysis could be taken much further by, for example, also considering the respective supplier system stacks (provided that access is granted), but the insights achievable based on the above assessment scope should create a sufficient level of enlightenment.

4. Assessment findings: Typical requirements and patterns of contractual reach

Leaving the highly unlikely scenario of 100% customer data handling compliance aside, assessment typically evidences that in relation to a representative sample of major IT service provider customer contracts, IT service providers agree to numerous customer data handling requirements without adequately considering the delivery implications and hence without delivering the service compliantly.

Therefore, the following general observations on the results of a customer data handling assessment can be made:

- Practically all customer contracts contain customer data handling requirements.
- Customer data handling requirements in general go well beyond – quantitatively and qualitatively – the mere contractual reference to applicable data protection acts.
- Typically identified customer data handling requirements include location restrictions, access restrictions to specific user types (eg, IT service provider

employees or pre-approved suppliers) and requirements to maintain customer data segregated from other customer data.

- At least 25% of the total of IT service provider-operated delivery systems processing customer data (often well over 1,000 systems in use for global service delivery, besides the systems controlled and operated by suppliers not integrated into the IT service provider system stack) breach – through their customer data handling – one or more contractual customer data handling requirements.
- Unnecessarily high numbers of IT service provider users have access to systems supporting service delivery of the contracts with access to customer data.
- Excessive numbers of IT service provider suppliers have access to, transfer or store customer data in breach of one or more customer data handling requirement(s).
- The contractual flow-down of customer data handling requirements to IT service provider suppliers is – in more than half the cases – only partial or even not given at all.
- The contractual consequences for breaching customer data handling requirements are material (ie, with a substantial percentage foreseeing the obligation to provide full indemnity and/or uncapped liability).

Dozens of different customer data handling requirements generally conform to one of a number of generic customer data handling requirement types, which are roughly ranked in order of frequency of appearance in customer contracts:

- Specific customer data types can be transferred to and/or accessed by only certain specified groupings of individuals. A typical user access restriction would be as follows: "Regarding data type(s) X, access shall be restricted to IT service provider full-time equivalents. IT service provider supplier staff shall not have user access." It is common for a single customer contract to contain more than five different user access restrictions.
- A requirement for IT service provider suppliers to be pre-approved by the customer – ie, access to customer data by a non-pre-approved supplier would constitute a breach of contract. Generally speaking, less than 10% of IT service provider suppliers are actually pre-approved by the customer. In complex global contracts it is common for IT service providers to make use of more than 500 international suppliers.
- Confidentiality obligations – these also constitute customer data handling requirements.
- Geographic customer data transfer restrictions – for example: "The IT service provider shall not transfer customer data (eg, sensitive, authority, bank or personal data) outside of geographical area X (eg, Switzerland, Japan, Bavaria or the European Economic Area)."
- Requirements for physical and/or logical segregation of customer data (eg: "The IT service provider will ensure strict physical and/or logical separation of customer's information, data and systems from that of its other customers

in order to prevent any unauthorised access to them as defined in customer policy X." This customer data handling requirement is increasingly being asked for by data security-sensitive customers.

- A requirement for the IT service provider to provide certain services from specific locations only (eg: "The IT service provider shall operate the customer service desk in Poland.")
- A requirement for notification of suspected and/or actual customer data handling breaches against contract or the law. Given the complexities of global service delivery, this restriction can turn out to be particularly onerous.

5. Typical causes of, and structural deficiencies leading to, low compliance

The complex and fragmented ways in which the services of an IT service provider are underpinned makes alignment with customer data handling requirements on major deals a complex and challenging goal. Legal, technical and operational processes and practices need to interlock and work seamlessly to ensure continuing compliance.

The following is a list of typical causes and structural deficiencies which lead to low customer data handling compliance within IT service providers.

- The IT service provider's approach to cost-optimising delivery as much as possible on the basis of standard products strongly contrasts with its business customers asking for more bespoke solutions with numerous customer data handling requirements. For example, changes to product design and design-and-build structures are required as customer data handling compliance is increasingly becoming a differentiator in the marketplace.
- Even if, on a contract-by-contract basis, compliant delivery was possible when the contract was entered into, unchecked operational in-life delivery changes can often lead to new customer data handling non-compliances. There appears to be a critical weakness in end-to-end processes of IT service providers, which means that relevant operational changes can be made without regard to the potential implications for existing contractual commitments (ie, customer data handling requirements) to customers. Adequate change control procedures to ensure compliance during the entire life cycle of the relevant customer contract are missing.
- Global sourcing (ie, the offshoring of activities supporting customer service delivery) leads to customer data being moved offshore, unchecked against customer data handling requirements. Such offshoring is often being signed off by finance and HR only (ie, without customer data handling compliance checks being performed), and is mainly driven by labour cost arbitrage considerations. Over the years, as technologically possible and commercially attractive as it is, offshoring appears to have eclipsed awareness of the need for customer data handling compliance.
- The IT service provider does not have arrangements in place to ensure that it understands what customer data it holds, and where and who has access to such data. For example, at bid stage (ie, pre-contractually), the team is not being provided with quality information on the potential global spread of customer data (in terms of user access, host locations, geographic data

transfers etc) to assess whether or not the proposed solution would comply with customer-desired data handling requirements. The same applies to contract managers when dealing with in-life service or delivery changes.

- Use of IT service provider suppliers for service delivery without obtaining prior customer approval as per the contract; sub-contracting of service delivery without or with only partial flow-down of customer data handling requirements to supply contracts; and inadequate in-life auditing of supplier contracts regarding flow-down of customer data handling requirements.
- IT service provider standard products are being designed without contractual or statutory compliance in mind, and they are being used in complex deals without considering compliance (ie, they are simply being assumed as fit for purpose by all sign-off authorities). In other words, whenever standard products are being used in an IT service provider – even, for example, as part of a wider bespoke solution in conjunction with third-party service components – they are not being checked against contractual customer data handling requirements, as it is assumed that the IT service provider's standard operating model automatically generates customer data handling compliance in relation to the use of standard products.
- Failure to provide role-based (or 'segregated') access control in IT solutions, effectively giving individuals uncontrolled access to customer data without considering the geographic access location or whether individuals are IT service provider full-time equivalents or third-party staff.
- No central data repository of contractual customer data handling requirements exists within the IT service provider to allow for change to control processes and for obligations management to be performed compliantly. For example, application owners have no means of responsibly and correctly responding to audits on authorised user access to their application(s). Individual application managers simply do not have the budget or resources to delve into hundreds of customer contracts (eg, every six months) to check on customer data handling compliance.
- Accountabilities and responsibilities at various stages in the processes and life cycle of the customer contracts (eg, critically at handoffs and handovers) are insufficiently set out and understood. Service delivery and legal bid sign-offs are granted largely in isolation, without holistically assessing the interdependencies of customer data handling requirements on service delivery and vice versa. Hence nobody feels accountable and/or reliable for relevant risk on an end-to-end basis. There is a disconnect between the IT service provider's bespoke contracts and its systems, network design and supply (internal and external) arrangements, due largely to the high level of complexity in the operational and delivery arrangements.
- Lack of clarity on objectives and incentives which can prioritise certain objectives above the need for customer data handling compliance – for example, counterproductive financial incentive structures which reward cost cutting via offshoring at the expense of compliance.
- The absence of a strong, clear and favourable 'tone from the top' regarding

the importance of compliance with customer data handling requirements and, more generally, of customer data handling compliance. Consequently, teams do not feel the need to ensure customer data-handling-compliant structures and processes.
- Lack of a corresponding compliance culture (ie, customer data handling compliance is being ignored with an expectation of impunity).

6. Specific measures to mitigate existing – and prevent future – risks of non-compliance

Truly transformational changes are required to tackle the customer data handling compliance challenge adequately. Given structural issues and cost/benefit inefficiencies in relation to the implementation of mitigation treatments for existing customer data handling risk, it appears much more promising for an IT service provider to focus on the prevention of further and future customer data handling risk build-up. In this context, prevention is more efficient and less costly than cure and backward engineering.

Improving how an IT service provider takes customer data handling requirements into account in its processes and practices, as well as clarifying accountabilities, not only reduces the risk of a potential contractual breach, but also maximises benefits to the business by delivering on its commitments – demonstrating the IT service provider value of 'doing what we say we will' and delivering excellence in customer service.

Set out in the remainder of this section are a series of possible organisational and cultural measures to mitigate existing – and prevent future – risks of customer data handling non-compliance.

6.1 Guidance towards achieving behavioural change

(a) *Customer data handling principles*

The customer data handling principles below support the overriding principles established in mandatory IT service provider internal policies:

- *Principle 1:* Any customer data handling requirements must be explicitly defined in customer and supplier contracts.
- *Principle 2:* The extent to which – and ways in which – customer data is to be accessed, processed, stored, transferred or destroyed by the IT service provider should be fully understood, documented and risk-assessed as early as possible prior to contract award or contract change.
- *Principle 3:* Any discrepancies between customer data handling requirements and what the IT service provider can actually deliver should be resolved prior to contract award or contract change (eg, by renegotiation of proposed customer data handling requirements or by changing the service design).
- *Principle 4:* Services for customers should be designed and delivered to comply with any agreed customer data handling requirements.
- *Principle 5:* Compliance with any customer data handling requirements should be maintained throughout the entire term of the customer contract.

Therefore, the in-life team regularly needs to assess and monitor the risk of any non-compliance with any customer data handling requirement in each contract or with applicable law.

- *Principle 6:* An IT service provider should cascade customer data handling requirements to all suppliers that will have access to customer data.
- *Principle 7:* Avoid generalised contractual provisions for data handling and data security.

(b) Compliance checklist for gatekeepers/authorisers of customer contracts

- Before your team makes any promises about data to the customer, remind them of the importance of customer data handling compliance to the IT service provider.
- Require those seeking approval to identify the IT service provider's legal, contractual and governance responsibilities in or relating to the contract concerning compliance with customer data handling requirements.
- Require the deal team to confirm that any necessary assessment of the IT service provider's ability to comply with the proposed customer data handling requirements has been completed and signed off by the relevant functions on an end-to-end basis, including reviews of supply chain and delivery arrangements.
- Require the deal team to confirm that they have drawn up a sufficiently detailed handover and in-life plan to address adequately compliance with the customer data handling principles (eg, by including a summary of key customer data handling requirements, identifying key deliverables and checkpoints, making any necessary improvements and communicating these changes across the IT service provider).
- Only authorise a customer contract with customer data handling requirements – or an amendment that could affect compliant delivery on such a contract – on a fully informed basis (as outlined above) and if it is consistent with the IT service provider's customer data handling principles and applicable law (taking advice from the legal, privacy and security teams as appropriate).
- If any proposed customer data handling requirement(s) or proposed change to a customer contract or to operational delivery arrangements could affect how, where or by whom the IT service provider delivers services to a customer, ensure that it is clear which customer and/or supplier contracts would be affected, what customer data handling compliance assessment has been made and whether the change would be consistent with any/all relevant customer data handling requirements.
- Require the deal team to document appropriate ownership and accountability for avoiding/mitigating identified risks in relation to compliance with customer data handling requirements and ensure you understand what that means for your own upstream and downstream authorisations.
- If the effective assessment or management of compliance with customer data

handling requirements necessitates some change to be made (eg, for processes to interlock better, inputs to be obtained or better communication across units), ensure this occurs before any approval is given or implemented, and this is signed off by the accountable owner.

(c) ***Governance process applicable to new bids and/or resigns, if service delivery currently not expected to be compliant with requirements***

If: (a) at bid stage, after having exhausted within the bid team all available technical, operational and contractual options to ensure that service delivery would comply with customer proposed customer data handling requirements; (b) prior to resign or an extension of an existing contract, after having exhausted within the contract team all available technical, operational and contractual options to ensure that service delivery would comply with current CDH requirements; or (c) in a public sector tender the bid or contract team reasonably believes, after having explored all risk mitigation and/or limitation possibilities, that service delivery in compliance with proposed (or current but to be renewed) customer data handling requirements is currently not likely to be achievable (eg, if changes to the contract cannot be secured in a case of public sector tendering), or that the IT service provider – if it were to contract as envisaged – would be left with a material risk of customer data handling non-compliance, then the relevant bid manager, with input from the deal lawyer and the solutions representative, shall – well in advance of signing – notify the lead operational owners of the issue (ie, the legal lead and the operations lead) with a brief customer data-handling risk assessment. In the notification, the operations lead shall be asked to confirm:

- he understand the issues and the customer data handling risks;
- the existence of a workable plan operationally to achieve customer data handling compliance;
- a committed timeframe to implement the plan; and
- a reasonable estimate of the implementation costs of such plan.

6.2 Other measures

(a) ***Resetting and proactively managing customer expectations***

Pre-contractually it is sensible to have an open discussion with the customer about the necessity of certain customer data handling requirements and also to clarify upfront the parties' respective contractual and statutory responsibilities in relation to customer data. The customer expectation must be managed in a way that it cannot reasonably expect to impose a multitude of customer data handling requirements on the one hand and, on the other hand, have an effective IT service provided on a global scale.

Experience shows that engaging openly and honestly at the earliest possible stages with the customer's data protection and/or security officer can be extremely beneficial. Any inconsistencies between the services the customer wants and the type of customer data handling requirements the customer thinks it wants should be addressed.

(b) ***Tone from the top***

It is fundamental for the right direction and tone to be set from the top, stressing the importance of customer data handling compliance. Any risk prevention activities will not be either effective or sustainable if they are not supported by a strong and clear tone from the top enforcing the importance of customer data handling compliance for the long-term economic health of the IT service provider.

(c) ***Mitigation of existing risk by renegotiating live customer contracts***

Given that any such renegotiation would necessarily include the acknowledgement of the IT service provider's contractual non-compliance with customer data handling requirements and also the identified material contractual consequences in case of breach, this (in its own right) is not a viable mitigation option unless and until the IT service provider can put forward appropriate negotiating positions which would be likely to include showing how the IT service provider could meet customer needs in different but perhaps equally acceptable ways.

(d) ***Data analysis tool***

A tool can be created to allow the bid teams and contract managers to establish – prior to committing anything to the customer – which of the systems within the system stack of the IT service provider actually would – in generic terms – process, hold or grant access to different types of customer data. Without such transparency it is hard to ensure customer data-handling compliance during service delivery.

(e) ***Process***

Changes can be made to the IT service provider's bid governance and contract management processes to ensure that customer data handling is duly considered.

(f) ***Clause family approach***

As the first step, a customer's proposed terms and conditions must be reviewed by the contract lawyers to identify any customer data handling requirements. These can be found anywhere in the contract (eg, offshoring, export control, subcontracting, security, data protection, in technical schedules, confidential information etc) and must be considered holistically (the 'clause family approach'). This is because if clauses with customer data handling requirements are reviewed independently, they may appear acceptable, but in the context of the totality of the relevant customer data handling requirements (the customer data handling clause family) they can be very onerous or have a significant impact on delivery.

(g) ***Product development that is customer data handling compliant***

As in the 'privacy by design' approach, which in systems engineering takes data protection considerations into account throughout the whole engineering process, customer data handling should be firmly built into the product development life cycle.

(h) *Standardisation*

Development and global rollout of generic positions, techniques and standard customer data-handling clauses for upstream contracting in the light of the IT service provider's delivery capabilities and operating models is necessary in order to ensure customer data handling compliance for new and possibly renewal customers.

(i) *In-life monitoring*

A mechanism should be introduced for regular monitoring of customer data handling compliance on customer contracts during the entire contract term.

In support of this purpose, and as a precondition for reliable *ad hoc* system customer data handling compliance checks, a comprehensive and searchable pan-IT service provider repository (eg, as part of an existing contract management system) should be created to: (a) identify, for each IT service provider system being used for service delivery, which generic customer data categories it processes; and (b) hold all customer data handling requirements mapped against relevant systems.

(j) *Training*

Target group-specific customer data handling compliance trainings of the commercial legal teams and other key technical and operational stakeholders.

7. Conclusion

The complexities of service delivery with customer data handling compliance are often being either underestimated or simply ignored in IT service providers. However, getting customer data handling compliance right can not only mitigate legal risk, but also translate into a strategic competitive advantage for the IT service provider in the marketplace.

In this context the legal/compliance function as 'owner' of the customer data handling requirements has a prominent and necessary role to play, but must recognise that customer data handling compliance can be achieved only: through close interdisciplinary collaboration between all functions involved in defining and delivering the service; with joint technical and legal leadership (but owned by legal/compliance); and with a strong and clear tone from the top of the IT service provider unconditionally mandating customer data handling compliance. A corresponding creation of awareness of the importance of customer data handling compliance, as well as a drive for cultural and behavioural change within the IT service provider, is a necessary precondition for achieving higher levels of customer data handling compliance.

About the authors

Constance E Bagley
Senior research scholar, Yale Law School
winninglegally@gmail.com

Constance E Bagley is a senior research scholar at Yale Law School. She was formerly professor in the practice of law and management at Yale School of Management, an associate professor at Harvard Business School, a senior lecturer at the Stanford Graduate School of Business and a partner at Bingham McCutchen. Her work focuses on law and strategy. Ms Bagley's books include *Managers and the Legal Environment: Strategies for the 21st Century* (8th edn, 2015) and *The Entrepreneur's Guide to Business Law* (4th edn, 2011) (co-authored with Craig E Dauchy). She is also a skilled public speaker and facilitator. Her clients include MassMutual Financial, PepsiCo, Microsoft, Prudential and CVS Health.

Ms Bagley received her JD *magna cum laude* from Harvard Law School, her AB with honours and distinction from Stanford University and an honourary doctorate in economics from Lund University.

Robert C Bird
Associate professor, University of Connecticut
robert.bird@uconn.edu

Robert Bird is an associate professor of business law and the Eversource Energy chair in business ethics at the University of Connecticut. Mr Bird's scholarship focuses on employment law, legal strategy, intellectual property, business and human rights. He is the author of more than 50 publications, including works in the *Journal of Law and Economics*, *American Business Law Journal*, *Law and Society Review* and the *Harvard Journal of Law and Public Policy*.

Mr Bird is the recipient of the Academy of Legal Studies in Business best international paper award, the distinguished proceedings award and the Holmes-Cardozo best overall conference paper award, among others. He was editor in chief of the *American Business Law Journal* in 2012 and 2013, where he designed and published the 50th anniversary issue of the journal's founding. He served as administrative editor, articles editor, senior articles editor and managing editor from 2006 to 2012.

Filip Corveleyn
Head of research and development, Tools4Legal GmbH
filip.corveleyn@tools4legal.com

Filip Corveleyn is a lawyer specialising in collective labour law project management. He has been actively managing large employment restructuring programmes for international clients for 14 years, as well as providing consultancy on legal project management. Mr Corveleyn has been recognised as an employment law specialist by Who's Who Legal. In the past he was a scientific researcher at the law department of the University of Louvain, where he read law and obtained his masters degree in European Tax law. He obtained his MBA degree at the Judge Business School/University of Cambridge.

He has published papers on legal innovation

together with Felix Rackwitz and presented at the Bucerius School of Law, Hamburg.

In 2015 Mr Corveleyn founded the legal start-up Tools4Legal together with Felix Rackwitz, as featured in the *Financial Times*.

Bruno Cova
Partner, Paul Hastings
brunocova@paulhastings.com

Bruno Cova is partner of global law firm Paul Hastings and chair of its Milan office. He focuses his practice on mergers and acquisitions, restructurings, securities law and corporate governance and corporate crises. In the field of corporate governance, he advises general counsel and boards of directors on governance reforms, legal risks and internal controls, regulatory and internal investigations.

Mr Cova has been general counsel of Eni E&P and Fiat Group and chief compliance officer of the European Bank for Reconstruction and Development. Immediately before joining Paul Hastings he served as chief counsel to the commissioner appointed by the Italian government to investigate Europe's largest financial fraud, at Parmalat.

He is also an officer of the International Bar Association Anti-corruption Committee and a member of the troika of experts advising the Corporate Governance Committee of Borsa Italiana on governance reforms.

E Leigh Dance
President, ELD International LLC
ELDance@ELDInternational.com

E Leigh Dance is president of management consultancy ELD International LLC, based in New York and Brussels. She is also founder and executive director of the Global Counsel Leaders Circle, an invitation-only forum of high-level corporate counsel and compliance leaders with multinationals.

Ms Dance helps corporate legal teams apply top global enterprises' best practice to improve legal function performance, structure, service delivery, governance, crisis management, professional development and provider management.

Her commentary on legal and compliance issues facing law firm and in-house leaders have appeared in *The Wall Street Journal*, *Financial Times*, *American Lawyer* and *Legal Week*. Ms Dance's book *Bright Ideas: Insights from Legal Luminaries Worldwide* (Amazon), compiles 26 original essays by industry leaders.

Ms Dance has international experience in global financial services, international public policy and development, with assignments in over 30 countries. She speaks English, French and Italian, holds an MBA in international management with high honours and a BA in international relations with honours.

Jochen Deister
Partner, DMZ Legal
jochen.deister@dmzlegal.com

Professor Dr Jochen Deister is a partner at DMZ Legal, a law firm with a focus on IT and privacy law. He holds degrees in German, French and Japanese law, and has specialised in IT and privacy law for more than 15 years. He began his legal career at Clifford Chance and has occupied various legal management positions at Amazon, Motorola and Avanade.

Mr Deister is also professor at the faculty of computer sciences at the University of Applied Sciences in Wiesbaden, Germany.

He founded and has served as director of the In-house Counsel Institute. He has run the Deister Institute for Negotiation Science for almost a decade and has trained and advised clients on negotiation and persuasion techniques. Mr Deister is a major contributor to the German standard for legal quality management.

Dennis Grabherr
Associate general counsel and vice president, Northern Europe, Hewlett-Packard Company
dennis.grabherr@hp.com

Dennis Grabherr is an in-house lawyer with more than 18 years of international leadership experience in multinational IT and telecommunications organisations. Most recently he joined Hewlett-Packard as associate general counsel and vice president for Northern Europe. He started his career working in private practice with Baker & McKenzie in Bogotá, Colombia, and then with Haarmann, Hemmelrath & Partner in Munich, Germany, and Warsaw, Poland.

He set up and ran the legal team for EQUANT's Central Europe, Middle East and Africa region in Frankfurt. Moving on to BT Global Services, he first headed the legal department for Germany, Austria, Central and Eastern Europe and Nordics. Thereafter, he was chief counsel for Latin America based in São Paulo and then set up and headed BT's global data governance function.

Wolf-Peter Gross
Management consultant, Law Firm Change Consultants
wpg@lawfirmchange.com

Dr Wolf-Peter Gross is a management consultant at Law Firm Change Consultants, a leading consulting firm for law firms and legal departments in Europe. He is a lawyer, systemic organisational consultant and business mediator. He has been general counsel in the telecommunications and system integration industries and has many years of experience as a managing director in international businesses. Since 2005 Dr Gross has been a consultant focusing on strategy, organisation, operations and change in professional service firms and law departments.

He is the author of several published articles and a member of the visiting faculty of GGS, the German Graduate School for Management and Law, Heilbronn, Germany.

Max Hübner
General counsel, PGGM NV
Max.huebner@pggm.nl

Max Hübner is general counsel at PGGM NV. He leads the legal and tax department, which acts as a law firm for PGGM NV and a business partner for PGGM's entities. He is also a lecturer at the Amsterdam University of Applied Sciences, a strategic adviser for law firms and general counsel and executive coach for legal professionals.

For more than 20 years Mr Hübner worked on legal matters in the field of law enforcement, governance, environment and financial markets. Since 1999 he has explored the nature of legal services and has introduced document assembly and legal workflow management and brought new concepts for legal services and pricing to the market. Based on his failures and successes, Mr Hübner has developed an approach for the transformation of legal departments.

Peter Kurer
Partner, BLR & Partners AG
Peter@kurer.com

Peter Kurer is a partner with the private equity firm BLR & Partners AG. He studied law and political science at the University of Zurich and the University of Chicago. He started his professional career with international law firm Baker & McKenzie, where he became a partner in 1985. In 1990 Mr Kurer became a founding partner of the Zurich law firm Homburger, where he headed the corporate law practice group. He specialised in mergers and acquisitions and corporate law, and served on a number of boards of public and private companies. In 2001 Mr Kurer joined UBS as general counsel and member of the group executive board. He served as the chairman of the bank during the 2008–2009 crisis and then retired.

Mr Kurer is now chairman of Kein & Aber, a Swiss book publisher; he sits on a number of boards and acts as independent adviser. He also writes and speaks frequently on M&A topics, corporate governance issues and legal and compliance risk management. His new book *Legal and Compliance Risk: a Strategic Response to a Rising Threat for Global Business* was published by Oxford University Press in February 2015.

Paul Lippe
Chief executive officer, OnRamp Systems
paullippe@legalonramp.com

Paul Lippe is chief executive officer of OnRamp Systems, the leader in using Watson and other machine-learning systems in order to analyse and simplify legacy contracts, manage complexity, improve quality and reduce costs for legal departments. The firm's Legal OnRamp system was first developed as a legal department productivity and collaboration platform for Cisco Systems.

Mr Lippe was general counsel and senior vice president for business development and corporate marketing at Synopsys, an electronic design automation company. He was also chief executive officer of Stanford SKOLAR, a medical digital library and e-learning company which was part of Stanford Medical School.

A graduate of Yale College and Harvard Law School, Mr Lippe speaks and writes regularly about the 'new normal' in law. Before law school he was special assistant to Senator Daniel P Moynihan (D NY) and chairman of the Colorado Air Quality Control Commission.

Abhijit Mukhopadhyay
President (legal), Hinduja Group
abhijit@sangamltd.com

Abhijit Mukhopadhyay, a qualified lawyer and chartered secretary from India and the United Kingdom, has been general counsel and company secretary in various multinationals in India. Mr Mukhopadhyay is currently president (legal) and company secretary for the Hinduja Group in London – a $15 billion multinational employing 89,000 people in 35 countries engaged in 10 business verticals. He is a non-executive director in five countries.

Mr Mukhopadhyay is vice chairman of the International Chamber of Commerce's Commission of Arbitration and Alternative Dispute Resolution in Paris, a member of the India Business Forum of Confederation of Indian Industry, an Advisory Board member, of the International Bar Association's LFM committee, European Advisory Board member of CPR Dispute Resolution and Faculty in the Global General Counsel Academy in London.

In 2010 Mr Mukhopadhyay was ranked in the top 50 legal professionals in India. His articles on legal issues have been published in India, France, the United States, Austria, the United Kingdom and Malaysia. He has spoken at seminars in India, Malaysia, Singapore, Germany, England, the United States, France, Sweden, Japan and Austria.

Felix Rackwitz
Managing director, Tools4Legal GmbH
felix.rackwitz@tools4legal.com

Felix Rackwitz was a partner and later on head of business development at a large German law firm for 12 years, working in their St Petersburg, Kiev and Frankfurt offices. He read law at the Universities of Marburg, Regensburg, Odessa and Kiel and obtained an MBA at the Judge Business School/University of Cambridge.

Since 2014 he has been active in start-ups in the legal sphere and founded the legal start-up Tools4Legal in 2015 together with Filip Corveleyn, which has been featured in the *Financial Times*.

Christian Rau
General counsel for Europe, the Middle East and Africa, DaVita Healthcare Partners, Inc
christiankhrau@yahoo.com

Dr Christian Rau is general counsel for Europe, Middle East and Africa of the US healthcare company DaVita, based in Amsterdam. He also serves as the director of the in-house legal function for the Bucerius Centre on the Legal Profession. He holds a German and US law degree.

Dr Rau has 20 years professional experience with Freshfields, Johnson & Johnson, The Linde Group and Davita, having been based in Berlin, Brussels, New Jersey, Munich and Amsterdam. He specialises in mergers and acquisitions, compliance, governance, US litigation and legal leadership.

His passion for developing and operating legal departments is demonstrated by the highly successful integration and operation of two distinct legal functions after the Linde–BOC merger. In the process, Dr Rau hired and developed dozens of lawyers in a newly-structured legal and compliance organisation, comprising more than 100 legal professionals in 18 offices across the globe.

Carsten Reimann
Chief executive officer, Xenion Legal
creimann@xenionlaw.com

Carsten Reimann is founder and chief executive officer of Xenion Legal, a startup providing lawyers on demand and developing next-generation legal solutions for corporate clients and law firms. He holds degrees in law and management from the Universities of Edinburgh and St Gallen. For more than 15 years Mr Reimann has specialised in legal management issues, including staffing and sourcing, while based in Brussels, Cologne, Frankfurt and London.

Mr Reimann was an attorney at Freshfields. He served as head of Nissan's Brussels office after having established Nissan's legal department for Central Europe, which was successfully certified according to ISO DIN 9001.

Mr Reimann also initiated the expert group on legal quality management at TÜV Rheinland and coordinated the project work on the standard for in-house legal departments.

Scott D Rosenberg
Corporate counsel, Project Leadership Associates
srosenberg@projectleadership.net

Scott Rosenberg has 25 years' experience helping law departments identify and translate practice management needs into strategic and actionable technology plans supporting operational best practices. Mr Rosenberg's work allows his clients to 'do more with less', creating a state-of-the-art technology platform while implementing successful change management strategies to ensure user adoption.

Mr Rosenberg served as senior manager of legal operations for Kraft Foods Group Inc and as managing director of Huron Consulting Group's legal business consulting practice. He started the corporate legal practice of Baker Robbins & Company. Mr Rosenberg is an expert in areas of legal technology and systems selection and implementation, including matter management, e-billing, document management, enterprise search, knowledge sharing, contract management, intellectual property and litigation support.

Mr Rosenberg is a lawyer and certified public accountant. He earned a BS in accountancy and a JD from the University of Illinois.

Paul Smith
Chairman, Eversheds LLP
paulsmith@eversheds.com

Paul Smith is chairman of Eversheds LLP. He is also a recognised expert on law firm partnering, convergence and innovation. He began developing this expertise as client partner for DuPont more than 10 years ago. In recent years, Mr Smith has focused on how the law firm and global corporate law department can work together effectively across multiple jurisdictions. He consults with many global corporate law departments on their structures, processes and practices to derive greater value from outside counsel. He put in place the Tyco convergence project in Europe, the Middle East and Africa, where Tyco consolidated most of its outside legal services from more than 250 law firms across 37 jurisdictions to one: Eversheds.

Legal Business magazine honoured Mr Smith as Lawyer of the Year, one of the most prestigious awards in the United Kingdom, in 2008. He was given this honour for his pioneering work in delivering new approaches to global client relationship management.

Christoph H Vaagt
Managing partner, Law Firm Change Consultants
CHV@lawfirmchange.com

Chris Vaagt is founder and managing partner of Law Firm Change Consultants – the consulting firm for law firms and legal departments – based in Munich, Germany. He holds a law degree and has worked as a consultant for various industries and as a lawyer in Munich, before turning to consulting for law firms and legal departments.

Before founding his own firm in 2005, he was a consultant with Hildebrandt International, a major US law firm consultancy. He has acted for major German, Austrian, Swiss and continental European Top 100 firms. He specialises in change management techniques, focusing on strategy and law firm culture.

Mr Vaagt is author of the first benchmark study of the German law firm market and edited the book *Law Firm Strategies in the 21st Century* on behalf of the International Bar Association.

Kent Walker
Senior vice president and general counsel, Google

Kent Walker leads Google's legal team and advises the company's board and management on legal issues.

He previously held senior legal positions at leading technology companies, including eBay, Netscape, AOL and Airtouch Communications. He also served as an assistant US attorney with the Department of Justice, specialising in the prosecution of technology crimes and advising the attorney general on management and technology issues.

Mr Walker graduated from Harvard College and Stanford Law School. He serves on the advisory boards of the Harvard School of Public Health and the Mercy Corps Social Ventures Fund.